The Dawn of Bohemianism

Pour me séparer du monde, répondit le peintre.

The Dawn
of Bohemianism

The *Barbu* Rebellion and Primitivism in Neoclassical France

George Levitine

The Pennsylvania State University Press

University Park and London

Library of Congress Cataloging in Publication Data

Levitine, George.
    The dawn of Bohemianism.
    Includes bibliography and index.
    1. Painting, French.   2.   Primitivist art—France.
3.   Painting, Modern—19th century—France.   4.   Avant-
garde (Aesthetics)—France.   I.   Title.
N684775.P68L48   759.4   77-13892
ISBN 0-271-00527-0

Designed by Glenn Ruby

Printed in the United States of America

To Eda

Once Again, and Always

Contents

List of Illustrations

Illustrations 1–14 follow page 36. Illustrations 15–53 appear at the end of the book.

1. François Boucher, *The Painter,* 1752, engraving by Marie-Madeleine Igonet (photo: Bibliothèque nationale).
2. Jean-Jacques Spoëde, *The Dean of Painters* (Beaunureau), engraving by J. Guélard (photo: Bibliothèque nationale.)
3. Etienne Jeaurat, *A Painter Moving,* 1755, engraving by Claude Duflos (photo: Bibliothèque nationale).
4. Anon., *The Drawing Teacher,* engraving (photo: Bibliothèque nationale).
5. Anon. (Anne-Louis Girodet ?), *The Great Ragpicker-Critic of the Salon of 1806,* engraving (photo: Bibliothèque nationale).
6. Claude-Nicolas Malapeau, *The Actor Dugazon in the Role of M. Fougère,* engraving. From Fabre d'Eglantine, *L'Intrigue épistolaire,* frontispiece, Paris, 1791.
7. Anon. (Johann Rudolf Schellenberg ?), *Portrait of Grimou,* engraving. From Henry Fuseli, *Geschichte der besten Künstler in der Schweiz,* Zurich, 1770, III, 15 (photo: Bibliothèque nationale).
8. Anon. (Louis Watteau de Lille ?), *Art Dealers, Restorers of Paintings, Paying Homage to the Good Thief,* oil on canvas. Musée Carnavalet, Paris (photo: Bulloz).
9. Anon. (Joly ?), *The Actor Joly in the Role of Lantara,* engraving (from Barré, Picard, Radet, and Desfontaines, *Lantara ou le peintre au cabaret,* frontispiece, Paris, 1809).
10. François-Louis-Joseph Watteau de Lille, *Lantara,* 1776, engraving by Laurent Guyot (photo: Bibliothèque nationale).
11. Charles-Joseph Traviés, *Lantara,* engraving by Jean Geoffroy (from Théophile Marion Dumersan, *Chansons nationales et populaires de France,* Paris, 1851, between pages 61 and 62).
12. Etienne-Maurice Falconet, *Apelles and Campaspe,* 1765, marble. Private collection (photo: Arlaud).
13. Charles Le Brun, *Dibutade,* engraving by François Chauveau (photo: Bibliothèque nationale).
14. François Maradan, *She Was Drawing, Seated on a Tomb,* engraving. From Charles Nodier, *Le Peintre de Saltzbourg,* frontispiece, Paris, 1803 (photo: Bibliothèque nationale).
15. Henri-François Riesener (?), *Portrait of Maurice Quay,* oil on canvas. Louvre, Paris (photo: Musées nationaux).
16. Jacques-Louis David, *The Sabine Women,* 1799. Louvre, Paris (photo: Bulloz).
17. Jean-Henri Cless, *The Studio of David,* drawing. Musée Carnavalet, Paris (photo: Archives photographiques, Paris).

Acknowledgments

I am happy to acknowledge that in undertaking this book I have incurred many notable debts. To the Graduate School of the University of Maryland and to the American Philosophical Society, I owe the generous assistance that provided me with research funds. My other obligations are too numerous to be given proper acknowledgment. Nevertheless, I should like to express my feeling of gratitude to all the curators and the staff members of public and private collections and libraries, who graciously showed me works of art, books, and manuscripts from their holdings and gave me the authorization to have them photographed or reproduced. I am particularly indebted to M. Jean Adhémar, Conservateur au Cabinet des Estampes of the Bibliothèque Nationale, Paris; M. Michel Guillot, Directeur of the Musée de Suresnes and Archiviste at the Archives Nationales, Paris; Mme Felkay, Conservateur des Archives de la Seine, Paris; Général Henri d'Avout d'Auerstaedt, Directeur of the Musée de l'Armée, Paris; M. Pierre Rosenberg and M. Jacques Foucart, Conservateurs des Peintures du Musée du Louvre, Paris; M. Jean Lacambre, Conservateur à l'Inspection générale des Musées classés et contrôlés; M. Alain Lévy, Conservateur de la Bibliothèque de Castres; Mme Marguerite Guillaume, Conservateur, and Mlle Monique Geiger, Conservateur Adjoint, at the Musée de Dijon; Mlle Denise Billas, Conservateur de la Bibliothèque de Grenoble; Mme Nouvel, Conservateur du Départment des Papiers Peints of the Musée des Arts Décoratifs, Paris; M. Coutarel of the Archives de la Préfecture de Police, Paris; and to Mme Koellisch of the Bibliothèque Paul Marmottan, Boulogne-sur-Seine. I cannot forget the invaluable help, advice, and encouragement that I received from many other people, such as M. Aimé Buix, M. Jean Carle, M. Alexandre Clavier, M. le Prince d'Essling, M. Gérard Heuillet, Professor René Huyghe, Professor Horst W. Janson, M. and Mme Marcel Lafond, and Professor Daniel Ternois. Thanks are also due to Miss Katherine Miller and Miss Kathryn Webster who assisted me in preparing and typing my manuscript, and to Mr. Glenn Ruby, Editor of the Pennsylvania State University Press, who helped with his pertinent criticisms and a variety of constructive suggestions. It is also important to recall here the many interesting conversations I had with several of my students, particularly Mrs. Melinda Curtis. In the case of this book, as always, I should like to express my deep and loving gratitude to my wife, Eda Mezer Levitine, who is responsible for the numerous translations from the French, and without whom my work would have been neither undertaken nor completed.

Introduction

Oddities of dress and oddities of behavior were far from alien to a post-Revolutionary Parisian society incessantly exposed to a variegated array of *Incroyables, Merveilleuses, Théophilanthropes,* and other *originaux.* Yet, surprisingly, the appearance of an outlandish new sect of young artists on the Parisian scene around 1800 seems to have succeeded in raising a few blasé eyebrows. These long-haired, bearded young men—wrapped in sheetlike cloaks and sporting white pantaloons, red waistcoats, turbans, and assorted rags simulating Grecian, Scandinavian (so-called Ossianic), and oriental garb—could hardly remain inconspicuous. In fact, with their heroic sense of dignity, forbearance, and gentleness, which they maintained despite constant derision and taunts from fishwives and street urchins, these earnest masqueraders added pathos to the nuances of Parisian eccentricity. Probably for this reason the picturesque sect, some thirty years after its extinction, was lyrically evoked as a "tribe of angels"; but, in their own time, the members of this "tribe" were more typically referred to as *Observateurs de l'homme, Illuminés des arts, Primitifs, Penseurs,* and *Méditateurs de l'antique.* The group seems to have had some preference for the last title, but, to avoid confusion and for the sake of conciseness, one can more conveniently refer to its members as *Barbus* (the bearded ones), since, despite its late appearance (1832), this somewhat satirical and possibly apocryphal designation is the one most often remembered and used today.

Because of their youthful fervor, singular bearing, esoteric tenets, and unusual aesthetic theories, the *Barbus* are one of the most appealing and intriguing subjects in French art history. In itself, the colorful nonconformity of this group was sufficiently striking to be acknowledged as a noteworthy dissonance in the Davidian era. However, the exceptional adventure of these young men and women—the latter occasionally called *Dormeuses* (sleepers), adorned with black crepe, veils, and wreaths of flowers—represented much more than an ephemeral ripple on the surface of the majestic lake of French Neoclassicism. Beyond the question of outward eccentricity, this episode finds far-reaching significance in the very fact that it took place.

The distinction between the *Barbus'* eccentric appearance and their inner motivation can be best characterized by a passage from an article in *Le Temps,* written in 1832 by Charles Nodier, a former member of the group, who by that time had become one of the guiding spirits of the full-fledged Romantic movement. Nodier recalled that "it was of little importance" for the members of the sect to "display themselves with the mantle of Agamemnon or the Phrygian cap of Paris, the veil of the widowed Andromache or that of the priestess Cassandra." In reality they were, as he said, filled with "other thoughts." Something of their true raison d'être, according to Nodier, is revealed in an exchange between Napoleon and the painter Maurice Quay, the leader of the *Barbus,* who was being interviewed by the First Consul as a prospective drawing master for his nieces. Taken aback by the strange attire of the young painter, Napoleon asked: "Why did you adopt a type of clothing which separates you from the world?" To which the entirely self-possessed, Agamemnon-garbed Quay pithily retorted: "In order to separate myself from the world" (NOD-TEM 441).*

This statement can be acknowledged as the first in a long succession of French artists' assertions of alienation, ranging from the Romantic period to the present day. If Nodier was correct, Quay's affirmation would have originally predated its literary counterpart, Alfred de Vigny's far better-known *Stello,* by some thirty years, although the two appeared in print in the same year. Naturally, as in most historical or legendary "firsts," the concept of Quay's daring declaration of independence could hardly have emerged Athena-like from the dogmatic godhead of the art establishment of the period. Thus it seems that, rather than undertaking a series of predictable parallels along the stations of the cross leading to the manifestos of the modern era, it would be more rewarding to explore the phenomenon of the *Barbus'* alienation in the context of the cultural panorama of their own time, and of the time that preceded them.

It is clear that a basis for such an approach should be sought particularly through an exploration of the deep changes that affected the position of the French artist during the second half of the eighteenth and the very beginning of the nineteenth centuries. However, such an exploration was undertaken neither by the scholars who came to be interested in the general question of the "artist's condition" (most frequently bypassing the *Barbus*) nor by the small number of those who had previously studied the particular problem of this sect. Thus in surveys devoted to nineteenth-century French painting, references to this sect are often confined to some diverting cursory comments, while the very few specialized studies addressing themselves to Neoclassicism or Romanticism tend to develop their considerations about the *Barbus* almost in a void, on the strength of semi-abstractions and rationalizations knit into the same well-known but pitifully limited source material.

Despite their intrinsic interest, a priori theories can add very little to the understanding of the problem: The *Barbus* cannot be studied fruitfully as an isolated phenomenon, for the century that preceded the appearance of the group represents much more than a vague "germinative" phase. The *Barbus* should not be seen as some kind of "culmination," but rather as a cultural expression of a fortuitous convergence, clustering, and crisscrossing of much earlier trends—trends which, independently of the sect, continue a simultaneous but separate evolution, diverging, coalescing, and diverging again, along their meandering paths leading toward the twentieth century.

* See the list of abbreviations following the text for the full titles of references appearing in the text.

In speaking of early trends, oversimplification must be avoided. For example, by considering only their "eccentricity," "unconventionality," or "Bohemianism," the *Barbus* might be readily dismissed as not really novel, since these labels could be properly affixed to countless earlier instances. Roman poets ridiculed in Horace's *Ars poetica* because they "take no pains to pare their nails or to shave their beards" and the much later and well-known cases of Caravaggio (1573–1610) in Italy, Brouwer (1605–38) in Holland, and Raymond La Fage (1656–90) in France are sufficient to underline this fact. While it is true that in France, in the midst of the Enlightenment, the most unusual biographical traits attributed to artists seldom match the bizarreness ascribed to their colleagues of other nationalities, or even to the French practitioners of earlier times, instances of strange behavior occur nevertheless. Before the *Barbus'* time, there was the suicide of François Lemoyne (1688–1737), who, haunted by Roman examples of "a beautiful death," stabbed himself nine times with his sword; the dark misanthropy of Jacques Autreau (1656–1745), who behaved like Molière's Alceste and described himself as "another Diogenes"; the obsessive philanthropy, Savonarolesque fanaticism, and monastic garb of Nicolas-Bernard Lépicié (1735–84); the gruffness and frugality of Etienne-Maurice Falconet (1716–91), who thought that he resembled Socrates and was prone to pseudo-Socratic mimicry; and the incredible indifference to health and appearance of Gabriel de Saint-Aubin (1724–80), who, instead of powdering his hair and washing his stockings, applied white drawing chalk to both.

There is little need to lengthen the random list of such tragic, bizarre, or comical examples of eighteenth-century French artists' oddities. Because of their historical accuracy (give or take a stroke of Lemoyne's sword), as well as their diversity, each occurrence of strange behavior emerged either as an isolated clinical case or as a separate instance of bizarre idiosyncracy. Since every historical period has produced some examples of this nature, they cannot be validly considered, either as a group or individually, as belonging to a repertoire of social and cultural types coined by their century. For this very reason—and this is a serious implication— none of these examples can be recognized as a convincing indication of a trend.

A study of trends shaping the artist's condition must of course take into account available documented facts. However, it can be argued that, independently of such facts, a process of change in the artist's position emerges as a recognizable factor only when it acquires a cultural silhouette, that is, when it projects an identifiable image born on the wings of art-historical legends and popular adages. This assertion is not limited to the art world. Thus, in the nineteenth century, the emergence of the images of the dull *bourgeois* and of the *nouveau riche* are as culturally meaningful as any statistics concerning the rise of the middle class. In different contexts in the same century, this idea applies, for instance, to the imagery of the "Wertherian" vogue of suicides, the *poète maudit,* and the demimondaine, or, during the eighteenth century, to the images of the *petit-maître,* the *abbé de cour,* and the *sans-culotte.* Freely borrowing from Plato's allegory, one could submit that in this particular cave shadows are at least as revealing and instructive as the shapes from which they are cast.

Admittedly, in a general sense, this concept is not entirely new. Ernst Kris, for instance, had already considered some of its implications in his *Psychoanalytic Explorations in Art* (1935), demonstrating the importance of what he called "biographical *formulae*," which recurred in ancient *lives of artists*. Such *formulae*, according to Kris, "may give us some understanding of how members of this group [artists] were regarded by their environment, what specific aspects characterized their position, and what specific qualities the public attributed to them" (65). This is essentially the approach that has often been adopted here in tracing the various trends that were woven into the fabric of the *Barbus'* phenomenon.

The purpose of this study, however, cannot be fulfilled through an analysis of "biographical *formulae*" found in the traditionally accepted *lives* alone. The nature of the subject—involving the kaleidoscopic imagery of the artist cast against the rapidly changing historical conditions, before and after the French Revolution—requires an extensive consideration of a largely unexplored peripheral and, often, anonymous body of sources, ranging from "serious" literature to vaudeville, scandal sheets, ditties, newspaper accounts, anecdotes, recorded rumors, and period clichés. Accepted opinions about the artist's profession flowed freely from the street to the amateur, to the Salon critic and the writer, and, again, to the street. Some of the most important aspects of this imagery (for instance, the social stigma attached to the manual side of the artist's work) were marked by anonymity and failed to appear in acknowledged biographies. The popular silhouette of the artist could be very different from his official "life": In the street, as a social class, artists seldom enjoyed a fully Olympian or Promethean stature.

It would be futile to pretend that it has been possible to unearth all the documentation one could hope to command in order to undertake such an exploration. Nevertheless, the material that has been gathered seems to establish some foundation for serious evaluation and perhaps a few conclusions. One uncovers, of course, some unknown aspects of what may be termed "the dawn of bohemianism" and "the birth of the modern image of the artist." But beyond this almost predictable significance—one thinks of the long succession of subsequent occurrences, ranging from the Nazarenes to the Hippies and Flower Children—the study of the *Barbus'* phenomenon also sheds some light upon a profound, little-understood social, cultural, and aesthetic crisis. Transcending its prophetic significance, this crisis is important in its own right.

In this study, which after all is concerned chiefly with a group of painters, the aesthetic connotations of the *Barbus'* many-sided activities are not unduly overshadowed by the legendary character of their aura. In this regard, I hope that related theoretical publications, patches of history introduced here for the first time, and, above all, examples of the *Barbus'* work, which I have been fortunate to locate and identify, will add to an understanding of the role played by this sect in the evolution of French painting at the turn of the century.

It can be seen that the problems under consideration have many textures and many layers, and I must confess that the title of the book, *The Dawn of Bohemianism: The* Barbu *Rebellion and Primitivism in Neoclassical France,* is, like most titles, unavoidably little more than a shingle. Neither the time-honored sequence of Rococo, Neoclassicism, Romanticism, nor a succession of well-established art-historical landmarks (i.e., Boucher's *Rising of the Sun,* 1753; David's *Oath of the Horatii,* 1785; Géricault's *Raft of the "Medusa,"* 1819) could provide a useful framework for this study. Often departing from famous names and recognized masterpieces in order to grope through long-bypassed recesses of the eighteenth and the nineteenth centuries, I was not always able to systematically follow a chronological order. It was also imperative, of course, to avoid ready-made structures that could involve the danger of built-in solutions. The discussion of this complex and often heterogeneous material had to be given sufficient elbowroom, and it seemed that the best organization would be a fairly loose thematic arrangement, introducing the *Barbus* after a consideration of the trends shaping the artist's condition. However, no method is entirely functional, no scholarship is totally objective, and no study is ever truly completed. Invoking these truisms, I would only like to express the hope that I succeeded in clearing the entrance to a little-known but inviting path, which other scholars will continue to explore.

Gloire aux Barbus!

I: The Image of the Artist

1

The Strength of Clichés

A study of a new historical phenomenon cannot be divorced from the situation from which this phenomenon arises. Without exaggeration, it can be stated that a familiarity with the eighteenth-century image of the artist is in every way as indispensable for the understanding of the *Barbus'* movement as a thorough knowledge of the conditions prevailing under the *ancien régime* is imperative for the understanding of the French Revolution.

The eighteenth-century image of the artist is rooted in a jungle of clichés, and historical clichés can be baffling. The brothers Goncourt observed in 1856 that "Bohemia has always been the state of grace in which French painting has lived" (*Les Portraits intimes du dix-huitième siècle,* I, 214), while only two years later, in 1858, Léon Lagrange remarked that "French art, unlike the Italian art of the XVIth century, has not known how to create for itself a splendid Bohemia in which to live its own life above and beyond social conventions" (*Joseph Vernet,* 1). Naturally the Goncourt made their statement to underline the lighthearted improvidence of Gabriel-François Doyen, while Lagrange, in his monograph on Vernet, expressed the antithetical opinion in order to provide additional relief to the bourgeois respectability of his own hero. The fact remains that in considering two important painters of the eighteenth century, two scholarly nineteenth-century studies—written about the same time—offer diametric characterizations of the entire course of French art history on the strength of contrasting clichés that seem to have been tailor-made for their respective subjects.

Yet neither the brothers Goncourt nor Lagrange should be too hastily accused of lacking scholarly candor. Surveys such as J. B. Salgues's *Des Erreurs et des préjugés répandus dans la société* (1811) and Gustave Flaubert's better-known *Dictionnaire des idées reçues* (published posthumously in 1881) show that clichés appear, disappear, and reappear through the centuries. The significance of their pervading presence at any given time is difficult to assess. Deeply immersed in every level of cultural life, they have been used almost unconsciously—as in the case of biblical or Shakespearean quotations—to demonstrate a particular idea, or its exact opposite. Clichés are crucial to the study of any era, but they are always colored by a historical perspective that can have many ramifications and can become incredibly tortuous.

For this reason clichés often reveal more truly the period during which they have been coined rather than any particular situation to which they may apply. Thus if one accepts the fact that the value of a cliché as a cultural cue is directly related to the moment of its appearance, one must conclude that the Goncourts' and Lagrange's notions of the wholly bohemian, wholly bourgeois character of French artists are neither true nor false. The Goncourts and Lagrange merely express two different and highly simplified views of *la vie d'artiste* that coexist—as clichés—in nineteenth-century culture.

Because of the distortions produced by such nineteenth-century stereotypes, a study of the eighteenth-century image of the artist must avoid as much as possible the apocryphal and historically misleading label of "bohemianism." Consequently, it must also shun, of course, an indiscriminate reliance on the accompanying syndrome popularized by Henri Murger's *Scènes de la vie de bohème* (1848) and surviving, in a "modernized" form, in the twentieth-century conception of the artist's lifestyle. Careless reference to these familiar nineteenth- and twentieth-century notions can easily obfuscate the *Barbus'* activities.

By refocusing the question beyond the distortions of later clichés, and considering the artist's image in the comparative safety of the eighteenth-century frame of reference, a change in the notion of his status becomes perceptible. In the eighteenth century, after countless ages during which they were confined to the condition of craftsmen and viewed on the same social level as carpenters, masons, or leather workers, the artists, to quote Claude-Henri Watelet (WAT-DIC I, 455), "are admitted into general society." And in order to be admitted to this society, that is, the circles of the upper bourgeoisie, men of letters, and aristocracy, the artist—for the first time in history—did not necessarily have to be a courtier, a renowned scholar, a recognized genius, or even a man of unusual talent. However, this view of general acceptance can be easily deceiving. To understand its true significance, the effect of the economic and social pressures to which artists were subjected in the midst of unfamiliar social milieus must be considered.

The profession of artist has never been known as an easy one. As early as the seventeenth century, Jean de La Fontaine, speaking of a painter in one of his *Contes, Les Rémois,* tellingly writes:

> A man honored in his profession;
> He was living off it: what more can one ask?
> It was sufficient for his condition.

> Homme estimé dans sa profession;
> Il en vivoit; que faut-il davantage?
> C'était assez pour sa condition.
>
> (La Fontaine, *Contes,* III, 3)

Although such early allusions to the artist's struggle in making both ends meet do occur, the notion of the artist's economic difficulties became a truism during the eighteenth century. Explicit variations on this theme can be seen in François Boucher's *The Painter (Fig. 1)* and Jean-Jacques Spoëde's caricature of Beaunureau, *The Dean of Painters (Fig. 2)*. In fact, the expression *gueux comme un peintre* (as poor as a painter) became a proverb (LEV-GRI 66). For instance, in his *Mémoires* (MAR I, 170), Jean-François Marmontel related his legal plea on behalf of an artist from Toulouse, in which he victoriously demonstrated the man's destitution by merely noting that he was a professional painter. The artists' poverty was a source of a variety of anecdotes and a fair target for humorous sallies. Some revealed a touch of gallows humor, such as Pierre-Jean-Baptiste Nougaret's story of a painter warming himself, during the winter, near the flames of a fire that is destroying his own house (LEV-GRI 66). More often pathos is masked by facetiousness and pitiless irony, as in Etienne Jeaurat's *A Painter Moving (Fig. 3)*, which shows an artist and his family being subjected to the recriminations of their creditors, a wine merchant and a baker's wife (see LEV-GRI 66–67). One can single out, for example, the often-quoted description of a technique of painting *in ramekin,* which, it is pointed out, has a very practical advantage, for the painters who use cheese as a medium in lieu of paint can, when needed, dine off their works (LEV-GRI 66).

Without meaningful statistics, is it most difficult to evaluate objectively the true state of the artists' economic problems in the eighteenth century in comparison with other periods. A few painters, like Jean-Baptiste Pierre, were born into wealth, and a few others, such as François Boucher, Joseph Vernet, and Maurice-Quentin de La Tour, succeeded in amassing considerable fortunes. Yet most artists were painfully aware of the ever-present threat of poverty, and on the whole contemporaries' comments suggested a situation of extreme instability. It is true that the recurring allusions to a pauper's end at the hospital often expressed a figure of speech or a form of dark humor. This is certainly the meaning of the seriocomic statement ascribed by the Comte de Caylus to Antoine Watteau, who is reported to have said: "As a last resource, isn't there the hospital? No one is turned away from its doors."[1] In fact, the admission to a hospital was not necessarily to be taken for granted. Jacques Autreau went so far as to write a poem, dedicated to the Cardinal de Fleury, in order to request the favor to be admitted to the hospital of the Incurables (*Œuvres,* 1749, IV, 181), and the Académie royale organized a special deputation to obtain the same privilege for Dumarest (*Procès-verbaux de l'Académie,* 1792, X, 185–86). It is known that twelve destitute artists died in the hospital of La Charité in 1778, the same year as the landscape painter Simon-Mathurin Lantara, about whom Pahin de la Blancherie writes: "He had the same fate as several of the greatest painters, he died of want" (LEV-GRI 67).

The extent of poverty among artists is impossible to ascertain, for most of the neediest among them—such as Ausselin, Boussard, Boutin, and the other destitute painters who died in 1778 in the hospital of La Charité—were also the least known. Contemporaries, acknowledging the artists' obvious economic problems, were often inclined to trace the causes of these difficulties to a rapidly growing profession.

Pierre-Charles Levesque, in 1792, speaks of the "mob which rushes into our schools of drawing" and of the "wretched life" awaiting most of these too numerous and often insufficiently talented future artists. He also points out that the number of individuals who were attracted to the profession of the arts "is growing nowadays in too great proportion, in comparison to the number of men who must enter other useful professions" (WAT-DIC II, 126–27). Similar observations had been made much earlier (1765) by Chardin. Describing the terrible fate awaiting the many would-be artists, this great painter, according to Diderot, said that "two thousand wretches break their brushes in a futile attempt to equal the worst painting exhibited in the Salon" (*Salon de 1765,* 1960, II, 57–58). The problem created by this situation became increasingly evident during the last years of the reign of Louis XVI. Indeed, the seriousness of the situation was noted by the government, and, in his *Compte rendu* of 1781, the finance minister Jacques Necker rhetorically exclaimed: "What need does the state have of a great number of mediocre painters, sculptors, and engravers?" (LEV-GRI 68). The aesthetic implications of this problem, which grew increasingly acute at the turn of the nineteenth century, were noted by Jean-François Sobry:

> This multitude of poor students who come to the Arts looking for a livelihood and who often only succeed in increasing their difficulties will only lead the Arts to an inevitable and rapid deterioration. The artists who are lacking in money, instead of following the inspiration of beauty, too often sell out to ignorance . . . they allow themselves to slavishly cultivate all the bad habits which can procure them some gain. (*Poétique des arts,* 1810, 480)

During the eighteenth century, despite repeated attempts to expose art students to other subjects, such as history, mythology, literature, and geography, the notion of the artist's ignorance remained as much a cliché as the notion of his poverty. References on this subject abound, shaded with varying connotations. Madame Roland, for instance, in her *Mémoires* (1864, 4), describes her father, the engraver-painter Gatien Philipon, in revealingly patronizing terms: "Without education, he had the superficial degree of taste and knowledge, which is given by the fine arts." The same attitude is reflected by Louis Petit de Bachaumont. Thus in a letter, striving to flatter the painter Pierre, this littérateur writes: "You have wit, you received a good education, you are lettered, you enjoy reading. . . . These are many advantages which you have over those who are engaged in the same career as you" (Goncourt, *Les Portraits intimes,* I, 84). Few eighteenth-century sources express the prevailing idea about the artists' lack of learning more graphically than the passages of Marmontel's *Mémoires,* in which he describes the artists he had met at Madame Geoffrin's celebrated Monday suppers. He writes: "With them [the artists] I was most careful to avoid displaying any literary knowledge alien to the fine arts. I had no difficulty in noticing that, although endowed with a native intelligence, almost all of them were lacking in education and culture" (MAR II, 102–3). This opinion is reflected in all of Marmontel's vignettes. Speaking of Carle Van Loo, for instance, he states that this artist "possessed to a high degree all the talent a painter can have without genius; but he was wanting in inspiration, and he had too little been exposed to the kind of studies which uplift the soul and fill the imagination with great objects and great thoughts in order to make up for this deficiency" (MAR II, 102).

The artists themselves realized their limitations in this regard. The sculptor Etienne-Maurice Falconet, for example, spent his life trying to compensate for the rudimentary education of his youth. Despite his family responsibilities, an active professional life, and serious career problems, he decided to study Latin when he was nearing the age of thirty, and, through strenuous autodidactic application, he became proficient enough to publish his own annotated translation of three books of Pliny the Elder's *Naturalis historia* (1772). Far from limiting himself to Latin, he also studied Italian and Greek, as well as religion and philosophy. Nevertheless, his feeling of inadequacy remains evident: In his introduction to his *Réflexions sur la sculpture* (1761), he remarks: "As for the literary side of my essay, since the style of an artist carries absolutely no weight in the field of letters, my mistakes in this realm will not be contagious" (in Levitine, *The Sculpture of Falconet*, 1972, 64). The same gargantuan hunger for knowledge and intellectual self-assertion is echoed in the behavior of the great pastel portraitist Maurice-Quentin de La Tour. He was an irrepressible *touche-à-tout,* studying a little bit of everything: mathematics, geometry, physics, poetry, philosophy, politics, and medicine. He became so vain of his encyclopedic knowledge that, to quote Marmontel: "He was humiliated when one spoke to him of painting" (MAR II, 103).

Regardless of the question of its validity, the artists' reputation for being poor and lacking education was undoubtedly related to the ancient kinship of their profession with that of the lowly class of artisans. Theoretically, the problem of this vexing relationship was satisfactorily solved in the seventeenth century, with the founding of the prestigious Académie royale de peinture et sculpture; but, paradoxically, the question insidiously regains some of its immediacy during the age of the Enlightenment. In large measure it is a consequence of the disarray created by the bitter struggle between the Académie royale, dedicated to the concept of nobility and the purity of the arts, and the Académie de Saint-Luc, which clung to many of the traditions and privileges of the medieval guilds. On the surface the liberation of French art from everything that gave to it what Abbé Laugier called "an air and a character of trade" (*Manière de bien juger des ouvrages de peinture,* 1771, 250–51) was finally completed with the closing of the Académie de Saint-Luc in 1776, followed by the publication of the *Déclaration du Roy concernant les Arts de Peinture et Sculpture* (*Procès-verbaux de l'Académie,* 1777, VIII, 284–85).

This proclamation was meant to erase the last vestiges of the ancient kinship between artists and artisans. It asserted officially that painting and sculpture belong to the liberal arts, that they are noble, and that they should be "perfectly assimilated to letters, sciences, and other liberal arts." It also stated that painting and sculpture should be totally independent of artisans' organizations, and that they should not be "confused with mechanic arts." Nevertheless, traces of the old confusion lingered on obsessively throughout the eighteenth century and beyond. In the 1762 edition of its *Dictionnaire,* the Académie française defined *artist* as one who practices an art "where genius and hand must concur" (LEV-GRI 71). Although echoing many earlier "noble" conceptions of the arts, this definition is revealing because, by including the apparently innocuous word "hand," it gave the seal of the academy's authority to the idea that manual skill—that is, manual work—was an integral and indispensable part of the artist's activity. One of the hidden social implications of this point of view is brought to light by the definition of the word *artist* in the 1777 edition of Diderot's *Encyclopédie* (III, 580): "Appellation which is given to workmen who excel in those mechanic arts which presuppose intelligence." In bringing the artists closer to the crafts and referring to them as "workmen," this definition seems to ignore entirely the liberalizing clarification of the *Déclaration du Roy,* which was promulgated the very same year.

A telling late eighteenth-century discussion of this issue appeared in the article defining the word *artist* in Watelet's *Dictionnaire* (1792). After contrasting the artist and the artisan in terms of liberal versus mechanic arts, the article states:

> Thus, today, a smith, a carpenter, a mason are called *artisans,* and the painter, the sculptor, the engraver are called *artists.* However, this appellation is given neither to the poet, nor to the musician. This distinction is probably derived from the fact that the previously mentioned *artists* use, in the practice of their arts, and introduce, in their works, materials and processes which, sometimes, seem to bring them closer to *artisans,* while the poet and the musician only rely on conventional signs which have no relation to what is called *manual* work. (WAT-DIC I, 128)

It is curious to observe that at the turn of the nineteenth century many artisans—cooks, shoemakers, tailors, hairdressers—began to usurp the title of artist. For instance, the *Journal du Commerce* (17 November 1805) noted that, since shoemakers were now known to make drawings like tailors, "it is understandable that these gentlemen have a reason to call themselves artists"; while the *Gazette de France* (21 November 1807), speaking of the hairdressers' pretension to look to the paintings of antiquity for inspiration, affirmed: "Thus, the artists of the past did not have more talent than a wigmaker of today," and the same newspaper related that a hairdresser was heard exclaiming, like Correggio, *"Ed io anche sono pittore"* (and I also am a painter). Despite their evident satirical tone—about 1800 the pretentiousness of "l'artiste décrotteur" (bootblack) was a standard joke (Jean-Baptiste Pujoulx, *Paris à la fin du XVIIIe siècle,* 1801, 98–99)—such statements clearly acknowledged the growing pretensions of certain classes of artisans. Somewhat later, Antoine Caillot, exalting the quality of industrial productions, stated: "The concept of industry makes, day by day, such fruitful and rapid progress, that it is difficult to distinguish the artisan from the artist. Indeed! Why should this latter title be given to a mediocre draftsman and be denied to a skillful workman?" (Caillot, II, 139).

Thus, after having been confused with artisans for such a long time, the "true" artists—despite their official "liberation" in 1777—faced, at the beginning of the nineteenth century, a new form of the same unpleasant problem, with artisans actively striving to be recognized as artists. A particularly graphic illustration of the new artist-artisan relationship can be found in the changing reputation of signboard painting as an art form. In the eighteenth century the signboard artists' lack of talent was proverbial. Their professional ignorance actually inspired a proverb-play of Carmontelle, *La Rose rouge* (CAR-PRO, 1822, II, 259–78), which portrays a signboard specialist who can only paint red roses for his customers' shops. A definite change took place at the beginning of the nineteenth century, and C. de Mery, in his comments about the play, spoke of the large size, complicated subjects, variety, and artistic merit of the shop signs of his time. He observed: "Sometimes the sign-boards are worth more than the whole shop" (CAR-PRO, 1822, IV, lxj–lxij). Some of the implications of this new development had already been noted much earlier by Pujoulx (14–15):

> I know in Paris ten shop signs showing more talent than the works of such and such a painter of the so-called academy. . . .
>
> A beautiful sign-board in the rue Vivienne, will stop more people, in the space of four years, than a beautiful painting of Raphael has succeeded in doing since the two and a half or so centuries that it has been created.

The author offers advice to the artist: "Painters who aspire to public exhibitions, do not scorn the sign boards." Pujoulx's conclusion foretells some of the concepts of twentieth-century environmental urbanism:

> If the shop keepers of the beautiful quarters of Paris were to spend for their sign-boards a quarter of what the outside decorations of their shops cost them, there would be streets which would be transformed into pleasant art galleries. It is a dream! perhaps some day it will become a reality: why not?

These ideas were not entirely novel, since a few great eighteenth-century artists, such as Chardin and Watteau, are known to have painted some highly admired signboards. But such examples are rare. At the end of the eighteenth century, few painters would have willingly accepted to undertake such lowly commercial tasks. Even those who, according to an anonymous English traveler, were "destitute of employment" and compelled to furnish "new patterns" for "the paper-maker" (*Paris as It Was and as It Is*, 1803, I, 508) would have considered Pujoulx's "dream" no more than a cruel reminder of the old confusion of artist with artisan.

Thus, like the profession of actor, the profession of artist remained stigmatized for a long time. No degree of individual success, collective praise, or dithyrambic proclamation of the nobility of the arts could quite free the artists from some clinging suggestions of manual work. It is hardly surprising that average middle-class families were reluctant—a feeling often still expressed today—to let their children choose this profession, and the arts were "by necessity, compelled to confine the recruitment of their young militia to the classes in which want and ignorance are generally the most apparent" (WAT-DIC I, 133). The obvious solution, suggested by Sobry, was to direct "towards the cultivation of the Arts only the individuals who were born with a certain amount of wealth and who were capable of providing by their own means for the expenses that such a cultivation demands" (*Poétique des arts,* 1810, 480).

Endlessly varying with an artist's individual case and with each change in the century's conditions, the significance of these themes—poverty, lack of education, and manual work—brought into focus the question of the artists' admission "into general society." This subject shows an evolution that can be illustrated by a comparison of two points of view: that of Chevalier de Valory (1763) and that of Watelet (1792).

De Valory's ideas were developed in an unpublished manuscript, *S'il est plus avantageux aux artistes de vivre dans la retraite ou dans le commerce du monde* (MS 202–1, Bibliothèque de l'Ecole des Beaux-Arts, Paris), which was read at two different sessions (1763 and 1764) of the Académie royale (LEV-GRI 72). After chiding the misanthropic artist who yields to his dark imagination in the isolation of his studio, Valory invites artists to join the proper society. His invitation is unreserved, and, according to him, no time was ever more propitious to grant to the artists "the honorable rank they must hold in society." He enumerates the many benefits to be derived from an exposure to society life, recalls flattering historical precedents, and reassures the artists as to the welcome they can expect to receive in such a milieu. The artists, he is certain, are "men who will know how to compensate by a superior merit what they might be lacking in the advantages of manners," and they "will feel more at ease with the great than those who have no other superiority than that of wealth" (LEV-GRI 72–73).

The ideas of Watelet appear in several of the articles of his *Dictionnaire.* According to him, there was no longer any real need to tempt the artist to join the society into which he had already been admitted and where he appeared far more often than in the past (WAT-DIC I, 454–55). Yet the question of society's acceptance involved some ticklish problems, since the artists were exposed to the dangers of a disorderly life, to which they were drawn more frequently than people from other professions (WAT-DIC III, 592):

> The artists' inclinations . . . are often such as to make it difficult for them to comply to social obligations to which *consideration* is attached, because their over-lively and ever-exerted imagination naturally leads to a taste of freedom, independence . . . even wantonness of the mind. (WAT-DIC I, 454)

The artists must fight these dangerous tendencies, and Watelet reminds them:

> Men, whose occupations or functions attract the attention of the society in

which they live, are compelled to honor their position by upholding the virtues and the *decorum* which are held in particular esteem by this society. (WAT-DIC I, 248)

Thus toward the end of the eighteenth century, Valory's idea that the artists' social shortcomings would be compensated by the superiority of their professional merit was no longer taken for granted. For Watelet these shortcomings, far from being limited to minor lapses in propriety, encompassed some built-in problems that were related to the very nature of the artists' character. This brought up a note of caution: The artists could claim the right to join the ranks of society only if they were willing to accept their obligation to conform to the highest recognized standards of conduct. Increasingly modeled by clichés and stereotypes, the artist's image came to be seen in a somewhat patronizing, distrustful, rather matter-of-fact light.

In considering this question of the admission "into general society," one must of course also keep in mind that most artists—except a few who, like the Chevalier Pierre, held a title of nobility—were commoners. For this reason, neither their talent nor proper behavior in society could always protect them from unpleasant experiences, such as the humiliating exclusion of the painter Joseph Vernet from his noble patron's dining table (Théophile Silvestre, *Les Artistes français,* 1926, II, 60). The well-known episode of Voltaire's bastinado, ordered by the Chevalier de Rohan as a punishment for the writer's presumptuous behavior, shows that writers and poets were very far from being exempt from the scorn of the aristocracy, and one might be inclined to assume that the common frustrations experienced by the creative men of plebeian birth would have strengthened fraternal links between artists and men of letters. On the aesthetic plane such relations were indeed taken for granted; thus the critic-littérateur La Font de Saint-Yenne noted, echoing the endless references to the Horatian *Ut pictura poesis:* "Everybody knows the perfect affinity between the painter and the poet" (*Réflexions,* 1752, 198). However, the constant contacts between writers and artists, and the deluge of mutually complimentary statements, should not be accepted without qualification as proof that this "perfect affinity" extended to the social sphere. As a group, men of letters admired—or felt bound to admire—the works and the talent of artists, but they rarely considered these comrades-in-arms to be their true social equals. Their expression of admiration tended to be tempered by a feeling of condescension.

In order to understand the implications of these condescending attitudes, one must recall that during the eighteenth century most of the art critics were recruited from the ranks of the literati: In other words, as a rule it was the men of letters who were to pass judgment on the works of the proverbially uneducated, inarticulate artists in various Paris exhibitions. Yet these exhibitions, most particularly those of the Salon, insured public visibility to their participants and played a crucial role in the artists' career.

During the second half of the eighteenth century, the Salon became an arena to which a group of artists approved by the Académie royale came "every two years to be thrown to the beasts," to quote Chardin (Diderot, *Salon de 1765,* 1960, II, 58). It should be pointed out that the literati held that since everyone had accepted the Horatian sisterhood of art and literature, there was no reason why art should be spared the attacks that traditionally and indiscriminately befell literature. On their side the artists, who were often defenseless against such attacks, continued to repeat that men of letters should be disqualified as critics, since only those who practiced art were competent to speak about it.

These differences were of course colored by self-righteousness and distrust. The characteristic standpoint of the men of letters was expressed by La Font de Saint-Yenne:

> Nothing then is more certain than the fact that an Artist will not create a name for himself without the help of advice and criticism. Those of his fellow-artists will not always be the most trustworthy. Most of them will judge the beauty and the mistakes in his works according to their own self interest, their reputation, or their passions. They will pass judgement according to a servile attention to the rules of their art, always cold and sterile. . . . Their judgement can also be inaccurate because of a routine comparison with their own style of painting, which is often mediocre and uniform. It is with a much higher degree of certitude that the feelings of a disinterested spectator can be presented, a spectator who does not wield a brush and can thus pass judgement according to a natural taste enlightened by principles. (*Réflexions,* 1752, 190–91)

The opposite point of view, the point of view of the artist, is illustrated by Falconet in his *Réflexions sur la Sculpture* (in *Œuvres diverses,* Paris, 1787, III, 1), originally read in 1761 at the Académie royale. This sculptor states:

> No one is more attentive than I am to the opinions expressed in this Academy. Artists have often been encouraged there to share their reflexions on our art with our fellow academicians. It has also been said at this Academy that an artist should speak about art only when he is holding a pencil or a roughing-chisel in his hand and that he should leave the discussion of our talents to the enlightened amateurs.

But Falconet's irony yields easily to anger. In *D'Un Passage de Racine fils* (in *Œuvres diverses,* Paris, 1787, III, 168), he writes:

> I do not intend to take to task all the littérateurs who have not felt the eloquence of painting nor all those who have wanted to belittle it, but I happen to be facing one whose ideas on art are so incorrect that I cannot prevent myself from speaking out.

His essay is enriched with a lengthy footnote in which he ridicules—in a highly detailed historically documented rebuttal—Racine's assertion that "the artists are better paid than men of letters" (III, 167–70, note a).

Predictably, in such expressions of scarcely hidden or frankly open professional antagonism, the men of letters most often maintained the upper hand. Their criticisms proliferated, and they were widely read. They appeared in periodicals such as the *Mercure,* the *Année littéraire,* and the *Gazette de France;* in collections of Parisian news and gossip, such as Bachaumont's *Mémoires secrets;* or in a variety of independently published books and pamphlets, usually bearing titles such as *Réflexions, Sentiments,* or *Lettres.* The artists, whose sensibility was naturally bruised by even the most sedate comments about their works, multiplied protests and grievances. In 1787, for instance, the Académie royale decided to publish, at its own expense, a paper, which was then read at one of its sessions, aiming to expose "the abuse of unjust criticisms" (*Procès-verbaux de l'Académie,* 1787, IX, 339). In an ineffectual attempt to temper the acrimony of such exchanges, the government advised the artists that a contemptuous silence was the best answer to the literati's unfair attacks (André Fontaine, *Les Doctrines d'art en France,* 1909, 253). However, from Charles-Nicolas Cochin's *Les Misotéchnites aux enfers* (1763) to Anne-Louis Girodet's *La Critique des critiques* (1806), the succession of biting satirical pamphlets written by artists against the critics shows that the artists could not be easily placated by this plea for equanimity. This warfare often erupted into caricature, as can be exemplified by two anonymous engravings: one satirizing the ignorance of the artists (*Fig. 4*), the other that of the critics (*Fig. 5*). Not too surprisingly, Madame Geoffrin invited artists and writers separately to her suppers, on two different days—the first on Monday and the second on Wednesday (MAR II, 83).

To the various causes of frustration undermining the eighteenth-century artist's incorporation "into general society" must be added the disappointments, misunderstandings, and hidden hostility to which he was exposed in his contacts with the man of letters. This natural comrade-in-arms, who too often proved to be a false friend, clearly believed that the artist, with his insufficient education and professionally embarrassing connotations of manual work, belonged to a different and somewhat inferior social and cultural sphere. Insidiously, the implications of this difference came to color some of the pre-Romantic stances that began to emerge during the second half of the eighteenth century.

One of these new attitudes, generically described by Paul Van Tieghem as the "romantic posturing at the brink of precipices" (*Ossian en France,* 1917, I, 282), is particularly interesting, for it inspired a long-lived art-historical myth: the legend of Joseph Vernet tied to a mast in a storm.[2] The original episode is supposed to have taken place in 1734, while Vernet was sailing from Marseilles to Rome. During the crossing his ship was caught in a frightful storm, and, despite the general alarm, the fearless young artist asked the sailors to tie him to the mainmast on the bridge so he could contemplate the raging sea. Independently from the question of its historical veracity, the story underwent a significant development. In the very early versions, for instance, in the account of Pitra, published by Grimm in December 1789 (*Correspondance,* 1881, XV, 555), Vernet is said to have risked his life in order to *study* the angry sea, and to have memorized his experience in view of his own famous seascapes. About 1800 the explanation of the artist's daredevilry began to change, and, according to Pierre-Simon Ballanche (*Du Sentiment considéré dans ses rapports avec la littérature et les arts,* 1801, 102), Vernet was eager, above all, to *admire* "this living picture of terror and energy," exclaiming enthusiastically, "Oh! how beautiful this is!"

Curiosity in the presence of danger is common to both versions; yet they diverge on one essential point. In the early accounts Vernet—like Pliny the Elder, who risked his life to observe the catastrophe of Pompeii from his galley—is guided by his love for study, his motivation essentially utilitarian. In the later versions the painter—like Ulysses tied to the mast of his ship to listen to the Sirens' voices—is spurred by an expectation of delectation devoid of any practical purpose. This contrast cannot be understood solely in terms of an opposition between eighteenth-century rationalism and early nineteenth-century romantic emotionalism. One must point out that eighteenth-century writers and poets, like Evariste-Désiré-Desforges de Parny, who exposed himself voluntarily to danger during a violent storm while sailing in 1773 for Brazil (*Œuvres,* 1826, I, 447–48), could indulge without ridicule in Ulysses-like posturing with no reason other than that of self-conscious pleasure in sensing danger and overcoming fear. However, because of the prevailing stereotypes, such unwarranted heroics were unthinkable for an artist in the eighteenth-century. He could expose himself voluntarily to danger only when justified by a reasonable and useful purpose of study, that is, by his professional probity, following the example of explorers like La Pérouse, or scientists like Dolomieu.

Thus in the second half of the eighteenth century, unusual and unexplainable acts, or new culturally fashionable excesses of behavior, such as the "romantic posturing at the brink of precipices" permitted to the writer or poet, were not permissible for the artist. Before 1800 he was neither expected nor allowed to transcend the norm of middle-class conduct in the "poetic" manner allowed to the man of letters.

2

The Artist's Tribulations
Told in a Light Vein

The popular notoriety of the *Barbus* was anything but a historical accident. During the eighteenth century, because of the increasing number of artists and the increasingly conspicuous evidence of their social problems, themes of *la vie d'artiste* overflow from the realm of specialized biographies into the general cultural and popular folklore. The signs of this phenomenon appeared early in the century, as, for instance, in a playful epigram of the poet Jean-Baptiste Rousseau, apparently inspired by an episode in Salvator Rosa's life (quoted in Nougaret's *Anecdotes des beaux-arts,* 1776, I, 455):

> A Painter in his hovel
> Was scandalously entertaining gentle Chérubine.

> (Avec scandale un Peintre en son taudis,
> Entretenoit gentille Chérubine.)

During the second half of the century, the artist as a subject or main character was increasingly growing in importance. Thus he appeared as a central character in the productions of the *foire* theaters such as Louis Anseaume's *Le Peintre amoureux de son modèle,* performed in 1757 at the Théâtre de l'Opéra Comique de la Foire Saint-Laurent (published in 1759). Clearly inspired by the tradition of the commedia dell'arte, this play portrays two artists, the old master Alberti and his young pupil Zerbin, in love with the same woman, Laurette, their model. The old painter is portrayed as touchy, bizarre, and unsociable, while the young man is lazy, indolent, nonchalant, and sneering. Predictably, in this amorous contest youth triumphs.

It seems that for some time the interpretation of the theme of the artist's life or of the artist's character had been searching for a definition. Thus in some popular plays the artist is a colorless character who above all tries to ingratiate himself with his patrons. In Rochon de Chabannes's *La Manie des arts, ou la matinée à la mode,* staged in 1763 (REP, *Théatre du second ordre, Comédies en prose,* XIII, 199–244), the painter Du Coloris is merely a parasite: with the musician Allegro, he plots to flatter and delude the wealthy would-be amateur,

Forlise, who, with his pretensions to connoisseurship, is depicted as a cultural *bourgeois gentilhomme*. In Carmontelle's undated *Le Portrait* (CAR-PRO I, 80–102), the portraitist Bernard submits to every kind of humiliation to please his sitter, the comtesse de Mineville. His portrait is in turn praised and derided. Finally, rejected by the comtesse, the work is purchased by an amateur, the baron d'Orban, who compares the portraitist to Rembrandt and who also happens to have a frame that exactly fits the dimensions of Bernard's painting.

Progressively the subject is imbued with prevailing feelings of sentimentality and morality. In Mme de Beaunoir's *Le Sculpteur ou la femme comme il y en a peu,* staged in 1784 (COL 80, *Variétés,* III, 159–244), the sculptor Le Doux is represented as a victim of the artists' inclination toward the vices of the lower classes. The talented but weak young man is led by evil friends into drunkenness: Having neglected his art, his career is on the brink of collapse. He is eventually saved from catastrophe through the devotion of his wife and the benevolent generosity of his patron, the Comte d'Artiphile. Clément, the hero of Carmontelle's undated *Le Peintre et le mendiant,*[1] has only one problem: poverty. He can no longer trust landscape painting, his specialty, for his livelihood because the merchants of decorative wallpapers leave no room for his art in the apartments of the wealthy. The story has the quality of a fairy tale. The painter is in love with Javotte, but he dares not speak to her because he is destitute. Walking in the Luxembourg Gardens, he encounters a beggar, Duchemin; and because of the kindness shown by the artist, the beggar—who is actually Javotte's very rich father—arranges Clément's marriage and assures the success of his career.

Occasionally the artist's vicissitudes are depicted in a totally unreal light. In the duc de Nivernois's undated *Le Peintre aveugle (Œuvres posthumes,* 1807, II), the artist's blindness, which is the result of his illness, is the very cause of his success. The hero states: "I think that it is fortunate that I have lost my sight; the uniqueness of a blind man who paints portraits with a good likeness has brought me more clients since my accident than I had during the course of my life" (18). This painter demonstrates the truth of the physiognomical science:

> I had understood . . . that each nuance of character has a corresponding nuance of physiognomy. . . . I have tried, when I became blind, to paint portraits according to the detailed description which was given to me of the mood and the qualities of the sitters. . . . Today I am able to catch the likeness of the sitter with greater ease and certitude than I ever succeeded in achieving with two very good eyes. (21)

Doubtless Fabre d'Eglantine's *L'Intrigue épistolaire* (REP, *Comédies en vers,* XVI) is the most influential play of the late eighteenth century to portray an artist: Staged in 1791, it was often still performed during the early nineteenth century. The story is a simple one. The old and wealthy guardian Clénard tries to force his young ward, Pauline, to marry him. Pauline, of course, is in love with a younger man, Cléri, the brother-in-law of the historical painter Fougère. Clénard, a procurator acting on behalf of Fougère's creditors, tries to attach the possessions of the impoverished and improvident artist. The latter is entirely indifferent to worldly affairs, maintaining that his profession is above the prosaic aspects of the law: "Has Rembrandt or Carracci ever been seized?" (143). He scorns portrait painting, which could have helped him to earn a livelihood, and he proudly remains a historical painter (*Fig. 6*):

> Learn, Madame, that in a portrait,
> A thousand opulent faces are not worth one muscle of the Horatii. (146)

Fougère is a good family man, but he places his artistic integrity above all other considerations. He offers the first example of the image of the artist, totally indifferent to the material side of life, who is immersed in his inspiration. Fougère remains one of the archetypes of the nineteenth-century conception of the artist, and as such he is mentioned by authors as different as Joseph Pain (*Nouveaux tableaux de Paris,* 1828, II, 90) and Honoré de Balzac (*Pierre Grassou,* 1839).

Aside from the images of the artist's servility, sentimentalized poverty, and proud, intransigent dedication to his art, the eighteenth century also witnessed the beginning of what might be termed the artist's "Dutch characterization." This trend seems to have corresponded to the "rediscovery" of Alexis Grimou (see LEV-GRI). Grimou's personality is almost completely mythical, and his eighteenth-century biographies were based mainly on apocryphal sources. It is true that many of Grimou's paintings are preserved, and there is little doubt that he actually lived in the eighteenth century (1678–1733); but, with the exception of a few dates, practically nothing is known about his life or character. One could not find a more perfect case of a real eighteenth-century artist solely known through an eighteenth-century legend.

Grimou's mythical personality begins to coalesce in the 1770s, after more than forty years of neglect following his death. The rare early mentions are scanty and impersonal; Dézallier d'Argenville's otherwise detailed *Abrégé de la vie des plus fameux peintres* (1745, II, 442) allots only seven words to Grimou, and Jacques Lacombe's *Dictionnaire des Beaux-arts* (1766, 319) gives him eleven lines. The extent and suddenness of later eighteenth-century interest in this painter is evidenced by the fact that he was brought to light by two different authors, almost simultaneously but independently from each other. Thus in 1770 Henry Fuseli—who believed Grimou to be Swiss—devoted thirteen pages to him in his *Geschichte der besten Künstler in der Schweitz* (III, 15–27), and in 1776 Nougaret—who considered the artist to be French—granted him eleven pages of his *Anecdotes des Beaux-Arts* (II, 229–39). The latter fact is of some importance: The article on Grimou is the longest biography in the French section of Nougaret's book (the two most respected painters of the French tradition, Poussin and Le Sueur, are allotted six and two pages respectively). The critics' particular notice of Grimou was also reflected in his selection as one of the three French painters (with Santerre and Watteau) whose art was characterized as "romantique"—for the first time in

French art history (1792)—by Pierre-Charles Levesque (in WAT-DIC V, 359). The late eighteenth-century biographers differ on a number of details, but they show unequivocal agreement as to the basic makeup of Grimou's personality.

Above all else, the painter is depicted as a drunkard of epic proportions, and, in an anonymous engraving in Fuseli's *Geschichte*, he is characteristically staged behind a bottle, clenching a wine glass (*Fig. 7*). His death came as a consequence of a Pyrrhic victory in a two-day-long drinking duel (Mme de Beaunoir's sculptor Le Doux is almost a teetotaler in comparison). The theme of drunkenness is a canvas against which the vivid details of Grimou's personality were woven. Showing a marked aversion for well-bred society, he preferred to associate himself with inebriated companions and was supremely unconcerned with the matter of proper dress. His paintings were highly demanded, but he was indifferent to the management of his affairs, worked only in spurts, and often gave to his friend the wine merchant canvases commissioned by paying patrons. As a result, he remained continually in debt.

Grimou had a passion for independence (equaling that of Fabre d'Eglantine's painter Fougère) and was totally unimpressed by the rank of his patrons. For instance, despite his lack of money, he destroyed an unfinished painting, commissioned by a minister of state, simply because he had become bored with it. Grimou's sense of independence, buttressed with unassailable self-confidence, extended to the most influential institution of his profession. While waiting at the Académie royale for the outcome of the meeting that was to pass on his admission, he had the opportunity to study the works submitted by another candidate. Outraged by what he saw, he decided immediately to join the rival, less prestigious Académie de Saint-Luc. The painter's conceit was such that when he walked at night through the insecure streets of Paris he shouted "This is Grimou" (LEV-GRI 62) whenever he heard a noise, firmly convinced that his fame guaranteed him safety.

Grimou's eccentricity, which is noted by practically all his biographers after his "rediscovery," seems to have been alien to the French art-historical tradition before the appearance of this myth. Thus the apocryphal personality of Grimou offers the first example of a French eighteenth-century artist considered as a truly bizarre individual and, more specifically, the first example of a French eighteenth-century artist fictionalized as a full-fledged eccentric in his own period.

Naturally Grimou's legend echoes, in a general way, the eighteenth-century literary interest in odd personalities, but this literary trend, exemplified in Diderot's *Le Neveu de Rameau* (1762), provides no precedents for the particular *kind* of eccentricity ascribed to the painter. It is useful to consider its sources: According to Grimou's major eighteenth-century biographers, most of their information was compiled from material supplied by various artists. But these artists, for instance, Jean-Georges Wille, P. Davesne, and Jacques-Fabien Gauthier Dagoty, belonged to a much later generation and could not have known Grimou personally. Most probably their stories stemmed from old tales, gossip, and jokes nurtured in the Parisian studios.

It is more than likely that Grimou's colorful atelier tradition was shaped by his well-established reputation as the "French Rembrandt." To a degree this reputation can be explained by some of Grimou's subjects and by some aspects of his style. But it must also be viewed in the light of the eighteenth-century attitude toward Dutch painting in general, and toward Rembrandt in particular. During this period Rembrandt's personality was often referred to as bizarre; Jean-Baptiste Descamps noted that the great Dutch painter was "very singular" (*La Vie des peintres flamands,* 1754, II, 87), and Nougaret stated that "like most talented people, Rembrandt was bizarre and very capricious" (*Anecdotes,* 1776, II, 7). In view of the lack of information about Grimou, it was tempting to endow him posthumously with some traits of the Dutch master to whom he had already been linked through his art. Thus speaking about Grimou, Levesque remarks: "He developed a distinctive style of painting, which, nevertheless, in some regard, is related to that of Rembrandt, and his character was not less bizarre than that of this great painter" (in WAT-DIC IV, 576–777). Grimou's aggressively plebeian, occasionally vulgar behavior could also find a model in Rembrandt, who, according to Levesque's same text, "associated only with common people, and found pleasure only in crapulous pastimes." Because of Grimou's many paintings of drinkers, which include several self-portraits, the parallel was probably developed to embrace other painters of the seventeenth-century Netherlandish school (Adriaen Brouwer, with his notorious reputation for drinking and leading a disorderly life, is particularly suggestive). Thus during the last quarter of the eighteenth century, Grimou's "Dutch" personality seems to have unfolded to mirror his "Dutch" art: In Fuseli's *Geschichte* he is depicted in a typical Dutch manner, framed by an arched window with a projecting sill (*Fig. 7*).

It appears that Grimou's myth echoed a contemporary fashion that sought to create fantastic "Dutch" or "Flemish" characterizations. In England William Beckford's *Biographical Memoirs of Extraordinary Painters* (1780) exploited a similar vein, offering bizarre and often comical biographies of nonexistent Netherlandish artists, such as Og of Basan, Watershouchy, and Sucrewasser. It is possible that this fashion was related to the popularity of Descamps's *La Vie des peintres flamands* (1754), but it is certain that it also paralleled the growing general interest in Dutch painting. After all, Rembrandt was mentioned with admiration both in Carmontelle's *Le Portrait* and Fabre d'Eglantine's *L'Intrigue épistolaire.*

About 1800 the "Dutch" fashion or trend, which was echoed in Grimou's myth, began to grow into an important semipopular literary genre. This is understandable, for Netherlandish "lives" provided biographers and littérateurs with historical personalities and colorful anecdotes that lent themselves more naturally than others to the spell of the clichés surrounding the image of the artist. An indiscriminate borrowing from such sources—as in the case of the legend of Grimou—could have appeared somewhat *outré.* But the oddity of Netherlandish "lives" could be easily mended and made more palatable to the French taste of the period with a few moralizing accents and some references to the current *sensibilité.*

These suggestions are clearly apparent in Armand-Louis-Maurice Séguier's *Le Maréchal ferrant de la ville d'Anvers,* a short play performed in 1799 at the Théâtre du Vaudeville (published the same year). Inspired by the biography of

Quentin Massys, this vaudeville was the first instance of a popular stage production introducing a historically known Netherlandish artist as its central subject.

The play underlines the social distance separating the artist from the artisan. The young Quentin Massys (renamed Robert) is in love with Augusta, the daughter of the painter Wanderwood; but Wanderwood—a successful artist who is proud of his noble profession—rejects this suitor as a prospective son-in-law because he is a mere blacksmith. Robert's willingness to become an artist appears unrealistic to Wanderwood, and having decided that Augusta should marry someone of his own profession, he organizes a contest to find the most talented young artist who could be worthy of his daughter. But guided by love, Robert, who had secretly mastered the art of painting, wins the contest by unexpectedly producing his portrait of Augusta.

Constantly glorifying the painter's profession—and actually exhibiting a real drawing of Greuze as a work of Wanderwood—the play multiplies disparaging comments about artisans. For instance, Wanderwood exclaims:

> Do you really think that a Painting can be made
> Like a night cap?   (*Le Maréchal ferrant,* 6)

He also wistfully alludes to the increasing number of people who try to become artists: "Soon there will no longer be any glory in the arts; everybody tries his hand at it" (8). Both Wanderwood and Massys are definitely, and proudly, "Netherlandish," but they are virtuous, solid citizens, neither drunkards like Grimou nor lost to the everyday world like Fougère. These characterizations are less colorful than those of the earlier plays and anecdotes of the century. However, the vaudeville contains some telling references to the failure of the untalented artist and to the stupidity of the incompetent critic: A painting of thistles by Vanderberg, one of Wanderwood's pupils, is devoured by an ass, which had been chosen by Vanderberg himself as the true connoisseur of his art.

A far lustier characterization of the artist can be found in *Teniers,* a very successful vaudeville of Jean-Nicolas Bouilly and Joseph Pain, performed in 1800 at the same theater (published an IX). Teniers (probably David Teniers II), who, despite his celebrity, is forced to sell his work at a low price, feigns death; and, as a result, the amateurs eagerly purchase his paintings at any cost.

While his wife manages his affairs in Brussels, Teniers hides incognito in a small village, where he assumes the fictitious personality of Dominique the house painter. Constantly drinking, and courting the wife of the local innkeeper, the artist leads a gay, carefree life. He does not hesitate to invoke historical precedents:

> Thus Callot, Tintoretto
> In turn knew how to paint and how to drink. (*Teniers,* 6)

While working as a house painter, Teniers competes with the ridiculous Duvernis, the untalented, comically pretentious, near-illiterate village dauber, to paint the signboard of the village inn. The victorious Teniers shows great generosity; he gives his signboard, without remuneration, to the innkeeper and buys a house for the village fiddler, who is in love with the innkeeper's daughter. Eventually the painter is rediscovered by the archduke Leopold, who lavishes his munificence on him (despite the fact that the artist does not act as a courtier), and the vaudeville ends with a *tableau vivant,* reproducing Tenier's *Village Fête.*

On the whole the story points to the artist's difficulties in being appreciated in his own lifetime, to the envy that surrounds him, to his pride, generosity, and strong inclination to indulge in drinking and in the other amusements of the lower classes.

The plot of *Teniers* directly recalls that of *Rembrandt, ou La Vente après décès,* written by Etienne, Morel, Servières, and Moras, which also appeared in 1800 in the Théâtre des Troubadours (published an IX). Here again an artist feigns death in order to be rediscovered and achieve success.

The two plays reveal, nevertheless, some significant dissimilarities. Rembrandt "has been subjected to all kinds of misfortune; he has never ceased to be a target for the injustice of his contemporaries" (*Rembrandt,* 3), and he is "a kind of an odd character, misanthropic and jealous" (28), obviously very different from the happy-go-lucky, merrily drinking Teniers. The choice of his profession is even questioned by his wife, who tells him that instead of becoming an impoverished painter he should have followed in the footsteps of his father, the miller. But notwithstanding the question of the artist's poverty, his posthumous rediscovery is presented more in terms of the just recognition of his talent than in those of a financial success. Reading the *gazette* [sic] that announces the false news of Rembrandt's death, his wife observes: "Hardly has he breathed his last breath that even his enemies are celebrating his memory and placing him in the ranks of the greatest painters" (3).

The vaudeville also alludes to the vexing problem of the artist's exploitation, which is intimated by the vulturelike Forbeck, the grotesque, hypocritical art dealer: "After all, what do I care about talent? I would easily buy for twelve hundred florins the worst possible painting if I were sure of being able to sell it for fifteen hundred tomorrow. The painter whom I consider the best is the one who has the greatest popularity" (19). The image of the poor, exploited, misunderstood, forgotten artist is emphasized here much more dramatically than in the vaudeville *Teniers.* Alluding to the writers' neglect of the painter, the opening lines of *Rembrandt* point out that while Scarron, Piron, Regnard, Dancourt, David Garrick, Frederick the Great, and Voltaire had inspired theatrical plays, "in these portraits, one cannot find Rembrandt, who could paint them so well" (2).

The concept of the neglected artist inspires some unexpected nationalistic remarks. Thus Surval, a French nobleman, observes with some melancholy: "The poor French will always be the dupes of charlatans of the entire world; a name ending in *i* or in *a* [a clear reference to Italian artists] is sufficient to turn everyone's head." For this reason:

> One rejects the genius
> Of which France was the cradle. (19)

Evidently this chauvinistic attitude does not apply to the Netherlands. Speaking about Gérard Dou's *Dropsical Woman,* Rembrandt, adopting an incongruously prophetic mode, evokes the glorious arrival of this celebrated masterpiece in the Louvre (1798) and associates it, rather erroneously, with the victories of Napoleonic arms:

> I see powerful sovereigns
> Adorning with it illustrious museums
> I see triumphant nations
> Placing it among their trophies. (25)

Despite the prevailing "Dutch" fashion, popular plays were not confined to the Netherlandish image of the artist. However, the appearance of artists from other nations is most often given a secondary importance. This is the case with *Le Tableau des Sabines,* by de Jouy, Longchamps, and Dieulafoy, which opened in 1800 at the Théâtre de l'Opéra-Comique (COL 74, *Vaudevilles,* III). For the sake of the plot, two of the characters disguise themselves as foreign painters, one pretending to be Italian, the other English. The play also includes Morose, a "real" English painter. In the first two cases the national characterization is limited to comical foreign accents; while in the third, the English origin is revealed by a sullen disposition, denoted by the name Morose, and by a tendency to indulge in unfair criticism directed against David's painting (*The Sabine Women*). The most interesting of such international vignettes is probably that of Morillos, the seventeenth-century Spanish painter introduced in Dieulafoy's *Le Portrait de Michel Cervantès,* presented in 1802 at the Théâtre Louvois (COL 48, *Comédies en prose,* IX). Morillos's nationality—colored by a sweeping characterization of Spanish art—is revealed through the ridicule cast on his predilection for gloomy subjects. Morillos states, for instance: "I am bringing to his [the duke of Lerme's] young wife, who is chagrined by the vapors, this little entombment of Christ in order to try to entertain her" (396). The play also contains a revealing statement that, bringing to mind Fabre d'Eglantine's Fougère, applies to artists of all nationalities. Thus Morillos's servant remarks:

> Painters have this in common with poets and musicians, that they are deceived more easily than all other men. Their mind is never of this lowly world; always busy with plans and fanciful ideas, they don't understand anything in the common affairs of life. (465–66)

This interest in foreign painters should not give the impression that French artists were forgotten. Given fictitious or anonymous personalities, French artists often appear in the comedies and vaudevilles of the turn of the nineteenth century. They are introduced in a great variety of roles, but in most cases they merely perpetuate established characterizations. For instance, in *Le Peintre dans son ménage,* by Jacques André Jacquelin and A. M. Lafortelle, performed in 1799 at the Théâtre des jeunes artistes and published the same year, the painter Aufinello (a pun for spirits-and-water) is almost a replica of Fabre d'Eglantine's famous Fougère. Predictably, numerous plays continue to repeat, with minor variations, the previously mentioned characterizations of the ignorant dauber, the rapacious art dealer, and the incompetent critic. However, the artist has now become a familiar stage character who can be given conventional or comical parts that are not necessarily related to his profession. Some of these roles are inconsequential caricatures, such as the painter disguised as a woman in *Le Beaunois à Paris,* a vaudeville by René-André Chazet and François-Denis Thesigni (reviewed in JD, 23 Pluviôse, an IX [12 February 1801]), or the insane painter of the anonymous and unpublished vaudeville *La Maison des Fous* (1801), who maintains that painting should be limited to only three colors (JD, 4 Floréal, an IX [24 April 1801]). Others belong to old theatrical stock-in-trade. In Jean-François Roger's *Caroline, ou Le Tableau,* performed in 1800 at the Théâtre français (COL 31, *Comédies en vers,* XIII), the painter Dubreuil, a knowledgeable art expert, is staged essentially as the traditional "family friend." Similarly, in Jean-Nicolas Bouilly's *Une Folie,* performed in 1802 at the Théâtre de l'Opéra-Comique (COL 64, *Opéras-com. en prose,* VII), Cerberti is a successful painter, but he is given the time-honored role of the rich old tutor in love with his beautiful young ward (who herself is in love with a dashing officer).

While a number of French artists of all periods—for instance, David (in *L'Intrigue épistolaire*) or Claude Lorrain, Joseph Vernet, and Pierre-Narcisse Guérin (in *Caroline ou Le Tableau*)—are mentioned in contemporary plays, none of these theatrical productions honors a real French artist with a central part comparable to the role granted to some Netherlandish painters. The appearance of a real, historically known French artist as a central character marks the turning point of the genre. Long before Jacques Callot (*Callot à Nancy,* vaudeville of Dumolard, 1813) and Jean Cousin (*Angéla, ou L'Atelier de Jean Cousin,* opéra by G. Montcloux d'Epinay and François-Adrien Boieldieu, 1814), this particular honor was given to the comparatively obscure eighteenth-century landscape painter Simon-Mathurin Lantara (1729–78).[2]

During the first third of the nineteenth century, Lantara inspired at least three different plays: in 1804, 1809, and 1831. Without doubt, the most important was the production of 1809, *Lantara ou le peintre au cabaret,* performed at the Théâtre du Vaudeville, which combined the talents of four specialists: Barré, Picard, Radet, and Desfontaines. The text was published twice (Paris, Fages, 1809, and in COL 73, *Vaudevilles,* II). Its plot is simple: Lantara, a destitute painter, discovers that his daughter and the son of Jacob, a wealthy art dealer, are secretly in love. Consequently the painter invites the merchant to lunch at the inn of the Jardin des plantes to discuss the marriage of their children. Jacob, who views such a marriage as a misalliance, disdainfully rejects the idea and leaves Lantara to eat his *déjeuner* alone with the model Belletête. The poor artist, unable to pay his bill, draws the portrait of Belletête and asks the innkeeper to sell this work for a *louis* to Jacob. But Jacob is willing to spend only twelve francs, and the artist, filled with indignation, tears up his own drawing. Later in the story Lantara makes another drawing, representing his daughter and her lover, that stirs great admiration and intensive bidding from Jacob and other art merchants. Finally, the painter sells this drawing to Jacob, to whom he promises the exclusivity of his production on the condition that the art dealer will agree to the marriage.

In this vaudeville Lantara is depicted neither as a dauber nor as a misunderstood artist. His talent is recognized by all, the uneducated innkeeper as well as specialized professionals such as art dealers. This talent does not protect him from poverty, but Lantara's destitution is the price he pays for his idealism, for he scorns money and refuses to prostitute his art:

> I would rather destroy my works a thousand times
> Than see them debased for an instant. (1809 ed., 29)

Idealism notwithstanding, Lantara exhibits deep rancor toward the people who exploit his talent, and retorting to Jacob, who criticizes his shabby appearance, declares with bitterness:

> . . . I would be a little less poor
> If you were a little less rich. (12)

This resentment against rapacious art merchants, apparent in some of the earlier vaudevilles, echoes an old tradition exemplified in an anonymous eighteenth-century painting (possibly by Louis Watteau de Lille): *Art Dealers, Restorers of Paintings, Paying Homage to the Good Thief (Fig. 8).*[3]

However, Lantara has many engaging qualities. He is a loving father, he is very sensitive, his word is sacred, he is not condescending to the lower classes, and he loves to sing. He is an appealingly improvident eccentric who is affected with only one vice, drinking, a weakness explained by his inherent melancholy. Lantara's characterization is not really modeled after Chateaubriand's René, but the play nevertheless is imbued with a subtle feeling of sadness, which is accented by the building of La Pitié—probably alluding to the painter's death in the hospital—depicted on the backdrop.

Lantara brings to mind old stereotypes and earlier theatrical characterizations: Indeed, this role is very close to being the French counterpart of the hero of *Teniers.* But while none of the traits of Lantara's vaudeville were novel in 1809, it was the first time these qualities had been brought together, combined in the same character, in order to depict a historically known French painter on the popular stage.

This "national" factor, as well as the growing nostalgia for the good-natured peacefulness, which was supposed to characterize the *ancien régime* in the midst of the uncertain times of the post-Revolutionary era, was the major reason for the great popularity of the vaudeville. Its success can also be explained by the play's Rostand-like mixture of lively wit and melancholy charm, the performance of the actor Joly (*Fig. 9*)—who gave to the role of Lantara "the drunkenness of an artist, almost a touch of nobility, with a sense of enthusiasm" (Dumersan, *Chants et chansons,* n.d.,

15)—and by the attractive music of Joseph-Denis Doche, which would remain popular through a large part of the nineteenth century and would be borrowed in two of Béranger's songs (*Le Printemps et l'automne* and *Qu'elle est jolie!*).

The success of the vaudeville does not explain, however, why its authors chose Lantara for its central role. After all, the eighteenth century offered a variety of other equally colorful candidates who could have provided a far better-known historical label for the first popular stage image of the French artist (Watteau, Gabriel de Saint-Aubin, etc.). Doubtless this choice was determined by a legend that, despite Lantara's obscurity, began to grow almost immediately after his death. In its general lines the artist's mythical characterization, which was initiated with the amateurs' compassionate rediscovery of his pitiful life, had been established by Bachaumont's widely read *Mémoires secrets* (XIII, 8 January 1779, 287–88):

> Lantara is one of those obscure and unhappy artists whose reputation becomes known only after death. He was born with the instincts of a genius . . . and only on the strength of his talent, without education, he had succeeded in reaching in his art an astounding perfection. . . . Ruthless masters sold his works, attributed them to themselves, and, not content in appropriating the profit, succeeded in thus making a reputation for themselves.

The legend was soon enriched with an anonymous quatrain—endlessly quoted in the nineteenth century—supposedly written upon the legal entry of the painter's death, in the hospital of La Charité:

> I am the painter Lantara
> Faith was my book
> Hope made me live
> And Charity buried me.
> (Registre de l'hôpital de la Charité, 22 December 1778)

This characterization corresponds to the spirit of an early portrayal of Lantara "from nature" by Louis Watteau de Lille (*Fig. 10*).

However, one can observe an evolution. The earliest biographical mentions, reflecting the vogue of "teary sensibility," merely spoke of a forgotten, cruelly exploited, destitute, highly talented, childlike autodidact. About 1800, under the influence of Sébastien Mercier's Zola-like naturalism, Lantara began to acquire a reputation of incredible improvidence, a fickle mind, sordid shabbiness, and overall oddity—a reputation so widespread that it was evoked in newspapers and pamphlets in reference to contemporary events. Undergoing a process of sentimentalization, the painter was eventually endowed with a personality à la Murger, a devil-may-care, drinking, lazy, poor, but merry, lovable bohemian (*Fig. 11*). About the middle of the century Lantara was recognized as the proverbial archetype of the bohemian artist.

The vaudeville, needless to say, played a crucial role in the crystallization of the Lantara legend, but it is clear that in portraying Lantara as their hero the authors chose a historically known painter whose apocryphal character embodied most conveniently the many clichés and stereotypes that shaped the image of the artist (Charles Blanc, article on Lantara, *Ecole française,* II, 1862).

On the whole, at the turn of the nineteenth century, two major popular images coalesce: Lantara and Fougère. Fougère, the artist totally lost in his art, will evolve into a bizarre and tragic silhouette, which probably influenced Balzac's *Le Chef-d'œuvre inconnu* and Zola's *L'Œuvre.* Failing to incite a comparable literary filiation, Lantara, the carefree bohemian, succeeds nevertheless in retaining much longer the original connotation as a truly popular stereotype.

3

The Artist as a Respectable Hero

Clichés notwithstanding, artists had every reason to preserve an appearance of social conformity and to maintain some regard for their own standing. It is obvious that few of them would have relished publicly corroborating, by their behavior, the embarrassing image that was beginning to form around their profession. Popular stereotypes, such as those characterized by Fougère and Lantara, could inspire amusement, astonishment, condescension, and even commiseration, but they could hardly command respect.

The situation involved a paradox, for the artists were aware of the unmistakable signs of the layman's growing interest in their profession. Despite disparaging or humiliating stereotypes, this interest was demonstrated concretely by the crowds invading art exhibitions; the increase of writings on art (ranging from scholarly studies and biographies to collected anecdotes and satirical pamphlets); and the previously noted increasing frequency and importance of the role given to the artist—as a subject—on the popular stage. In fact, the practice of the arts came to enjoy a certain fashion in the *comme il faut* circles. For instance, the *Journal des Dames et des Modes* (5 July 1806) noted:

> Never have young men been so slandered and never have they followed so sensible a line of conduct. Little by little, they are giving up music and dance for the sake of less frivolous arts. Today, their time is divided between painting and chemistry. Painting, especially, is in fashion, and there is no young man of good taste who after buying his high quality paints and brushes at the *Palette de Rubens* in the rue de Seine . . . does not flatter himself to have brought back from there the talent of David, Vincent, or even that of Rubens himself.

This fashion involved both sexes, and the same newspaper adds: "Today young ladies are given a box of assorted paints and crayons, just as twenty years ago, they would have been given a work-basket." Explaining the increase in the number of drawing teachers, Caillot points to the fact that

> for the last twenty-five years, a general need to study the art of drawing has been in evidence not so much in view of a pleasant distraction than as a means

to fully appreciate the great artists' masterpieces of engraving, painting, and sculpture. And most fathers enjoying a certain financial comfort would think that they had given their children an incomplete education if they had not provided them with the opportunity to learn how to draw a landscape or some heads. (II, 261)

On a different plane, the increasing interest in the artists' profession can be illustrated by the account of the funeral of the painter Jean-Baptiste Greuze, published in the *Journal des Débats* (28 March 1805). Commenting on the disappointing fact that the ceremony attracted only a small number of artists and friends, the writer remarks that the artist's hearse was "almost always surrounded with very little luster" and asks:

> Can one find a more effective way of honoring genius than to inspire a noble emulation, to encourage talent, to see a crowd of the most prestigious men of the state hastening to accompany to the grave the remains of these privileged beings whose lives were a blessing of Providence, a source of glory for mankind?

The article concludes with a reference to historical precedents, such as the ultimate honors paid by Francis I to Leonardo da Vinci and the homage given by the British lords to the remains of Sir Joshua Reynolds.

The early nineteenth-century elite's changing attitude toward the artists' profession was also reflected in the discussion of Joseph-Jérôme-Le Français de La Lande's list of famous people who died during the year 1806. This list followed the order of the relative importance of various professions, and artists were given the sixth place, after scientists, physicians, politicians, military men, and littérateurs. Aside from the surprising fact that artists were included at all in such a categorization, it is even more curious to note that La Lande's placement of littérateurs and artists at the bottom of his list was indignantly challenged by the *Journal de l'Empire* (1 January 1807).

Such discussions of ranking and, for that matter, any kind of rank—except perhaps the very first—could not have been particularly soothing to artists. They painfully realized that the generally increasing interest in their profession, now officially assimilated into "letters, sciences, and other liberal arts," did little in reality to shield them from the daily mortification of popular stereotypes. The artists were undoubtedly ready to accept as a credo the most exalted conceptions of their profession (such as Goethe's *Künstlers Apotheose,* which appeared in 1790, or the passage in Leonardo's *Paragone,* where the Renaissance master affirmed that it was fitting to call painting "the grandchild of nature and related to God") and to extend the notion of the quasi-divine nature of their creativity, beyond painting, to all their other specialties.

Omitting the legend of Saint Luke (who was supposed to have painted the portrait of the Virgin from nature), the glorification of the artists' profession could be suitably expressed in a number of subjects borrowed from classical antiquity. It is certain, for instance, that the miracle performed by Venus for the benefit of the sculptor Pygmalion, which gave life to one of his statues with which he had fallen in love (Ovid, *Metamorphoses,* X), the incredible honor paid to Apelles by Alexander the Great, who rewarded his favorite painter by yielding to him his favorite concubine (Pliny the Elder, *Naturalis historia,* XXXV) (*Fig. 12*), and the touching story of Dibutade, who invented drawing and clay modeling by outlining on a wall the shadow cast by her lover (Pliny the Elder, *Naturalis historia,* XXXV) (*Fig. 13*) offered well-known themes celebrating the immortality of the arts in an amorous context. During the eighteenth and nineteenth centuries, such episodes of the art-historical golden legend—in which the triumph of love paralleled that of the artist—were multiplied ad infinitum in the visual arts, literature, and drama. It is true that here and there one can observe variants conceived independently from any question of love. Thus François-André Vincent revived, in 1789, the essentially "professional" theme in *Zeuxis Choosing as His Models the Most Beautiful Maidens of Crotona* (Louvre); in 1800 Jean Broc decided to represent an equally "professional" theme in *The School of Apelles* (*Fig. 24*); and in 1806 Nicolas-André Monsiau depicted a "society" scene in *Aspasia Conversing with the Most Famous Men of Athens* (Louvre), a group that includes Phidias and Parrhasius. However, such subjects were comparatively rare: Most classically inspired iconography devoted to the arts was endowed with erotic resonance. For these reasons and because of the somewhat mythological fame of the artists of antiquity, these themes could hardly alleviate the social anxieties that permeated the profession at the turn of the century.

The art of what was often called the "modern" period, that is, the art history of comparatively recent times (beginning with the Renaissance), seemed to offer a far greater number of unexplored possibilities for the glorification of the artist. In fact, a few examples of this approach appeared in the sixteenth and seventeenth centuries, for instance, Federico Zuccaro's *Apotheosis of the Artist,* executed in 1598 for the Palazzo Zuccari, or Giorgio Vasari's decorations for the Sala di Cosimo il Vecchio, representing Cosimo with Donatello, Ghiberti, Fra Angelico, and other artists.[1] In France Vasari's idea was borrowed by Jacques Sarrazin. In the cenotaph of the Prince de Condé, commissioned in 1648 for the Church of Saint-Paul-Saint-Louis (now in the Musée Condé, Chantilly), he introduced a *Triumph of Fame* (a bronze relief), bringing together Gaston d'Orléans, Condé, Raphael, Correggio, Bernini, and Michelangelo, whose hand rests on Sarrazin's arm. But these early examples remained generally unnoticed, and, rather surprisingly, the first French example of a notably dramatic episode in the life of a "modern" artist was provided by Charles Eisen's *Signorelli Painting His Dead Son* (exhibited in 1752 and 1762 at the Académie de Saint-Luc, and in 1783 at the Salon de la Correspondance). Eisen's conception, derived from Vasari, suggests some kinship with the tragic mode of the legend of Parrhasius, who is said to have painted the torture of Prometheus, using as a model a live slave being devoured by a real vulture

(Nougaret, I, 195), and the even stranger apocryphal accounts asserting that either Michelangelo (Nougaret, I, 308–9) or Giotto (Salgues, III, 49) would actually have crucified a man in order to paint the crucified Christ. Despite the fact that Eisen's *Signorelli* has disappeared, it is important to remark that it shows that a French painter—long before the pictorial dramatizations of artists' lives produced by an Englishman such as John Hamilton Mortimer (in 1776)—chose to depict the pathetic theme of the artist's superhuman, indeed inhuman, devotion to his art. This is the very type of subject that will inspire, much later, Léon Cogniet's *Tintoretto Painting His Dead Daughter* (1843, Musée de Bordeaux) and, under various forms, will reappear in Gustave Flaubert's *L'Education sentimentale* (1869) and Emile Zola's *L'Œuvre* (1886).

In glorifying the artist by showing the unique character of creative genius, Eisen's *Signorelli* implicitly stresses the artist's alienation from the accepted range of human feelings. Such a theme could not of course have provided a satisfactory channel for the social aspirations of the arts. A more universally understandable assertion of the importance of the artist's status appeared in François-Guillaume Ménageot's *Leonardo da Vinci Dying in the Arms of François Premier* (1781, Amboise, Hôtel de Ville). This deathbed definition of the artist's triumph will be used repeatedly at the turn of the nineteenth century. Nicolas-André Monsiau, for instance, applied this formula in *The Death of Raphael* (1804, now lost), as did Pierre-Nolasque Bergeret in the *Honors Rendered to Raphael After His Death* (1806, Malmaison, Château). In these compositions the death of a great artist is endowed with an importance that recalls the death of a philosopher, like Socrates, or a military leader, like Du Guesclin. But above all, the great artist is glorified here by the exalted rank of his mourning patrons and friends (the king, the pope, etc.), rather than by his own creative achievements. Beyond the deathbed theme, countless episodes inspired by the life of famous "modern" artists appeared in a variety of interpretations, revealing the great man's proud simplicity (Monsiau's *Poussin Accompanying Cardinal Massimi to the Door,* 1806, now lost), the assertion of his talent in adverse circumstances (François-Marius Granet's *Stella in Prison,* 1809, Pushkin Museum, Moscow), or his amorous life (Ingres's *Raphael and the Fornarina,* 1814, Fogg Art Museum, Harvard University, Cambridge).[2] But such subjects acquire an anecdotal quality, alien to that of a triumph, which echoes, with increasing frequency, the clichés surrounding the "low" image of the artist.

The pleasure and reassurance that artists could derive from triumphant or edifying episodes which they could find in the lives of their great antique and "modern" predecessors found little justification in the popular culture of the 1800s. It is true that the artist's image was not always totally disfigured by clichés and that, on occasion, he was depicted in conventionally favorable terms. Nevertheless, when the artist was not depicting himself and when he was not personally directing the glorification of his own profession, he was seldom given heroic, fashionable, or flatteringly attractive roles. A telling example of what could be considered, in a

1. François Boucher, *The Painter*, 1752, engraving by Marie-Madeleine Igonet.

2. Jean-Jacques Spoëde, *The Dean of Painters* (Beaunureau), engraving by J. Guélard.

3. Etienne Jeaurat, *A Painter Moving,* 1755, engraving by Claude Duflos.

4. Anon., *The Drawing Teacher*, engraving.

5. Anon. (Anne-Louis Girodet ?), *The Great Ragpicker-Critic of the Salon of 1806*, engraving.

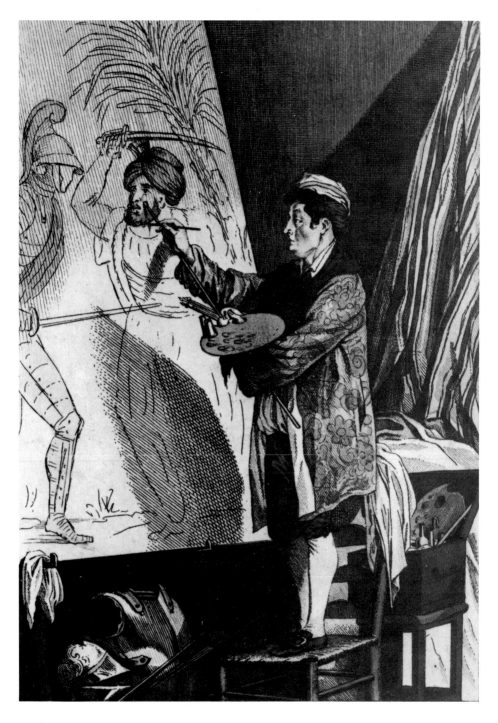

6. Claude-Nicolas Malapeau, *The Actor Dugazon in the Role of M. Fougère,* engraving. From Fabre d'Eglantine, *L'Intrigue épistolaire,* frontispiece, Paris, 1791.

7. Anon. (Johann Rudolf Schellenberg ?), *Portrait of Grimou,*
engraving. From Henry Fuseli, *Geschichte der Besten Künstler in der
Schweiz,* Zurich, 1770, III, 15.

8. Anon. (Louis-Watteau de Lille ?), *Art Dealers, Restorers of Paintings, Paying Homage to the Good Thief,* oil on canvas. Musée Carnavalet, Paris.

9. Anon. (Joly ?), *The Actor Joly in the Role of Lantara,* engraving (from Barré, Picard, Radet, and Desfontaines, *Lantara ou le peintre au cabaret,* frontispiece, Paris, 1809).

Je suis le peintre Lantara ; L'Espérance me fesait vivre,
La Foi m'a tenu lieu de livre, Et la Charité m'enterra.

10. François-Louis-Joseph Watteau de Lille, *Lantara*, 1776, engraving by Laurent Guyot.

11. Charles-Joseph Traviés, *Lantara*, engraving by Jean Geoffroy (from Théophile Marion Dumersan, *Chansons nationales et populaires de France,* Paris, 1851).

12. Etienne-Maurice Falconet, *Apelles and Campaspe*, 1765, marble. Private collection.

13. Charles Le Brun, *Dibutade,* engraving by François Chauveau.

14. François Maradan, *She Was Drawing, Seated on a Tomb,* engraving. From Charles Nodier, *Le Peintre de Saltzbourg,* frontispiece, Paris, 1803.

popular sense, a "pleasant" characterization of the artist is provided by Colonel de Francarville, the leading man in *Fanchon la vielleuse* (produced in 1803 at the Théâtre du Vaudeville, COL 73, *Vaudevilles,* II). The idea of the plot somewhat recalls that of Molière's *Le Sicilien ou L'Amour peintre* (1668). In the immensely popular *Fanchon la vielleuse,* produced by the authors of *Teniers,* the wealthy, wellborn colonel assumes the fictitious personality of the painter Edouard in order to win the love of Fanchon, the beautiful, successful, wealthy, generous, but low-born hurdy-gurdy player. Edouard displays many wonderful qualities, such as honesty, courage, and wit, but while courting Fanchon, he asks:

> How can it be that you, who are living in affluence, surrounded by esteem, sought after by the most brilliant men of Paris and of the Court, have chosen me, who must make my livelihood with nothing but my paint brushes? (*With emphasis*) For, after all, I am nothing but a painter? (204–5)

Edouard's characterization as a painter goes beyond this conventional allusion to the difficulties of his profession. Thus one wonders what artists in 1803 may have felt when reading the description of this character: "He must show the man of quality under the guise of a young painter carried away by a passion for which he will make the greatest sacrifices" (174).

Another example of social ambivalence, even more significant than the painter in *Fanchon,* appears in the characterization of Maurice in the vaudeville *Le Peintre français à Londres,* written by Barré, Radet, Desfontaines, and Bourgeuil (produced in 1802 at the Théâtre du Vaudeville). The French painter Maurice, working in London, borrows money from Durocher, an art dealer, to pay his gambling debts. However, the painter is unable to repay the merchant: Consequently Durocher, in order to force Maurice to work for him, tries to have the artist imprisoned. Meanwhile, the wealthy Lord Solnen asks Maurice to paint the battle of Aboukir (an English victory over the French) for a large sum of money; but the painter, whose fame rests on his painting of the battle of Boulogne (a French victory), patriotically declines such a treasonable commission. Maurice's affairs are settled when he agrees to paint Lord Solnen's portrait.

While habitual gambling is more acceptable than habitual drunkenness, it must be noted that in a few cases the interest of the artist as a "leading man" was brought out independently from any references to social flaws, debts, or rapacious art merchants. An illustration of such an unorthodox conception is provided by *Le Peintre français en Espagne, ou le dernier soupir de l'inquisition* (performed in 1809 at the Théâtre du Vaudeville), written by Barré, Radet, and Desfontaines, three of the four authors of *Le Peintre français à Londres.* In this play the French painter Merval, disguised as a Castilian, is involved in a series of adventures related to the French invasion of Spain and the consequent insurrection in Madrid (1809). His attitude is fiercely patriotic; in fact, he is almost a military hero, and he confronts the myrmidons of the Spanish inquisition, as well as secret English agents. In the finale he paints the allegory of the victorious French eagle and sings:

> When he consecrates the memory
> Of brave soldiers, the honor of Frenchmen
> The painter shares their glory and their success.
> (*Le Peintre français en Espagne*, 4)

Le Château et la Chaumière, ou les arts et la reconnaissance (performed in 1807 at the Théâtre du Vaudeville), written by the very same Barré, Radet, and Desfontaines, proves that the artist's moral excellence does not necessarily have to be measured solely by his patriotism or courage. Thus in cases of financial success, *les enfants des arts* are also capable of showing an uncommon degree of gratitude and generosity. After the French Revolution, the evil steward of the noble emigré family d'Arminville, held in great affection by its former vassals, tries to sell their château for his own profit in the absence of his former masters. Thereupon three young artists (a painter, a sculptor, and an architect), who, as orphans, had been sheltered and raised in the château, and who later, by their talent, earned considerable fortunes in Rome, return to the home of their early youth. Realizing the intent of the steward, they repay the kindness of Madame d'Arminville, now a widow living in a humble cottage, by buying back for her her ancestral abode. Because of its political innuendos—the story could have been construed as an allusion to the exploitation of the victims of the Revolution by ruthless speculators—the performance of this edifying play was forbidden by the police until the Restoration (1814, also its date of publication).

The very few conventionally respectable or flattering characterizations of the artist appearing on the popular stage tend to suggest a political tinge: The Colonel de Francarville, disguised as the painter Edouard, is essentially an aristocrat of the *ancien régime;* the painter Maurice happens to be in London when France is at war against England; the painter Merval is in Spain as a witness of the Napoleonic invasion; and the three grateful artists, who save the Château d'Arminville, arrive in France at the time when the question of avaricious speculators had become an important issue. However beguiling, none of these characterizations ever reveals any signs of the "culturally fashionable" qualities of the literary heroes depicted in contemporary novels and poems. More specifically—in terms of popular imagery—the most engaging, patriotic, courageous, and generous artist is never allowed to be afflicted with a discernible case of the *mal du siècle.*

Popular culture did not remain immune to this "romantic malady," and its symptoms conspicuously studded contemporary melodramas and secondary novels. But these popular forms, overflowing with strident or teary emotionalism, rarely, if ever, included the artist in their cast of characters. The image of the artist, relegated to light comedy and to the vaudeville by the propagators of popular culture, did not seem to tempt "serious" writers. Thus before 1800 there was nothing in France that could be compared with German literary works such as Wilhelm Heinse's *Ardinghello* (1785) and Ludwig Tieck's *Franz Sternbalds Wanderungen* (1789). In fact, before a few well-known novels of Balzac (*La*

Maison du chat qui pelote [1829], *La Vendetta* [1830], *Pierre Grassou* [1839], etc.), there is only one French portrayal of the artist as a "serious" literary hero: Charles Nodier's *Le Peintre de Saltzbourg* (NOD-SAL, 1803, 21–76).

The significance of this book should not be underestimated. German authors such as Heinse and Tieck projected their fictitious hero-artists into a Renaissance milieu and depicted them as active "professionals" who were concerned above all with aesthetic questions. Admittedly, the background of Charles Munster, the central character in *Le Peintre de Saltzbourg,* is not developed beyond the fact that he is a German artist, although there are some vague references to his political exile from Bavaria and an allusion to his past friendship with the late Werther (probably Goethe's hero). However, Munster's choice of literature (Klopstock, the Bible, and *Ossian*) indicates that he is a well-educated contemporary of Nodier. Munster is actually inactive as a painter, and his ideas about his profession are limited to a few perfunctory utterances about the difficulty of artistic creation. For instance, commenting about the lack of sensitivity of the great majority of people, he states: "The artist bemoans the weakness of his resources and curses his canvases and his palettes, when he observes so many inimitable shades, so many fleeting aspects, so many varied expressions in the great picture of the magnificent Creation" (NOD-SAL 52).

The emotional outpouring of Nodier's painter has little to do with his profession per se. Restlesslessly wandering through moonlit woods, ruins, chapels, and graveyards, he ceaselessly broods, moans, and cries; he constantly evokes his tragic, impossible love for Eulalie—apparently also an artist *(Fig. 14)*—who during his absence married another man (she loved Munster, but she believed that he was dead). The tone of Munster's lamentations can be illustrated by the following passage:

> At twenty-three years of age, I am cruelly disillusioned by all earthly things and I have fallen into a great contempt for the world and for myself; for I have seen that there was nothing but affliction in nature and that there was nothing but bitterness in the heart of man. . .
>
> Whirling in an ocean of anxiety and suffering; when one hardly has begun to find relief from so many violent emotions, when one has hardly begun to rectify exaggerated opinions:—here comes death swift and unexpected, embracing you in her rigid arms and lulling you to sleep in the silence of the tomb! (NOD-SAL 37–38)

Le Peintre de Saltzbourg overflows with lyrical expressions of pseudo-philosophical melancholy, modulated between the tone of Jean-Jacques Rousseau's *Confessions* and that of Edward Young's *Night Thoughts.* In addition, the book offers pathetic deathbed scenes, funerals, storms, a suicide, an awesome flood, and the account of Munster's progressive insanity, culminating in his drowning near a monastery. In terms of characterization it is quite obvious that the portrayal of Nodier's tragic painter is essentially a combined pastiche of Goethe's Werther and Chateaubriand's

René. Paradoxically, for this very reason, *Le Peintre de Saltzbourg* must be acknowledged as a minor landmark: It is the first appearance in France of a fictitious contemporary artist cast as a full-fledged pre-Romantic hero.[3] It will be seen later that the exceptional character of Nodier's conception can be more fully understood in the context of his allegiance to the *Barbus*.

Le Peintre de Saltzbourg symbolized the total integration of the artist into the highest levels of the culture of his time—more clearly than the legend of Vernet, which after all is limited only to the extraordinary episode of the artist's behavior during a storm. Nodier's fiction suggests that the artist does not need to nurse any sense of social inferiority, for he is no longer tolerated or accepted merely because of his talent: Independently of any question of his profession, he has been fully and unequivocally absorbed in the mainstream of contemporary culture, at its highest fashionable level, as the equal of poets, military heroes, and all those distinguished men of undefined calling who are so often given the leading role in "serious" literary productions.

Despite the number of its subsequent editions (1820, 1831, 1832, 1840, 1850, etc.), Nodier's book does not seem to have attracted much attention at the time of its first publication. Yet it is certain that it is possible to find some unusual examples of French artists who did not wait for Charles Munster to adopt, in real life, an analogous culturally fashionable stance. For instance, Anne-Louis Girodet, writing to his friend François Gérard, allowed himself a wide range of lyrically melancholy notes borrowed from Rousseau and Goethe:

> I would have been born, my friend, under the most unlucky of all stars if heaven had not given me your friendship. Keep it alive, it will soften the bitterness which fate is preparing for the rest of my life. At the very moment when I am writing to you, I have just quarreled with my family. Young, inexperienced, and, above all, full of good faith, I was naïve enough to believe that my parents were my natural friends. . . . It is very hard, my friend, to learn to know society only in order to despise it, and, therefore, to flee from it; it would be much better to remain a child forever. I would rather be deceived by men than to be forced to hate them. (30 December 1789)[4]

Naturally the resemblance of Nodier's literary fiction to the epistolary mimicking of Girodet is not particularly remarkable, since both were derived from the same well-known models. But it is important to note here that at the turn of 1800 the fashionable image of the melancholy hero, which both Nodier and Girodet tried to conjure, was specifically associated with that of the artist.

Admittedly, at the beginning of the nineteenth century, it was not difficult to encounter artists, like Girodet, or like Gérard, Gros, Fabre, or Guérin, who displayed exquisite manners and dressed with great elegance and conservative taste. Sporting modish attitudes, some of them were lionized in the most exclusive and sophisticated salons and were quite capable of delivering with great proficiency learned Latin quotations and witty repartees. Several artists, such as Pierre-Luc-

Charles Cicéri, the renowned theatrical decorator, Pierre Duval Lecamus, the popular genre painter, and Mme de Mirbel, the successful miniature artist, opened their own salons. The salon of Gérard enjoyed particular prestige. Mme de Bawr wrote that every Wednesday evening Gérard's apartment "was filled with people who had distinguished themselves in the arts, in letters, in sciences, and with notable personalities from all countries" (*Mes Souvenirs,* 103). Gustave Jal noted that "the distinguished foreigners who came to Paris give importance to the honor of being received at M. le Baron Gérard's salon" ("Les soirées d'artistes," *Le Livre des cent-et-un,* 1831, I, 137–38). In fact, a few of these artists could have easily provided a model for Balzac's highly polished, ambitious, and successful Théodore de Sommervieux, the *peintre-homme du monde* (*La Maison du chat qui pelote,* 1829). However, such social accomplishments and ambitions failed to dent in any discernible measure the deeply rooted popular image of the artist's profession.

It is almost superfluous to add that the various decorations and the titles of nobility that were periodically bestowed on artists, such as the *ancien régime's* Order of Saint-Michel or the baronies of the Napoleonic and the Restoration periods, did little to influence the artists' prevailing popular image. J. Lucas-Dubreton, for example, quotes a passage from an unidentified play, in which a viscountess, speaking about the devaluation of aristocratic titles during the Restoration, disdainfully states: "Baron, this is a title which is fitting only for a painter's wife."[5] One wonders what the barons Gérard, Gros, or Regnault felt upon hearing such snobbish—but clearly typical—utterances!

The appearance of "new" legends did not change the situation. Artists had never been successful in launching a myth, inspired by a contemporary fellow member of their profession, that could compete with caricatures, such as those of Fougère and Lantara. The story of Jean-Germain Drouais (1763–88), the favorite pupil of David, is a case in point. His career, much more compelling than that of Vernet, seems to offer all the necessary ingredients for the creation of a myth of a heroic anti-Fougère. Drouais, like the comical character of Fabre d'Eglantine, was known for his total and exclusive devotion to his painting, but Drouais was born into wealth, remained unmarried, attracted everyone's admiration for his handsome looks, and achieved exceptional early success without arousing his peers' envy. Yet neither these unusual factors nor the painter's "romantically" untimely death in Rome at the age of twenty-four, neither the competition organized for the monument built in his honor in the church of S. Maria in via lata nor the altar erected to his memory in David's own house, proved to be sufficient to capture the public's imagination. Almost mystically evoked by biographers and critics,[6] the nostalgic image of a contemporary young French painter—who was believed to be destined to become a new Le Sueur or a new Raphael—was evidently less arresting in the public's mind than stereotyped vaudevillian silhouettes.

Condescension lurked everywhere. On 27 September 1806, for instance, the Ministry of General Police issued a bulletin on the subject of an exhibition, which foretold the *Salon des refusés* of 1863.[7] The patronizing tone is unmistakable:

> A few paintings could not be accepted for exhibition in the Musée Napoléon [Salon], some, because they were not ready on time, others because they did not deserve this honor. . . . [The authors of the paintings in the latter group] request the authorization to open a special room to exhibit their works. . . . The representative of the State is willing to authorize this new exhibition. The critics will do justice to the pretensions of the mediocrity. The good artists, on the contrary, will be encouraged by the acclaim they will receive.—Permission to be granted.

All in all, the artists' basic problem at the beginning of the nineteenth century is probably best stated in a passage of Pujoulx's *Paris à la fin du XVIIIᵉ siècle* (220). Discussing the difficulties of guessing anyone's profession, the author of this important social chronicle of the turn of the century (1801) remarked:

> Artists have always had something special; and by this word, I mean true artists. There is no one who, upon meeting Greuze for the first time, did not exclaim: he is either a crazy man or a painter!

At that time Greuze was seventy-five years old, but it is obvious that Pujoulx's observation could have been applied to any artist of this period.

II: The Saga of the *Barbus*

4

Dramatis Personae

In Part I, I attempted to sketch the context of the *Barbus* phenomenon, showing that, at the turn of the nineteenth century, the profession of the arts had not succeeded in quenching its endless thirst for social respectability and complete cultural recognition. The French Revolution, which made so many new things possible and feasible for the first time, brought no change in the artist's fate. The references to Olympian precedents, the halfhearted tributes of the popular stage, the first appearance of the artist as a melancholy hero in "serious" French literature, the cultural dandyism of a few successful artists, and the official awards and titles did not cleanse from the profession's image the conspicuous stains of denigrating stereotypes. At the same time, and most frustratingly for the artists, the public continued to show unequivocal signs of interest in every aspect of their activities. The artists' social and cultural position—subjected to a contradictory pattern of acceptance and rejection, accented by embarrassing popular clichés—was becoming increasingly ambiguous and unendurable. Thus, in a not too surprising reaction, this false and ambivalent situation led the artist to grasp for a new identity, apart from that of all other contemporary professional, cultural, and social groups. The advent of the *Barbus,* illustrating the most extreme stance in this search for identity, can be considered one of the most interesting manifestations of the evolving pattern of the artist's image.

The very nature of the problems surrounding the long-forgotten *Barbus* unavoidably determines the approach that must be adopted in a study of the group. In this regard it is important to keep in mind that the particulars of most of the *Barbus'* careers were marked by varying shades of obscurity, and it is certain that no individual *Barbu* ever basked in the limelight of worldly recognition so long as he tried to remain a true *Barbu.* Thus, as in the case of a play in which most actors are cast as self-effacing spear carriers, it can prove to be useful to take a look at the *Barbus'* background before the rise of the curtain. The sect required no formal enrollment; thus, in the absence of any "official" register or any complete listing of names, the identification of individual members of the group as *Barbus* must rely on contemporary references and later reminiscences. Although such material does not always cast sufficient light upon the nuances that divided true sectarians from their sympathizers and friends, this problem, which is somewhat complicated by the fluctuations of the *Barbus'* membership, can in most cases be resolved in the context of the sources.

Despite the *Barbus'* apparent indifference to special titles and to hierarchy, Maurice Quay and Lucile Franque, two members of their "tribe of angels"—a poetic designation later coined by Nodier (NOD-TEM 446)—were thought by their comrades to be more angelic than the others. Indeed, angelic is not too rhapsodic an adjective, for the ecstatic admiration these two young people inspired among their fellow sectarians had an aura of hagiolatry.

By all available accounts, Maurice Quay's personality was the most arresting of the *Barbus* group. Culling their analogies from the pantheon of western civilization, a few of Quay's contemporaries came very close to openly acknowledging his status as a demigod. According to their descriptions, his physical appearance was a composite of Antinous, Hercules, and Myron's *Jupiter,* while his intellectual and moral makeup evoked Moses, Pythagoras, Mohammed, and Jesus Christ. Parenthetically, it must be admitted that these qualities are not apparent in the gaunt, sensitive, and somewhat restless features recorded in a portrait attributed to Henri-François Riesener (*Fig. 15*). It is probable that this portrait shows the young Quay before the full development of his personality, and that he subsequently changed. Whatever the case, we are told that at the highest point of his reputation his talents almost matched those ascribed superhuman traits. As a poet he surpassed Chateaubriand, and he simply had no rival in his own time; as a painter he equaled Apelles and Poussin, and his talent aroused the fear of his teacher, Jacques-Louis David.[1]

This extraordinary man left frustratingly little discernible trace in the world. One is almost tempted to think that Nodier expressed Quay's own wish to perpetuate an aura of mysterious aloofness when, writing about his fellow sectarian's death, he stated: "Do not ask common people about Maurice Quaï: the future will be deprived of his name" (NOD-TYP 75).

What do we know about Maurice Quay? All sources seem to agree that he died of consumption, and a footnote of Delécluze asserts that he was born about 1779 and died in 1804.[2] It is impossible to verify the accuracy of the first date, but it is certain that the second is incorrect. The minutes of the police interrogation of Nodier (21 December 1803), brought about by the publication of his anti-Bonapartist *Napoleone,* refer to Quay's death and clearly imply that it occurred between June 1802 and December 1803.[3] Available information provides no further clarification on these questions of dates, but recently consulted documents, which I had the good fortune to discover in the Archives of the city of Puteaux, near Paris,[4] the Archives of the Departement de la Seine,[5] and the Archives nationales,[6] shed some new light on the "mystery" of Maurice Quay's life. His full name was Pierre-Maurice Quay (the spelling Quaï, used by Nodier and Delécluze, never occurs in the documents of the painter's family). His father, Jean-Maurice Quay, and his grandfather, François-Maurice Quay, belonged to a family of Savoyard gardeners who came to Puteaux from the province of Genevois (on the border of Switzerland) sometime before the mid-eighteenth century. In 1774 Jean-Maurice, who established himself in Paris as a nurseryman, married a young girl named Margueritte Simon, and they had two children: a daughter, Margueritte-Denise, and a son, Pierre-Maurice (our Maurice Quay). Margueritte-Denise, somewhat older than her brother, married an obscure artist, Jean-Baptiste Garnier, who was appointed Pierre-Maurice's surrogate guardian (Pierre-Maurice was still a minor) at the time of his mother's death in 1795.

Pierre-Maurice Quay's family lived at 16 rue de Clichy, in the rather bucolic and unfashionable *quartier des Porcherons* (corresponding to what is known today as Montmartre), in a house adjoining his father's nursery. The house is described in great detail in the inventory written in 1796, a year after the death of Pierre-Maurice's mother. This description gives a vivid idea of Pierre-Maurice's childhood and early adolescence, which he spent in his father's nursery among laurels, orange, and a variety of other boxed fruit trees, or in his father's small house, which contained worn devotional books, a considerable portion (eighteen volumes) of the 1775 edition of Voltaire's *Œuvres,* and some unidentified works of art (one painting and sixteen engravings). After the death of Pierre-Maurice's mother, life became increasingly difficult, and his father, plagued by debts and forced to sell his land, eventually died in lonely poverty in 1819.

Pierre-Maurice Quay's humble, artisanlike heritage and his early and close contact with an artist (Jean-Baptiste Garnier, his brother-in-law and surrogate guardian, who lived on the same street) can perhaps explain the future *Barbu*'s limited education, his interest in aesthetic questions, and his enrollment in David's studio (probably in 1796).[7]

Lucile Franque's talents must have been nearly as exceptional as those of Maurice Quay, for it was repeatedly suggested that—had she wished it—she could have become either the Michelangelo of poetry or the Ossian of painting. Her personality was marked by deep intelligence, idealism, warm generosity, solemn melancholy—unpredictably giving way to a childlike gaiety—and an unusually graceful bearing. This exceptional young woman was said to evoke the classical figures appearing on Greek vases, as well as Raphael's *Saint Cecilia,* Ossian's Malvina, Sterne's Elisa, and Rousseau's Julie. There was something uncommonly sweet, ethereal, and mysterious about her (NOD-TYP 75–76), and this poetic mood is unmistakably reflected in her self-portrait (*Fig. 34*).

Her life, which is far better documented than Quay's, was of course somewhat less poetic than her personality. Lucile was born in Lons-le-Saunier (Jura) on 13 September 1780. Her given Christian name was Marguerite-Françoise-Lucie, but probably Lucile sounded more elegant.[8] Her father, Jean-Joseph Messageot, a former cavalry officer decorated with the high military order of Saint-Louis, was a postmaster. After his death his widow, *née* Marie Françoise Clerc, who was left with three children—a son and a second daughter in addition to Lucile—married Claude-Antoine Charve, judge at the Tribunal of Lons-le Saunier. After the births of the Charves' son and daughter, Lucile became the oldest child of a family that, in addition to a brother, Xavier (destined to become a naval officer), and a sister,

Fanny (who was to marry Anne-François Tercy and become a minor writer), also included a half-brother, Louis-Maximin (the future husband of Lucile's daughter), and a half-sister, Désirée (the future wife of Charles Nodier).[9]

Having shown strong literary and artistic inclinations at an early age, Lucile was sent to Paris, where she began to work under an unknown master.[10] While studying painting in the capital, the young provincial developed a romantic relationship with Jean-Pierre Franque, a student of David, who was a friend of Maurice Quay and one of the first full-fledged *Barbus*. A careful study of documents reveals that Lucile gave birth to a daughter, christened Isis-Mélanie-Chrisotémie-Laodamie, on 15 September 1799,[11] more than two years before her marriage to Jean-Pierre Franque on 10 January 1802.[12] Afflicted with consumption, she died in Chaillot, a Parisian suburb, on 23 May 1803.[13] She was not easily forgotten, however. Sixty-four years later, Mme Mennessier-Nodier, the daughter of Nodier as well as Lucile's grandniece, would write that Lucile's "short passage on earth had left a luminous trail like a vanishing star" (*Charles Nodier,* 90).

The consideration of the *Barbus'* rank and file brings their legend to somewhat less mystical heights. In this regard, the careers of Lucile's husband, Jean-Pierre Franque, and his twin brother, Joseph-Boniface, suggest less glamour but a stronger sense of professional purpose.

The twins were born on 11 August 1774 in Buis-les-Baronnies (Drôme),[14] a small rural town spread at the foot of the Mont Ventoux, which has remained famous since the time it had been climbed by Petrarch. Their father, Jean Francou (a name with a strong provincial resonance, later changed into Franque by the twins), a husbandman, and their mother, *née* Marguerite Signouret, resided on the farm of Sans-Regret perched on the top of a steep hill. Until very recently it was still possible to see some of the twins' early drawings, preserved on the rocks nearby. According to local folklore, these drawings attracted the attention of a nobleman traveling through the region—one is reminded of the discovery of Giotto by Cimabue—and Caze de la Bove, the Intendant of the Dauphiné, decided to send the two boys to Grenoble to study art at the expense of the provincial government.[15] I have recently discovered that in this city the twins were enrolled in the Ecole gratuite de dessin, directed by Jacques-André Trelliard, painter to the king: The two brothers studied at this school for at least two years, from 1786 to 1788, and were trained to become engravers.[16]

In 1792, during the revolutionary period, it was decided that the twins' education should be assumed by the départment de la Drôme. Consequently their case was brought to the attention of the Assemblée nationale in Paris, which, "impressed by their work and their poverty," placed the brothers Franque in David's studio and allotted to them a pension of 2400 *livres* for four years, with an additional sum of 600 *livres* for their traveling expenses.[17]

The twins were welcomed by the famous painter, who, declining any kind of remuneration, expressed his gratitude to the Assemblée nationale for having been chosen "the first teacher of these young men who can be justly called the children of the nation since they owe everything to it!"[18] In David's studio the two brothers seem to have been considered the most promising students of the generation following that of Girodet, Gros, and Gérard. Thus David offered to the twins free lodging in the area of his studio, in the Louvre, and asked Jean-Pierre to help him in the execution of *The Sabine Women*.[19] From this point on information dwindles. As previously mentioned, in 1801, Jean-Pierre married Lucile Messageot. By that date he had already left the Louvre: He was living in the abandoned building of the convent of Sainte-Marie, in Chaillot,[20] and, most probably, already dissociated from David's studio. Things must have been difficult, for in 1803 his wife's death certificate describes him as a "marchand de tableaux." But neither Jean-Pierre nor Joseph-Boniface had abandoned painting, and from 1806 on they regularly exhibited their works in the Salon, becoming fairly successful and acquiring distinguished patrons that included the Maréchal Masséna and Napoleon's family.

Toward 1812 the careers of the two brothers part. Joseph-Boniface went to Italy, spending some time in Florence working for one of Napoleon's sisters, Elisa Bacciochi, princess of Lucca and Piombino. On 10 September 1813, she appointed him professor of drawing at the Academy of Carrara, where he arrived on 23 January 1814. However, because of the political events leading to the decline of the Bonaparte family, he was unable to perform his teaching functions and he left Carrara. Eventually he went to Naples, where he assumed a professorship at the academy in 1823.[21] After directing the Academy of Naples for ten years, he died there in November 1833. His long sojourn in Italy did not prevent him from working for eminent French patrons, such as the duc de Berry, and from exhibiting occasionally in Paris. Jean-Pierre gave private lessons,[22] continued to exhibit very regularly in the Salon (until 1853), and acquired a measure of prominence (in 1836 he received the decoration of the *Légion d'honneur*). Modestly but diligently, he contributed to the huge projects of historical decorations at Versailles and at Saint-Cloud, and in 1860 he died at Quintigny (Jura), in the country house of his wife's family.[23]

What is known about the career of Jean Broc suggests that he was as serious-minded and as energetically industrious as the brothers Franque. He was born on 16 December 1771 at Montignac (Dordogne), a small town of Périgord, which later became famous because of the prehistoric cave of Lascaux. His father, also named Jean, and his mother, *née* Marguerite Granger, belonged to a family of small shopkeepers and tailors; it is certain that the future *Barbu*'s lineage, without being quite as rustic as that of the twins, was marked by a comparable inconspicuousness.[24]

Broc's childhood and adolescence are clouded in obscurity. It is known that he served in the Republican army during the wars of the Vendée, and that he entered David's studio sometime before 1798, after having been released from his military obligations, through the intercession of the famous poet Jean-François Ducis.[25] In this studio Broc seems to have acquired a special reputation for his pride and strong faith in his own talent. Somewhat worried by the young man's attitude, David is reported to have given him some warning advice on this matter: "You think you are blessed with genius; but beware, it does not grow by itself in the head, and it must be cultivated. . . . Keep telling yourself that you are not yet a man of genius!" (DEL-DAV 50). Apparently self-confidence did not prevent financial difficulties, and probably for this reason Broc shared, from time to time, the brothers Franque's small apartment in the Louvre, where they lived through their master's generosity (DEL-DAV 71).[26] As one of the oldest students of David, Broc tried to establish useful contacts—Gérard drew the portrait of Mme Broc in 1800 (Louvre) —and resolutely strove to achieve recognition. Thus he succeeded in entering a few of his paintings in the Salons of 1800 and 1801, and in both years he received a *prix d'encouragement.* In 1801 he left the Louvre, cutting the umbilical cord that attached him to David's studio.[27]

During the Imperial period Broc enjoyed a degree of success and was the recipient of a few minor official commissions, as in the case of his participation (1805) in the decoration of *la Salle des Maréchaux* in the palace of the *Tuileries,* for which he executed the portrait of the Maréchal Soult. He continued to exhibit until 1833, but his star appears to have waned and his success becomes, more often than not, a *succès d'estime.* To supplement his livelihood, he opened his studio to students and provided designs for a type of wallpaper, called *tableaux-tentures,* engraved by Mader and printed by Dufour (1820).[28] Nothing is known about his private life with the exception of the fact that he had a daughter, Alina (Aline), who in 1835 married General Joseph Dwernicki, a member of a wealthy Polish family. At an undetermined time Broc settled with his daughter's family in Galicia, where he died, almost totally forgotten, about 1850.[29]

The family background of Antoine-Hilaire-Henri Périé was far more socially prominent than those of the Franque twins and Broc. He was born in Castres (Tarn) on 30 May 1780; his father, Hilaire-Jean-Pierre, and his mother, *née* Marie-Magdeleine-Françoise Senauver, belonged to a well-to-do, highly respected, and highly educated family of parliamentarians of the Languedoc. In fact, Hilaire-Jean-Pierre Périé, who replaced his own father as *Conseiller au Sénéchal* of the city of Castres, was a poet of some reputation and the winner of a prize at the celebrated *Jeux-Floraux* of the Academy of Toulouse (1785).[30]

Because of his family's standing, it is plausible to believe that Antoine-Hilaire-Henri Périé received a good general education. But because of his precocious fascination for drawing and painting, his father entrusted the growth of his budding talent to local artists, first in Castres and then in Toulouse. Eventually, responding to the young man's insistence, his father sent him to Paris and enrolled him in David's studio. It can be seen that, if one is willing to forget the questions of financial resources and family relations, Périé's beginnings somewhat parallel those of Ingres. It is impossible to ascertain the length of time Périé studied under David, but it is known that in 1799 he was definitely a member of the famous studio and that he was very close to Maurice Quay. After leaving David at an undetermined date, Périé succeeded in exhibiting some of his works in the Salons of 1810, 1812, and 1822. He did not attract great attention, but he met famous Parisian littérateurs such as Charles Nodier, and it is obvious that he was well received in certain cultured circles of the capital. This explains his marriage to Amélie-Julie Candeille (1823?), the then celebrated actress, playwright, and writer who was formerly an intimate friend of Girodet. Périé befriended many members of the literary milieu of the Languedoc, such as Jean-Antoine Gleizes and Auguste de Labouisse-Rochefort. In 1826, perhaps because of a reputation established through these connections, the painter was invited to become the director of the archaeological museum in Nîmes (Gard), as well as the director of the Ecole de dessin in the same city. Consequently he and his wife moved to Nîmes, where he died on 12 September 1833.

The same honorable mediocrity marks the life of Guillaume-François Colson (1785–1850).[31] He entered the studio of David at a very early age and, according to Delécluze, later gave some proof of his talent. However, the author also writes that Colson destroyed his career "through the unshakable stubbornness with which he clung to the sect of the *penseurs* or *primitifs*" (DEL-DAV 92). If this is true, Colson's tedious and pretentious historical and religious paintings (exhibited from 1812 on) represent a much later phase of the artist's development.

The *Barbus'* group also included far more shadowy figures, barely discernible in the limbo of history. Some have recognizable names. This is the case, for instance, of the two brothers Hue, Horace (Horace-Joseph?) and Alexandre-Laurent, sons of the well-known seascape specialist Jean-François Hue (1751–1823), who was one of the most successful followers of Joseph Vernet.[32] Horace's life is still enveloped in total obscurity.[33] However, it is certain that Delécluze included a "Hue *fils*" in his list of David's students (DEL-DAV 416); and it is known that Alexandre-Laurent (1779–1858?) received some early training under his father (most probably it was this Alexandre-Laurent who was enrolled in David's studio), that he exhibited landscapes in the Salon (from 1810 to 1842), and that he was appointed as a drawing teacher in the lycée of Versailles. The case of the brothers Hue is paralleled by that of Fabre d'Eglantine *fils*. Despite the fact that his father was a well-known playwright (the author of *L'Intrigue épistolaire* and the creator of Fougère), as well as one of the most controversial personalities of the Revolution, the information on Fabre d'Eglantine *fils* is scanty.[34] It is known that with the support of Nodier (1801–3) he fiercely defended the memory of his father, who after his death (he was guillotined in 1794) was accused of being an informer and an embezzler (AUL II, 228, 233–34; IV, 495). In addition, all that is known is that the young Fabre d'Eglantine *fils* studied at the prestigious Ecole du Génie maritime and that he was involved in the design of the disembarkation barges that were supposed to be used in the Napoleonic invasion of England. After having worked as a maritime engineer, he practiced as a civil engineer in Arles (Bouches-du-Rhône) and died in Versailles in 1840.

Even less is known about other *Barbus,* who in the absence of a famous father or any kind of recorded achievements left only a name to posterity. Because of the lack of identifying Christian names and the careless misspellings, even surnames can create confusion. For instance, it is possible that Jenier (NOD-LAR 23) and Peniez[35] refer to the same individual (perhaps the painter Pagnès, who was still living in 1817[?]). The same question of quasi-homonymy arises in the case of two other similar names, Prault (NOD-LAR 23) and Grault (NOD-EST 25), which most probably designate the same person (possibly the engineer Marcel Prault-Saint-Germain).[36] The problem of identification of course becomes unfathomable in regard to discreet references, such as "Augustin D." or "S****" (DEL-DAV 92–93).

It is often equally impossible to determine the creative "specialty" of each *Barbu*. It is known, for instance, that Fabre d'Eglantine *fils* was admitted to the Ecole polytechnique, which required some skill in drawing as well as some familiarity with Latin literature (AUL III, 591). While one might suspect that as a future engineer the young man was naturally leaning toward drawing, it is also possible that he nurtured a parallel interest in literature. In this regard, one must keep in mind that the *Barbus'* membership was by no means confined to those engaged in the visual arts. Since the two "archangels" of the group, Maurice Quay and Lucile Franque, were known both for painting and poetry, it is not surprising to discover that two other sectarians, Jean-Antoine Gleizes and Charles Nodier, had dedicated themselves exclusively to writing. Because of their many publications, Gleizes and Nodier achieved far greater public prominence than any other member of the *Barbus* group.

Jean-Antoine Gleizes (1773–1843)[37] (*Fig. 35*) was truly a fellow countryman of Antoine-Hilaire-Henri Périé. Like Périé, he came from the département du Tarn, and he was born in the small town of Dourgne (little more than a large village, a few miles from Castres). His father, Denis Gleizes, a lawyer, and his mother, *née* Marie-Anne Faucos, were well-to-do and owned considerable land in the region.

Jean-Antoine Gleizes's early education was far stronger than that of any other member of the *Barbus'* group with the exception of Fabre d'Eglantine *fils* and Nodier, and he was admitted without difficulty to the nationally famous medical school in Montpellier. However, he did not remain there for long, for his initial exposure to medical training determined almost at once a lifelong philosophical attitude. Repelled by anatomical dissection, Gleizes developed an overwhelming aversion to all forms of dead flesh, a mystical dedication to a vegetarian diet, and a strong inclination for solitude. This attitude was enhanced by an idealistic philanthropy, esoteric religiosity (he was a devout Christian, but he believed in metempsychosis), and his disillusionment with the sanguinary excesses of the Revolution (which he had welcomed at first).

In 1794 he married Aglaé de la Beaumelle, the daughter of an eighteenth-century writer who was propelled to celebrity for involuntarily inciting Voltaire's satirical wit. After leaving medicine Gleizes, who was planning to teach history, undertook a program of humanistic studies at the Ecole normale in Paris. However, probably because of his moody disposition, he eventually abandoned this project and returned to his native Pyrenean region. He spent most of his life there with his wife, at her château of La Nogarède (Ariège), which, because of Mme Gleizes's hospitality, social grace, and literary interest, became a true "salon" of sophisticated conversation and culture.

The amenities of this pleasant life did not prevent Gleizes from exerting considerable energy in proselytizing his vegetarian faith, and for this purpose he corresponded extensively with a number of eminent literary figures of his time: Chateaubriand, Justin Girod-Chantrans, Louis-Pierre Anquetil, and, of course, Nodier, his fellow *Barbu*. He was a true vegetarian fanatic; since Mme Gleizes did not share his belief, he decided to eat alone and was often subjected to ridicule. Gleizes left a considerable number of publications—to be considered in a subsequent chapter—in which the influence of Bernardin de Saint-Pierre and of Chateaubriand is combined in a quasi-religious vegetarian preaching.

Charles Nodier (1780–1844), previously mentioned as the author of *Le Peintre de Saltzbourg,* was one of the most influential figures in nineteenth-century French literature. He was known as an amateur entomologist, an ardent bibliophile, a witty critic, an inventive essayist, and, especially, as the entertaining author of numerous *contes* such as *Trilby* (1822) and *La Fée aux miettes* (1832). But in French literature Nodier's name has an additional, perhaps more significant meaning: He is chiefly remembered as the initiator and the guiding spirit of the romantic *Cénacle* of the Arsenal, which brought together virtually all the noteworthy literary (and some artistic) talents of the period, from 1824 to 1844.

Because of the considerable volume of scholarship that has been devoted to Nodier in recent times, it might be sufficient in the context of this study to sketch very briefly the early phase of his life.[38] Jean-Charles-Emmanuel Nodier was, in a literal sense, the contemporary as well as a fellow countryman of Lucile Franque: He was born the same year (1780), in Besançon, within a stone's throw of Lucile's Lons-le-Saunier. He was the son of Antoine-Melchior Nodier, a teacher and lawyer who was elevated to judgeship under the Revolution, and his almost-illiterate housekeeper, Suzanne Paris (Charles was legitimated in 1791). Before entering the Ecole centrale of Besançon in 1796 (where he remained for only a year), the young Nodier had already received an extensive educational foundation, further strengthened by Girod-Chantrans, a learned friend of the family who informally acted as his tutor. Nodier's gargantuan reading cemented this foundation.

The effervescence of the revolutionary period and his father's Jacobinic prominence thrust the young Nodier into the public arena at an incredibly early age: Produced as a sort of child prodigy, he was already making official patriotic speeches when he was eleven years old. Far from resenting this kind of exposure, the young man, becoming aware of his talents, immersed himself in literature and political plotting. Thus at the age of sixteen, guided by his imagination, he organized the secret literary society of *Philadelphie,* for which he invented a set of rituals in imitation of the Freemasons.

Soon after, through Judge Nodier's influence, Charles was appointed assistant librarian at the Ecole centrale of Besançon. His position allowed ample time for other activities, and the young man began to write prodigiously on a variety of literary, scientific, and political subjects. He continued to write in Paris, where, beckoned by a friend, he arrived in December 1800. Leading an erratic existence, Charles, for several years, traveled back and forth from the capital to Besançon. In 1803, because of his seditious poem, *La Napoleone,* he was arrested and imprisoned for thirty-six days. Even after his release, secured by his father's intercession, he continued to be suspected by the police. This state of affairs did not impede Nodier's wandering life, which was devoted to writing and conspiring. In 1808, during his peregrinations, he was befriended at Dôle (near Besançon) by the family of Judge Claude-Antoine Charve, the stepfather of Lucile Franque (who had died five years before). That same year, he married Désirée-Liberté Charve, Lucile's half-sister.

From the time of Nodier's marriage, his career no longer directly relates to the subject of this book. It is sufficient to say that Nodier's astounding productivity as a writer, his charm and wit as a raconteur, his political acumen, and his boundless ambition eventually brought about his celebrity. In 1824 he was appointed chief librarian at the Arsenal—the site of the famous *Cénacle*—and in 1833 he was elected to the French Academy, the official apex of any nineteenth-century writer's career.

To have a fuller idea of the *Barbus'* circle, one must keep in mind that it also involved a number of important sympathizers including Paul Duqueylar (1771–1845) and Jacques-Nicolas Paillot de Montabert (1771–1849). These sympathizers never became full-fledged members of the group, and they can be best considered in subsequent chapters in the context of their respective contributions to the movement.

5

The Birth and Early Development
of the Sect

David's studio had a central role in the birth of the *Barbus;* but it must be remembered that the sect's membership was not exclusively limited to this great painter's students, or even, for that matter, to artists. It is also useful to keep in mind that, geographically, the sect's adherents came from widely distant regions of France, and that in regard to social standing their families ranged from the highly cultured to the uneducated, and from the wealthy to the nearly destitute—professing varying shades of political beliefs scaled from royalism to Jacobinism. A powerful unifying factor can be traced to the question of age. At the beginning of their movement (1797), all the *Barbus* were very young: In that particular year the oldest among the known members of the group was twenty-six and the youngest only seventeen. However, the age factor per se can determine neither the relative date of an individual *Barbu*'s active appearance on the scene nor the duration and the depth of his involvement in the movement. Because of the general lack of precision that characterizes such matters, one is often compelled to interpret and to correlate fragmentary data that must be gathered from miscellaneous sources.

The most extensive information on the group's beginnings can undoubtedly be found in Delécluze's *Louis David, son école et son temps* (1855). Etienne-Jean Delécluze (1781–1863) was known as a prolific writer, historian, translator, and critic (in art as well as in literature) who organized his own very influential *Cénacle* in direct competition with Nodier's. However, long before asserting his reputation as a man of letters, Delécluze, determined to become a painter, had enrolled in David's studio at the age of fifteen. Being a considerate and unassuming young man, he rapidly established pleasant relations with all the members of the illustrious atelier.

Delécluze's book is essentially devoted to David, introducing the *Barbus* only as an accessory element. The material about the *Barbus* brought out by Delécluze can be subdivided into four categories, set apart by different origins and different dates: Delécluze's own extensive account of his experiences in David's studio, which was published for the first time in his book, is scattered through the entire length of the text (referred to here as DEL-DAV); a reprint of his much earlier (1832) recollections *Les Barbus d'à présent et les Barbus de 1800,* originally published in the seventh volume of the *Livre des Cent-et-un* (DEL-BAR); a reprint of Nodier's *Les Barbus,* a brief article that had originally appeared in *Le Temps* (5 October 1832) (NOD-TEM); and a reprint of a still earlier piece by Nodier, *Deux beaux types de la plus parfaite organisation humaine,* which was first published in his *Essais d'un jeune Barde* (1804) (NOD-EST).

Delécluze appears to have been a well-informed and unbiased eyewitness, and, generally speaking, his vivid and detailed description of David's studio is most probably historically accurate. However, one must keep in mind that the related events had taken place approximately sixty years before the publication of his book, and about thirty years before the appearance of his article in the *Livre des Cent-et-un.* No amount of objectivity could have shielded the writer from occasional inaccuracies. One instance of Delécluze's lapses of memory can be singled out to illustrate the danger of an uncritical reading of his text. The case is particularly important, for it bears upon the sect's chronology, the respective role played by some of its best-known members, and the reliability of other sources. In his text of 1855 Delécluze wrote that he had seen Nodier, in the Louvre, "more than once . . . going up and down the little wooden staircase leading to the room above the studio of the *Horatii,* where, by all appearances, he was going to preside over the meetings of the *penseurs* or *primitifs"* (DEL-DAV 73). In the context of the book it would appear that Nodier was one of the early leaders of the *Barbus,* and that he had joined, on a number of occasions, Maurice Quay and the brothers Franque in their Louvre apartment, on the entresol, above the studio in which was placed David's celebrated painting of the *Horatii.* In the same context it would also appear that Nodier's visits to Franque's apartment had already been occurring at the end of 1796, before the time Delécluze had officially become a member of David's atelier and when he was still receiving his first art lessons in the studio of the *Horatii,* from one of the master's advanced students (DEL-DAV 27). Evidently Delécluze confuses dates and facts. Nodier's life (with the exception of the *Barbus* context) was scrutinized by a number of literary historians, and it is definitely known that the writer did not come to Paris from Besançon before December 1800 (see Oliver, *Charles Nodier,* 26). Thus the *Barbus'* gatherings in Franque's apartment could not possibly have included Nodier before that time, and consequently the writer could hardly have been in a position to preside over the early meetings of the sect in the Louvre. Nodier probably did attend some of these meetings after December 1800, but the facts indicate that Delécluze can be more fully trusted with his descriptions than with specific dates.

Nevertheless, one can well believe that Delécluze would have remembered the approximate time of the beginning of his studies in the Louvre (end of 1796, beginning of 1797) (DEL-DAV 17, 49). Everything considered, one can safely state that the birth of the *Barbus'* movement coincides with the phase of David's studio that followed the events of Thermidor (27 July 1794), that is, the end of *la*

Terreur. After a brief imprisonment, related to his involvement in the excesses of the *Comité du Salut public* and to his friendship with Robespierre, David was given his freedom and the right to resume his profession. His Jacobinism was largely forgiven, and he began to work on the composition of *The Sabine Women* (*Fig. 16*), with which he symbolized the spirit of national reconciliation. He was doing his best to erase his image as a fanatic revolutionary: He dressed conservatively, displayed an *ancien régime* urbanity, and tried to help, whenever possible, the former émigrés who came to his studio. Thus, paradoxically, the *Barbus'* aesthetic radicalism was born in David's studio in the midst of an atmosphere of congeniality and relative relaxation.

The group of students who worked in David's studio at that time was not as rich in talent as the earlier generation of Gérard, Girodet, and Gros, and the other successful young artists who had been trained under the master before the Revolution. With the notable exception of Ingres and perhaps of some lesser known but gifted painters, such as François-Marius Granet and Auguste de Forbin, few of the students of this post-Revolutionary group were destined to leave a significant mark on the history of French art.

Within the framework of studio teaching, these new students fell into three different classes, corresponding to the relative stages of their professional training: the young beginners drawing from plaster casts; the more advanced pupils drawing from live model; and the seniors, who were allowed to paint. To these categories one can add the group of a few students who had in fact completed their training cycle, but who, for various reasons, still lingered around the studio. At the time of Delécluze's arrival in David's studio, the brothers Franque belonged to the latter group, and the other future *Barbus* were variously assigned to the three basic categories: Broc was already painting; some very young would-be sectarians, such as Guillaume-François Colson, were still drawing from plaster casts; while Périé and Maurice Quay were working from the live model and were about to be promoted to the painting easel. The busy atmosphere of David's studio is captured in a drawing of Jean-Henri Cless, which shows the young painters at work, and the master (wearing a hat) engaged in a "critique" (*Fig. 17*).

Quay's advancement to the category of painters is related in Delécluze's description of David's critique of his students' works:

> He [David] came to Maurice Quai: "You can paint also, Maurice," David said. "You have made here a very good study. If this man chooses to, he will go far, he loves nature and has a good understanding of the antique." (DEL-DAV 63)

Delécluze gives a description of the "early" image of Maurice, which probably corresponds to Riesener's portrait (*Fig. 15*):

> Tall, thin, his hair and beard black and bushy, his burning eyes, and his expression, passionate and yet kindly, had an imposing and at the same time an

attractive quality. There was, in this man, something which recalled Mahomet and Jesus Christ, two beings for whom, as a matter of fact, he had a profound veneration. Agamemnon [Delécluze is referring to Maurice], a very witty young man, had a fluent, easy, elegant manner of speaking; and whether this quality was natural to him or acquired, he always betrayed in the choice of his words, the structure of his phrases, and in his frequent use of similes and of most colorful metaphors, the slightly grandiloquent style that can be observed in the speeches and the writings of Orientals. Nevertheless, his conversation was solid, substantial, and varied. (DEL-BAR 423)

At the beginning Maurice's oddity was confined to his beard. Delécluze writes: "As long as his talent was only in its infancy, he did not profess openly the strange opinions on the arts and on the manner in which he claimed they should be practiced, which he was to assert later" (DEL-DAV 70). He seems to have first won his fellow students' goodwill by "the loftiness of his ideas and the sincerity of his soul." When he heard, for instance, that his comrades had nicknamed him *don Quichotte* (long before he was called Agamemnon), he surprised and impressed everybody by saying with great dignity that he was quite honored to be compared to Cervantes's idealistic knight

> for whom he nursed a respectful admiration and whom he considered, although on an immensely different level, in the same category as those who, like Jesus Christ, were born to do great deeds and to be mocked by men. Thus, irony, which, as a matter of fact, he endured rather graciously, was the flaw which gave him the most unfavorable opinion of the character of those who allowed themselves to yield to it. (DEL-BAR 426)

Maurice's admiration for the moving image of a self-sacrificing benefactor of humanity who is met with the derision of the populace led him to express politically dangerous, still-unpopular ideas. Thus upon hearing a burlesque story referring to Jesus Christ in a facetious manner, the young artist, after having angrily reduced his sacrilegious fellow student to silence, retorted:

> What an extraordinary thought indeed, he said. . . . To invoke Jesus Christ for the purpose of a joke! Hasn't any one of you ever read the Gospel? The Gospel! It is more beautiful than Homer, than Ossian! Jesus Christ in the midst of fields of wheat, silhouetted against a blue sky! Jesus Christ saying: "Let the little children come to me!" Can you find subjects for painting that are greater, more sublime than those? Idiot, he added, with a tone of friendly superiority to his comrade who had made the joke, why don't you buy the New Testament and read it before speaking about Jesus Christ? (DEL-DAV 78)

Maurice resolutely rejected the appellation of Jesus Christ for himself (NOD-TEM 443). To appreciate the courage of the statements related by Delécluze, one must recall that Napoleon's reestablishment of Catholicism as the official religion of

France was in the future: The *Directoire* society was still permeated with the revolutionaries' active hostility to the Church, its tenets, and its traditions.

It must be stressed that, for Maurice, true greatness was very rare indeed. He refused to recognize it even in the most traditionally admired historical leaders, such as Pericles, whom he called merely "another Louis XIV," whose century "already smelled of decadence" (DEL-BAR 422). This discriminating sense of greatness, joined to an imperious disdain for mediocrity and superficial wit, was equally reflected in Maurice's aesthetic sensitivity. On certain occasions he could lose his temper, as in the case of the behavior of Auguste de Forbin, who, in collaboration with Pierre-Henri Revoil, another of David's students, had written a vaudeville, *Sterne à Paris,* which was performed at the Théâtre du Vaudeville, (22 January 1800). De Forbin did not confine his talent to the stage, and his propensity for giving free rein to improvising vaudeville couplets in David's studio had a way of provoking Quay's Homeric wrath (obviously he was unwilling to identify himself with Fougère, Teniers, or Lantara!). Shouting "Old Pompadour!," he would repeat with a tragicomical insistence "Vaudeville! Vaudeville!" while attacking furniture and painting boxes in the studio with a cane or a broken piece of easel (DEL-DAV 82–83). The half-serious, half-playful spirit of Maurice's atelier prankishness is echoed in a later, anonymous lithograph depicting a confrontation between a marquislike exponent of the Rococo tradition and a number of youthful champions of classical art affecting the attitudes of the warriors of David's *Sabine Women (Fig. 18).* In fact, Quay's distaste for eighteenth-century mannerisms was not limited to the vaudeville, and he could ferret out parallel flaws in the pantheon of classical literature. A mere mention of Euripides spurred Maurice to exclaim: "Euripides? Vanloo! Pompadour! Rococo! It's like M. de Voltaire!" (DEL-BAR 426).

Such a stern sense of perfection necessarily limited the number of masterpieces that could be worthy of Maurice's approval. According to Delécluze:

> As for literature, he [Maurice] found true, solid, unquestionable merit only in the Bible, the poems of Homer and of Ossian. He brought everything back to these three masterpieces and paid attention to other writings only insofar as they were more or less influenced by these three literary monuments. (DEL-BAR 425)

He loved to read passages from Ecclesiastes aloud to his friends, and Delécluze confessed to have been deeply impressed by the "tender and yet majestic artlessness" of one such reading. On this particular occasion Delécluze in turn asked Maurice if he wished to hear some beautiful passages from another book:

> Yes, he told me at once, read me a passage from Homer, but in Greek. . . . I immediately took a volume of Homer and read to him, in Greek, the admirable description of the storm, in the fifth Canto of the *Odyssey,* which I was then studying. I read it to him as though I were certain that he could understand; and he, for his part, listened with all the attention and the evident satisfaction of someone who might have had a thorough understanding of the

Greek language. When I finished, he seemed moved. He got up; and, gravely placing his hand on my head, he said to me in a tone of voice which expressed gratitude and, at the same time, sorrow at not seeing me more enthusiastic: Poor child! Thank you! but you do not know your own happiness! (DEL-BAR 426–27)

Maurice Quay, of course, did not know any Greek (he read Homer in French translation), and the scene described by Delécluze is the almost exact antithesis of Molière's "pour l'amour du grec souffrez que je vous embrasse."

In Maurice Quay's order of admiration, Homer was to be placed below the Bible, and the Bible was surpassed by Ossian. According to Delécluze, Maurice told him "with the authority and the enthusiasm of a prophet":

> Homer is admirable; but Genesis, Joseph, Job, the Ecclesiastes and the Gospel are far superior to the books of Homer, that is certain. But, I am telling you (he added, with even more forcefulness), Ossian is far greater than all that! and here is the reason for it: he is much more sincere, listen well! he is more *primitive* . . . Homer? Ossian? he asked himself, the sun? the moon? That is the question. In truth, I think that I prefer the moon. It is simpler, greater; it is more *primitive*! (DEL-BAR 428)

Maurice's glorification of the "Celtic," or "Erse," poems, which about 1800 were attributed to the legendary third-century Gaelic bard Ossian—actually a forgery concocted by the eighteenth-century Scottish poet James Macpherson—was anything but unusual. The Ossianic vogue, based on the French translation of Pierre Le Tourneur and given additional impetus by Bonaparte's admiration, was very much in the air.[1] Comparably simple explanations can be suggested for Maurice's admiration of Homer and the Bible: the former, obviously reflecting the prevailing Neoclassic cult, and the latter, echoing the Old Testament "sublimity" of the widely read writings of Edward Young, imitated by Nicolas Gilbert and announcing Chateaubriand's *Génie du Christianisme.*

In varying degrees Maurice's literary taste was shared by practically everyone in David's studio: What is really unusual here is not so much the nature of the choice but the intensity of the admiration. In fact, the far-reaching consequences of Maurice's enthusiasm transcended the question of literary merit. Thus in a speech delivered to his fellow students, Maurice declared (as quoted or paraphrased by Delécluze):

> As for the thoughts that we reformers must continually entertain in our minds and our hearts, we could not derive them from sources that are too *primitive* and too pure. They can be found in Homer, then in Ossian, but especially in the Bible; it is in the scenes and the depictions of the primitive people among whom these books were written that we shall find what we need to regenerate our souls and our minds and give a lofty usefulness to our talents, when they will be perfected. (DEL-DAV 91)

Maurice's search for the purity of a *primitive* fountainhead—which was the essence of his admiration for Homer, Ossian, and the Bible, although this order of preference seems to have changed from time to time—represented the key element of his thinking and of his sensibility. Not surprisingly, this factor also dominated his attitude toward the visual arts and toward what might be loosely called his philosophy of life.

Delécluze associated the formation of the *Barbus'* concept of primitivism with their reaction to David's painting of *The Sabine Women*. In his article of 1832 he implied that this reaction occurred, in 1799, at the time of the exhibition of the finished painting (DEL-BAR 421). But this information could not be entirely accurate, since *The Sabine Women* had been seen in an unfinished state, at the beginning of 1797, by several of David's students, including Jean-Pierre Franque (who was helping in the execution of the painting) and Delécluze himself (according to his own statement), long before the date of its official exhibition (DEL-DAV 187–88). Delécluze's account of 1855 is probably more reliable in this regard:

> The master [David], on the point of starting his painting of *The Sabines,* and feeling more than ever attracted to the works of antiquity, had come to restrain his admiration for modern works so much, that he proposed to use as models only the Greek works which were considered to have been executed in Phidias' time. Among the reliefs, he sought those which had the oldest style; he did the same for medals, and he particularly praised the natural quality and the elegance of line of the figures painted on the so-called Etruscan vases. . . . The master's opinions, exaggerated by his pupils, even by the most intelligent ones, are soon misrepresented by the foolish ones. . . . That is what happened in this case, when he said about his project of the *Sabines*: "Perhaps I have shown too much anatomy in my painting of the *Horatii*; in this one, the *Sabines*, I will hide it with more care and more taste. *This painting will be more Greek.*"
>
> The latter words . . . struck the imagination of the young students and especially of Maurice, and, inspired by this statement, they claimed that David had only foreseen the road to follow, that the principles upon which the arts were practiced had to be radically changed; that everything which had been done since Phidias was mannered, false, theatrical, horrible, vile; that the Italian masters, even the most famous ones, were stained by the vices of the modern schools; that it was indispensable to abstain from looking at any of the paintings of the Grande Galerie, and that in the gallery of the antique, one had to lower one's eyes and walk without stopping by the Roman statues and even by those which had been done in Greece since Alexander the Great. (DEL-DAV 71–72)

Delécluze's text of 1832 suggests an attitude which foreshadows the twentieth-century Futurists' iconoclasm:

According to him [Maurice Quay], in order to cut short the pernicious doctrines and prevent the propagation of bad taste, one should have preserved only three or four statues from the museum of the antiques . . . and set fire to the gallery of paintings, after removing, at most a dozen productions. (DEL-BAR 424–25)

It is impossible to verify the accuracy of the statement attributed to David, which was supposed to have determined the *Barbus'* rebellion. But there is little doubt that almost from the very beginning it was widely believed that their extremism was inspired by some of the great master's pronouncements. Thus in discussing Paul Duqueylar's *Ossian Chanting His Poems* (1800; *Fig. 23*)—a painting by a *Barbu* sympathizer, which was greatly admired by Maurice's friends—the critic Charles-Paul Landon chastised the members of the new sect in the following terms:

. . . young students, faithful echoes of certain innovators who, after having erroneously interpreted the opinion of a famous master [David] and after having distorted his own words, go proudly repeating everywhere not what they think, for they cannot think anything by themselves, not what they have heard said by a famous artist [David] whose opinion is authority—they did not understand him—but rather what they think they have heard; they create from it a new, ridiculous doctrine, but they will certainly fail with their proselytes.[2]

What was, in fact, this "new, ridiculous doctrine"? Dismissing almost all of the productions of the modern era, Maurice Quay maintained that the artist should concentrate his admiration on Greek vase painting, statues, and bas-reliefs of the most ancient style (DEL-BAR 425). Pre-Phidian Greek, Etruscan, and Sicilian vase painting provided the best examples of what might be called "simple," "grandiose," and, especially, "primitive" (DEL-BAR 421):

The basis of his [Maurice's] doctrine was to observe the antique and to work only from nature; but he considered imitation only as a very accessory means and for him the only true artistic goal could be reached only in the most sublime beauty. (DEL-BAR 425)

Maurice's harmonization of imitation and beauty is further amplified in another section of Delécluze's book:

In practice, one should only aim at expressing the highest beauty; thus Maurice encouraged his followers to cease working in David's studio if the model did not seem beautiful to them; he advised them to paint only figures of six feet, and, still for the sake of capturing beauty, prescribed light shadows, so that too sudden a transition from light to dark would not destroy the harmony of forms, which always happened, he added . . . with these vile Italians. (DEL-DAV 72)

Considerable evidence suggests that Delécluze tended to oversimplify Maurice's ideas when he attributed to him, with a touch of patronizing irony, a pictorial ideal of some kind of neo-Greek archaistic gigantism, conceived in a manner recalling

Flaxman's shadowless style. It will be seen that the *Barbus'* notion of primitivism came to include non-Greek historical periods, such as the Italian Quattrocento, as well as stylistic approaches that could be reconciled with chiaroscuro. Nevertheless, one cannot doubt that Greek archaism was very much at the roots of the early aesthetic attitude of the sect. From this point of view, it may be noted that, aside from the reference to David's statement about *The Sabine Women,* Delécluze brings up another factor that is supposed to have played a role in the shaping of the *Barbus'* stance: the triumphant arrival in Paris of the Italian war spoils (27 July 1798). These treasures included some of the most celebrated examples of Renaissance painting (for instance, Raphael's *Transfiguration*) and of Classical statuary (such as the *Belvedere Apollo* and the *Laocoön*). This event, giving additional impetus to the prevailing Neoclassical interest in the art of antiquity, stimulated many scholarly writings on the causes of its perfection. Somewhat paradoxically, this fascination for the question of sources and origins gave birth to a point of view that placed "the most simple composition derived from an Etruscan vase above the works recently brought from Italy" (DEL-DAV 210).

It will be seen later that the growing importance of archaic art at the end of the eighteenth century cannot be summarily explained away by the repercussions of the French military conquests. However, Delécluze's account of this episode gives a clue to the chronology of the development of Maurice's sect. He links the arrival of Bonaparte's Italian spoils to the increased bitterness of the *Barbus'* criticisms of *The Sabine Women,* which resulted in David's dismissal of Jean-Pierre Franque as his assistant in the execution of this painting and in the break of the master with the members of the rebellious sect—following a sudden increase of its influence on the population of the studio (DEL-DAV 210). Consequently one can surmise that the basic position of Maurice's followers, as a unified group, had already been fully formulated by 1798.

The followers of Maurice—who, one might recall, considered himself a reformer—were not united by aesthetic opinions alone. Delécluze states that Maurice's ideas on art "were only the corollaries of other loftier, more serious ideas," which he discussed with his closest adherents in the Franques' apartment (DEL-DAV 72). Having never been invited to this inner sanctum, the writer relates what he heard from Nodier. Thus according to Nodier, who is supposed to have attended several *Barbus* sessions in the fateful apartment (but not before 1800), "it was a question of nothing less than of a reform of society based on a plan, not precisely similar to that of the Saint-Simoniens, but of the same type, and which had to begin with a change of costume" (DEL-DAV 73). Apparently Nodier never kept his promise to divulge more information on this matter. Delécluze himself recalls that Nodier joined Maurice, Broc, and the brothers Franque in meetings held in the famous Louvre apartment (DEL-DAV 27, 71), and, having no direct knowledge, he speaks very vaguely of Maurice's moralizing and of his "*humanitarian* utopias" (DEL-DAV 89). Fortunately, however, the writer kept in his memory Maurice's initial act that committed him to a proselytizing activism:

Soon it was not enough for Maurice to spread his doctrine by means of conversations which took place in the room of the studio of the Horatii, or in the students' studio, after the work of the day; he let it be known to his fellow sectarians "that it was necessary to speak loudly and to walk courageously, head high; that it was true that David had started the great work of artistic reform, but that the incertitude of his character and the lack of scope of his ideas had been the cause of his political downfall and did not give him the energy necessary to complete the revolution which had to be achieved in art. He added that, so long as models of bad taste such as those taken from Italian, Roman, or even Greek art, going back to but excluding Phidias, were to be admitted in the schools, there was no basis for hoping that any amelioration would be felt in the studies; that, as for him, he would begin to hope for the return of simple, sincere, that is *primitive* taste only when he would see all these so-called masterpieces . . . burned and destroyed (those are his very words) [one might recall that this iconoclastic idea was already mentioned in Delécluze's text of 1832]. This day will come, my friends, do not doubt it, he cried out in his enthusiasm; but it is necessary to hasten this moment by spurring the conversion of those who are still plunged in error. Thus, to fulfill this mission, we must act with daring and courage. . . . I have decided that in a few days from now, I shall shed these shabby clothes which I am wearing like all the men of our century. Already, as you can see, I have let my hair and my beard grow; a large white tunic is being readied now and I shall wear it under a wide blue cloak, and I shall wear only buskins on my feet. But I can read doubt in your eyes; you think that I, like a faint-hearted man, have had this clothing prepared to adorn myself with it in the obscurity of our small room and only in your presence? Do not be deceived; next *décadi,* you will see me dressed in this manner in the Tuileries, strolling among those stupid bourgeois who will be blushing because of the ugliness and the shabbiness of their modern garb. Soon, you will follow my example, I do not doubt it, and I must tell you that my good friend Périé, who is here, making noble use of his fortune to further our great aims, has had a complete Phrygian costume made for himself, after that of the marble Paris which is in the museum, a garb he intends to wear while accompanying me in the stroll which I described to you. Yes, my friends, it is time to give a practical and serious goal to art and to enclose the great and eternal truths in the envelope of beauty, so that they may be accepted with pleasure, even with alacrity, and so that they sprout and fructify in the heart of man. . . . As citizens, it is of the utmost importance that we first alert the eye of the important reform we want to undertake; and nothing, in this regard, is more effective to favorably dispose the eyes and the minds of men than to don this admirable Greek *primitive* costume which creates such a majestic and such an elegant effect." (DEL-DAV 89–91)

Delécluze's description of Maurice garbed as Agamemnon reveals a mixture of amazement and admiration:

As for his costume which consisted of a large tunic coming down to his ankles and an ample cloak with which he covered his head in case of rain or sun, it was very simple, and I have seen few actors, without even excepting Talma, who could wear this type of clothing with more grace and ease than my friend Agamemnon. (DEL-BAR 423)

One might suspect that Périé liked to exhibit himself in the street even more assertively than Maurice, for the former's "Paris" seems to have been more frequently noticed and described than the latter's "Agamemnon." The most reliable description of Périé can be found in a hitherto unpublished note jotted down by Mme Aglaé Gleizes (Jean-Antoine Gleizes's wife) during a trip to Paris in the spring of 1800:

Hil:P [Hilaire Périé] is dressed in so extraordinary a manner that even in Paris he is booed or followed in the streets. Long white trousers which go up to the armpits, yellow shoes closely molding the foot, held by straps, a red waistcoat tied in the back and with a very low neckline showing really very little or no shirt, a long beard, short hair, and then a piece of red cloth thrown over the shoulders: such is the costume for which 7 or 8 young men would give their life and by which they attract attention under the name of *méditateurs.* Today, a young man [who] was following Hilaire for half an hour finally approached him and said to him enthusiastically: when two men meet, they must jump at every chance of seeing each other. You are one of these rare beings with whom I sympathize and whom I did not hope to find in Paris.[3]

Although differing in several details from Mme Gleizes's description, the Phrygian costume of the statue of Paris, reproduced in Landon's *Annales du Musée* (1802, III, pl. 63), can give some idea of Périé's attire *(Fig. 19).*

The reaction described at the beginning of Mme Gleizes's note was evidently more typical than the one that appears at the end. The *Chronique scandaleuse de l'an 1800* (92–93) confirmed that Périé-Paris, as well as the other oddly garbed *méditateurs,* offered a ready target for popular derision:

Citizen Perrier [Périé], a student of David, is the Don Quixote of *the love for the antique.* He can be seen in all the streets, dressed in a Greek or Roman fashion, with a beard and a large cloak. The fishwives, when they meet him, do not spare him insults, little boys are running after him, dogs bark at him; all this does not shake his determination. If only he showed a great talent besides! but he shines only by his eccentricity. He belongs to the new sect of the *illuminati of painting.* The members of this sect lock themselves up in a dark place, and wait, in order to work, for the moment of inspiration. Most of them could wait a long time.

One day, he met a Greek, from the land of the Greeks, for there are several kinds. The latter seeing his extraordinary costume, asked him if he was his compatriot: no, answered Perrier [Périé], I am French.—Then you must come from Egypt.—No, *I come from home.* . . . The other man, surprised, begged his pardon and went away saying: the French must be *great Greeks,* since they even fool the people of the land.

In 1800 the term *Greek* was vulgarly used to designate cheats and deceivers, and the concluding pun of the *Chronique scandaleuse* obviously alludes to the Grecian-garbed Périé's supposed lack of candor. Périé always remained sensitive to this type of accusation. It is true that he was rather vain and, according to the *Biographie castraise* (III, 124), "he often confessed that he secretly enjoyed showing himself off in public, dressed in this attire draped *à l'antique,* which flatteringly revealed his beautiful body." However, he resolutely rejected any innuendo that cast doubts on his sincerity. Thus in 1826 he was compelled to set right a letter by his wife, Mme Périé-Candeille, to the writer Labouisse-Rochefort, in which she facetiously spoke of the *Barbus'* false beards:

> I cannot allow to stand unchallenged the history of my beard, without objecting to the word *false* which my wife has used so lightly. If ever a steadfast purpose, good faith, and natural sincerity have guided someone's conduct, these were the qualities which incited us to singularize ourselves in 99. The only thing which was lacking in all this was what the world calls common sense; but since this time, my razor has made so many sacrifices to convention that I must be absolved from having had the folly of conducting myself according to my reason.[4]

The date 1799 mentioned by Périé had a special significance in the rabidly reactionary perspective of 1826 (the period of the Bourbon Restoration). Actually the precise dating of the first appearance of the costumed *Barbus* in the Parisian streets was the specific purpose of the "false beards" passage of Mme Périé-Candeille's letter to Labouisse-Rochefort. Making a point to dispel any possible confusion between the politically motivated garb of the revolutionaries of 1793 and the innocent disguises of the *Barbus* of 1799, she wrote:

> As for the innovations that a few young students of the school of David thought, *pour l'amour du Grec* [reference to Molière], to introduce in the French costume, six years after the change which the Cannibals of 93 had already so brutally brought to it, the malevolence which clings only to the analogies of evil, might confuse these two dates, and I think that none of the scatterbrains, who then, were walking around with a false beard on their chins, would like very much to recall this fact, on the old reminiscences of which a real beard has since grown, grown again, and grayed.[5]

Mme Périé-Candeille's clarification is justified by a persistent tendency to confuse the classical costume with Jacobinic opinions. Thus in 1831, recalling the revolutionary period, the duchesse d'Abrantès wrote in her *Mémoires* (I, 140–41):

> Young men were roaming in the streets, like true *sans-culottes,* with a little tunic, a cloak, or rather an ample toga; for, one borrowed from all types of

republics, that is in order to do evil, and *Lycurgus was teaching how to burn castles.*

There is little doubt that she was referring to Maurice's group, for she added:

> The artists, the men of letters spoke only, dreamt only of the republic. One could see young men, dressed entirely in the Greek fashion . . . and, walking gravely, wrapped in their white togas edged with red, stopping near one of the entrance gates of the Louvre, discoursing, under this portico, about the interests of the state. They did not laugh, held their chin in their hand, greeted people with a nod, and actually tried to play the old Romans, even the young ones, as best they could; and do not think that there were only two or three young fools, there were at least three hundred! [The duchess d'Abrantès erroneously claimed that these events occurred at the end of 1794, during the Revolution.]

The same confusion occurred, one year later, in Charles Lenormant's "Du Costume parisien, et de son avenir":

> I would have hardly spoken of the competition that the students of David gave to the *carmagnole* [a short jacket worn by the Revolutionaries] and of the Greek costume which they dragged in the mud of the Halles quarter, if this costume had not marked the beginning of the wonderful extravagance of feminine attire during the *Directoire.* (*Le Livre des cent-et-un,* 1832, VII, 14)

It must be observed that the type of costume worn by the *Barbus*—it can probably be recognized on a diminutive figure of Antoine-Maxime Monsaldy's view of the Salon of 1800 (*Fig. 22*)—despite its extravagance, was not entirely unfamiliar to the Parisian scene at the end of the eighteenth century. Many authors described the antiquarian excesses of the time. For instance, Delécluze, speaking of the *Directoire* period, wrote:

> The new government of the Directoire, undoubtedly with the thought of effacing all memories of the Revolutionary costume, so hideous and so slovenly, has decreed for the representatives of the people, for the members of the Tribunat and of the Conseil des Anciens, a costume which approximates as closely as possible the antique attire, so as to satisfy and even to flatter the prevailing taste.

Recalling the celebration of official holy days, the same author added: "One could see . . . processions of extras of the Opera, dressed as priests and priestesses of antiquity" (DEL-DAV 184–85). Contemporary newspapers often point out the excesses of classical fashion in everyday life. They relate, for instance, the tragic death of a woman wearing a light costume *à la grecque* on a cold winter night (JD, 9 March 1801), or the amusing determination, shown by dressmakers, fashion merchants, and hairdressers, in imitating classical models (*Le Moniteur,* 16 January 1805). Mme Vigée le Brun's *souper grec,* organized toward the end of the reign of Louis XVI, shows that this vogue was anything but new and that the *Barbus'* attire could hardly have appeared truly outlandish around 1800 (*Souvenirs de Madame Vigée le Brun,* I, 67–71).

In this regard, even the *Barbus'* beards were really not sufficient to explain the public's derision. It is true that beards were uncommon, but such capillary ornaments did not necessarily incite hilarity or antagonism. It is interesting to note that a police report (24 November 1800) describing the "Greek priest" Isaïe Carus stated that he achieved success and celebrity "because of his beard, his magnificence, and especially because of his extraordinary figure."[6] Thus the populace's scoffing hostility could not be solely directed against the strangeness of the *Barbus'* costume and the incongruity of their beards.

Above all, the *Barbus* sported nonconformist ways that did not correspond to the type of nonconformity usually ascribed to artists. It was obviously laughable and irritating to watch the goings-on of a group of young would-be artists who seemed to do their best to break away from the prevailing stereotypes of Fougère and Lantara, not only by flaunting their scorn for such popular imagery, but also by presumptuously pretending to reform society with a display of an odd masquerade.

It is important to realize that the barbs cast against Maurice's followers castigated them as *artistes manqués* as much as ridiculously garbed eccentrics. Thus the allusions to the *Barbus'* lack of talent and their lack of industry, found in the *Chronique scandaleuse,* also recurred in *Le Petit Arlequin au Muséum.* After having detailed the "méditateurs'" attire (almost identical to that of Périé) and having described them as "a few young men hardly out of school who are pretending to have formed a sect," the anonymous author observes: "They do not work, talk little, meditate a lot, and spend a long time in front of a painting in a state of ecstasy which borders on stupidity."[7]

The arrogance of such an attitude could not be easily condoned in an atmosphere marked by the growing Napoleonic concern with civic order, discipline, and usefulness. The *Journal des Débats* stated (8 March 1800): "The political factions are slumbering, literary cabals are awakening; one is no longer plotting in the clubs against political tranquility, one is plotting against taste in the literary coteries and in the museums." The word "museums" is revealing, for the statement could not possibly refer to officially recognized artists. It appears that Maurice and his cohorts, without being accused of political machinations, were suspected of having conspired against "good taste," that is, the accepted aesthetic norms (the sect's "humanitarian utopias" remained largely unnoticed). This suspicion could not have been based only on the pronouncements and the costumes of the *Barbus.* Their "activism," far from being confined to questions of taste and aesthetics, also unequivocally asserted the cultural importance of the artist. In telling his friends that "it was necessary to speak loudly and to walk courageously, head high" (DEL-DAV 89), Maurice Quay was inviting them to cast off the humiliating clichés fostered by popular imagery and the vaudeville (for which, it was seen, he was nursing an intense hatred). For the first time in history, the artist was asked to step out of his studio in order to change the course of established culture. This was not merely a question of regaining the dignity supposedly enjoyed by Athenian, Roman, and Renaissance artists. The artists were actually asked to assume openly the role of leaders and reformers—the term "réformateurs" is specifically used by Maurice (DEL-DAV 91). Despite the fact that this role had little to do with politics per se, the new image of the artist as *l'homme révolté*—an image that appeared disturbingly incongruous at the turn of the century—stirred incomprehension and hostility in French society.

It is impossible to name all the students of David who came under the influence of Maurice between 1798 and 1800 (from the date of the arrival of the Italian spoils—which corresponds to the open criticism of *The Sabine Women*—to that of the final break between David and the members of the sect). According to Delécluze's text of 1855, the members of the "aristocratic" party of the studio, which included Moriez, Ducis, Roland, de Forbin, de Saint-Aignan, and Granet, and those of the "pious" group, especially Fleury-François Richard and Pierre-Henri Revoil, were deeply moved by Maurice's religious statements (DEL-DAV 79). Others, such as Paul Duqueylar, Adolphe Lullin, and Jacques-Nicolas Paillot de Montabert, acknowledged the truth of Maurice's primitivist credo without, however, going so far as to assume the *Barbus'* attire or to imitate their odd behavior (DEL-DAV 94–100). Despite the duchesse d'Abrantès's assertion that at least three hundred "young fools" adopted the Grecian costume, the only art students who are known to have wholly accepted the demands and the consequences of Maurice's preaching during the period of David's studio were the brothers Franque, Broc, Périé, Colson, and a few others to whom Delécluze discreetly refers with initials.

The break between David and the rebellious students did not take the form of an outburst. Stressing David's discretion, Delécluze states:

> Without creating a scandal, he [David] found the means of letting it be known to those of his disciples to whom his lessons were not suitable not to disturb the studies of their former comrades. (DEL-DAV 122)

Despite this break, many *Barbus* seem to have lingered around David's studio at least until the end of 1800—the time of Nodier's first visit to Paris. This fact appears to be confirmed by Delécluze's reiterated assertion that Nodier attended several meetings of the sect in the brothers Franque's small apartment (which, as previously mentioned, he could not possibly have done before December 1800).[8]

It is conceivable, of course, that Nodier encountered some *Barbus*, perchance, while visiting the Parisian museums, but it is more plausible to surmise that he was introduced to the sect by Lucile Franque. It is known that upon his arrival to Paris the young writer dutifully called on a number of his fellow countrymen from the Jura. This group could have very naturally included Lucile, who, after all, was the stepdaughter of Judge Charve, one of the colleagues of Nodier's father. Thus the writer probably was already acquainted with Lucile's family prior to his Parisian trip, and she may have been referred to him as one of the persons from whom he could receive some guidance in the capital. Nodier made two sojourns in Paris during the time of the *Barbus'* heyday: first, from December 1800 to March or April

1801, and a second time from October 1801 to late spring 1802. All in all, however, his direct contact with the group of Maurice Quay could not have exceeded twelve months. This contact of course had an intermittent character, since during this period the writer was most energetically involved in a variety of literary projects and social activities.

But, despite the lack of continuity of Nodier's participation in the *Barbus'* movement, his appearance on the scene (probably during the winter of 1800/1801) was an unquestionably influential event. He was bringing to the sect the enthusiasm and the imagination of a well-read, highly talented young writer, an irrepressible penchant for esoteric pursuits and conspiracy, and a firsthand experience of clandestine associations. The latter factor had a very personal meaning for the writer, for, in Besançon (1796), long before he came to Paris, he had already founded the secret society of the *Philadelphes. La Philadelphie* was an association of friends (including Charles Weiss, Charles Pertusier, Luczot de la Thébaudais, and Jacques-Joseph Oudot), which combined the playful, occasionally prankish aspects of a college fraternity with the mysticism and the rituals of a lodge of Freemasons.

The philosophical orientation of the rites of this small, short-lived organization can be surmised from a charter (composed of twenty-five statutes) written by Nodier.[9] Exalting the loyalty of its members toward one another, this association was devoted to friendship, concord, probity, and help to the needy. Its meetings were dedicated to moral and literary discussions. The brothers' insignia was a ribbon "bleu de ciel," worn around their necks, and a special importance was attached to the sign of the pentagon, to the number five, and to secrecy.

Article 14 of the statutes, describing the ritual prescribed for the initiation of new members, gives a hint of a solar cult:

> He [the new member] will be initiated only on the fifth day of each month, at five o'clock in the afternoon and he will utter, turning towards the sun, the following words: I swear before God and the sun to be inviolably attached to my brothers, helpful to all the unfortunate, kind to all men, to be faithful to the law which binds us and never to reveal its secrets.

At the end of its existence, the association acquired an active anti-Jacobinic bent, culminating in the *Philadelphes'* nocturnal dismantling of a guillotine erected in Saint Peter's Square in Besançon. Initially, however, their intentions were completely apolitical (as stated in article 6 of the statutes). According to Marguerite Henry-Rosier, many of their discussions were directed toward finding a harmonious formula for life and rediscovering "the innocent happiness of the first ages."[10] At the time of Nodier's first trip to Paris, *La Philadelphie* was about to disband, but he always kept alive a fond memory of these youthful dreams. Remembering this period, he wrote that it was easy for him then to fly "on the mystical wings of Swendenborg's angels" (*Souvenirs de la Révolution et de l'Empire,* II, 27).

Jean-Antoine Gleizes discovered the *Barbus* a few months before Nodier, during the summer of 1800. On the strength of the previously quoted note written by Mme Gleizes, there is little doubt that this contact was established through Jean-Antoine's friendship with Périé, whom he had known since the days of their early youth in the region of Castres, the old center of religious rebellion and Catharist heresy. Obviously Gleizes was not disturbed by Périé's eccentric costume when he met his friend again in Paris, since, according to his wife's notes, all three paid a visit together to the exhibition of David's *Sabine Women* two months later.[11]

Like Nodier, Gleizes most probably soon became one of those men who, "without being strangers to the arts, did not practice them," with whom, according to Delécluze, Maurice held conversations devoted to lofty ideas that transcended art theories (DEL-DAV 72–73). In this regard Gleizes's contribution was at least as important as that of Nodier. First of all, he brought to the group his fanatic faith in vegetarianism. For him vegetarianism was the very essence of the original meaning of Christianity, true morality, virtue, and philosophy, as well as the indispensable prerequisite for man's health, strength, beauty, intelligence, and, in the final regard, redemption.

According to Gleizes, vegetarianism was justified by anatomy (shape of teeth, etc.).[12] Man's constitution reveals a deep inner harmony with vegetal life, for vegetables contain the ingredients of all the humors of the human body. Indeed, vegetal life has a mystical significance; it forms the great ladder linking earth and heaven. Conversely, in eating animal flesh, man is enclosing death within himself: The eating of meat is the source of all vices. It causes the destruction of natural goodness, wisdom, and justice, and it is the origin of ugliness, disease, and of the brevity of our life. In religious terms the suppression of the murder of animals was the reason for the coming of Christ, and one cannot be both a Christian and a meat eater.

Speaking about man before the Fall, Gleizes, basing himself on ancient poets such as Ovid and Virgil, as well as on Genesis, asserted that our first parents lived on the milk of the earth, that is, on the herbs and the fruits, which in those times were found in great abundance. In order to bring man back to his original state of innocence and happiness, one must place him, again, in his primitive world. This primitive world cannot be re-created without vegetarianism. To illustrate his theories, the author evoked the ancient sects founded by Pythagoras, Epicurus, and Zeno, as well as the example of great historical and mythological reformers and benefactors, such as Buddha, Osiris, Orpheus, and the American Indian sages.

Gleizes's views, which he would later expand profusely in *Thalysie* (1821) and *Le Christianisme expliqué* (1830), had already been essentially formulated in *Les Nuits élyséennes* (written in 1799 and published in 1800) shortly before he joined Maurice's sect. But this book is not devoted exclusively to the glories of vegetarianism: It was conceived as a sort of a *poème en prose,* which—announcing *René*[13]— is lyrically saturated with melancholy, solitude, and an undefinable anxiety summoning the *mal du siècle.* Gleizes's originality is seen in the transposition of these well-known, preromantic *états d'âme,* from Gothic ruins and moonlit graveyards, into the setting of an oriental desert. Its geographic location is left unmentioned, but for Gleizes the desert appears to have been the last refuge for the beautiful, dignified, and virtuously innocent primitive humanity:

> It is there that one can see man with his original traits and his primitive form: there his glance is proud and his gait is free; he strides as the foremost being of all creation and examines in turn the sky and the earth. (*Les Nuits élyséennes*, 36)

The simple, free life of the oriental desert is thus equated with the ideal of the primitive man, an idea that even extends to the symbolic clothes, a "white tunic," adopted by Gleizes's hero: "With what pleasure I shed my Asiatic garb and donned the simple clothes of solitude and of the desert! For me they were the first symbol of home in this land" (75).

In the context of the contribution of Nodier and Gleizes, it may be pointed out that Delécluze's description of the *Barbus'* activities in the studio of David (before the end of 1800) contains no direct references to esoteric rituals, secrecy, vegetarianism, or oriental nostalgia. These elements will become apparent in the next stage of the sect's development, in Chaillot—outside of David's circle—a stage that seems to have remained unknown to Delécluze.

6

Chaillot: The Later Development and the Disappearance of the Sect

In the eighteenth century and at the turn of 1800, the hill of Chaillot, which today is one of the most elegant quarters of Paris, held very little attraction for the curious traveler (*Fig. 20*). A popular guidebook laconically informs the tourist that the area offers "nothing noteworthy" (*Le Pariséum,* 1809, 391). It is true that this hill had inspired a minor play by Toussaint-Gaspard Taconet, *Les Ahuris de Chaillot* (1766), that it became the site of the *Conventionnel* Tallien's luxurious *Chaumière de Chaillot* (1794), and that it was honored with a brief visit (1811) by Napoleon, who was planning to build a palace for le Roi de Rome on this location. But, all in all, about 1800 the hill was a vast, rather wild suburban no-man's-land. Speaking of this area, Louis Madelin wrote in *La Colline de Chaillot* (1926, 40–41):

> The old roads were nothing but potholes . . . the neglected estates were turning into virgin forest and . . . many of the abandoned houses of former noblemen might well have concealed counterfeiters behind their rotting doors. In fact, this suburb, poorly administered, poorly supervised, had become a *refugium peccatorum.*

One might add that the police reports of the period frequently spoke of a variety of illegal goings-on in the area, ranging from vagrancy and smuggling to political conspiracy: In 1803 Georges Cadoudal, while plotting his unsuccessful attempt to assassinate Napoleon, chose Chaillot as a hiding place.

The *Barbus* adopted for their principal meeting place the deserted Convent of the Visitation de Sainte Marie. It was a large ecclesiastical complex—vacated under the Revolution and falling to ruin—that stood at the foot of the hill of Chaillot, in the midst of a maze of quarries, abandoned gardens, decaying houses, and over-grown paths. The convent had been founded by Henriette d'Angleterre (1651), the daughter of Charles I of England, and it was within the confines of its walls that Bossuet read his famous *oraison funèbre,* dedicated to this queen. The old stones still echoed with the memory of other historically eminent occupants and visitors, such as two of the most famous repentent favorites of Louis XIV, Marie Mancini and Louise de la Vallière, and the most celebrated highwayman of the early eighteenth century, Louis-Dominique Cartouche. A police report (1 April 1801)[1] offers some authentic details on the condition of the convent at the turn of the century:

> Making my police rounds, and walking up the street which leads to the quai de Chaillot, by the former convent of the Dames Ste Marie, I noticed that an opening of approximately six or seven meters had been cut into the garden wall of the former convent of the Dames de Ste Marie in Chaillot, which gave free entrance to everybody in said garden; upon entering there, I noticed that, in this garden, there were different vaults and old buildings without any doors, which, at night, could be used as a refuge for vagabonds, thieves, and people with evil designs, that, in this garden, there were two stone staircases with different levels leading to several buildings and to a large terrace, with a view on the Champs de Mars, communicating on the same level with all the buildings of the said Abbaye de Ste Marie in Chaillot, which are huge and for the most part without doors or windows.

According to the same report, some workers who had been in the garden of the convent told the police officer that the land was in litigation and legally attached, and that the creditors of the present owner [the citoyen Lafontaine] were planning to divide it and sell it in separate lots. Another report states that the garden of the convent was about to be partially cleared to open a new street leading to the top of the hill.[2]

The reference to vagabonds, thieves, and "people with evil designs" was not unjustified. On 15 April 1800, long before Georges Cadoudal and his associates had rented a house near this site in order to plot the assassination of the First Consul (September 1803), the police discovered in the complex of the convent the opening of an underground passage equipped with a 300-meter system of pipes designed to smuggle distilled alcohol from Chaillot to Passy (Aulard, *Paris sous le Consulat,* I, 15 April 1800, 271). It is most unlikely, of course, that the *Barbus* were involved either in the smuggling of alcohol or in Cadoudal's conspiracy. Since it can be assumed that Maurice's followers would not have had the imprudent curiosity to watch the installation of illegal pipes and the subsequent smuggling operations, and that they would not have had the foolhardiness to remain in the convent during the police's intensive combing of the area, which took place after the discovery of Cadoudal's hiding place, it is possible that these two events mark the chronological limits of· the *Barbus'* sojourn in Chaillot. It is difficult to be more specific, and one must rely on the available data: the police report about the break in the wall of the convent's garden, 1 April 1801; the announcement of Lucile's marriage, 6 January 1802 (the convent was given as the legal address of the groom); Nodier's correspondence (all letters referring to Chaillot were written in 1802); and the legal record of Lucile's death on 23 May 1803 (Chaillot was indicated as the legal residence of the deceased). All this points to the fact that the sect had been active in the area from the middle of 1801 to the spring of 1803.

For this period Nodier's correspondence replaces Delécluze's book as the most important source of the *Barbus'* history: The chronology of these letters, most of which were published by Alexandre Estignard (NOD-EST) and Jean Larat (NOD-LAR), can be established from their context. According to this correspondence, the composition of the sect was undergoing some fluctuation. Périé, Colson, and Broc, for example, are not mentioned by Nodier (Broc, who was actively exhibiting in the Salon, seems to have left the group). However, in addition to old-time regulars, like Maurice, the brothers Franque, Lucile, and the comparatively new members, such as Nodier and Gleizes, the ranks of the sect seem to have been increased by a few neophytes, who were not connected by Delécluze to the *Barbus*. The identity of some of the new members, for example, the brothers Hue and Fabre d'Eglantine *fils,* is fairly well established. Others, such as Jenier, Peniez, Grault, Prault (Prault-Saint-Germain?), and Jenny (?), are little more than shadowy silhouettes. It is known that Jean-Pierre Franque, Lucile, and very likely Maurice Quay actually resided in Chaillot, but this was not necessarily true for all the members. In one letter Nodier wrote that for two months he had been spending his *days* in the midst of the *méditateurs* at Chaillot (NOD-LAR 23), and in another letter he said that he had been prevented from seeing Maurice for ten days (NOD-EST 29). Such statements, as well as other facts, suggest that a number of *Barbus* were commuting, as Nodier had been, between Chaillot and Paris.

It is evident, nevertheless, that for Maurice's followers Chaillot represented much more than an occasional daytime refuge from the vices and vulgarities of the capital, where in Nodier's words: "All passions . . . reach such extreme heights that one is led to become a scoundrel or a madman" (NOD-EST 22). Speaking of Chaillot, the writer stated that the members of the sect "lived in common" (NOD-LAR 23), and, conveying a semi-ecclesiastical note, he described the convent as the group's "place of retreat" (NOD-EST 22). This connotation is also unmistakably suggested by the appellation "Port-Royal des Méditateurs"—alluding to the famous seventeenth-century abbey of the followers of the heretical Jansenist doctrine—which, according to Nodier, was ironically given to the Convent of the Visitation de Sainte Marie by the society's wits of the time (NOD-EST 28).

Referring to the purpose of the *Barbus'* "retreat," Nodier wrote to Charles Weiss, his friend and former *Philadelphe:*

> Have you heard anything about this society of painters and poets to whom common people referred as the *Illuminati of the Arts,* who were more generally called the *Observers of Man* and who had unassumingly named themselves the *Meditators of the Antique?* You must have often heard of these young men who took pride in having resurrected among themselves the beautiful forms, the beautiful customs, and the beautiful clothes of the first centuries; of these artists who wore the Phrygian costume, who ate nothing

but vegetables, who lived in common, and whose pure and hospitable life was a living picture of the golden age? Well, I have found them. (NOD-LAR 23)

Thus it appears that Maurice Quay and his followers were attempting to establish in Chaillot something that amounted to a private utopian society. It is hardly necessary to note that the old dream of utopia, continually recurring throughout the eighteenth century, was very much alive at the turn of 1800. Yet, amid the vast expanse of utopian systems which could have been known to the *Barbus,* a utopian group of artists and poets represented a most unusual variant on the theme. To my knowledge, before the *Barbus* this particular concept of utopia was exemplified only in the single case of one German novel: Wilhelm Heinse's *Ardinghello und die glückseligen Inseln* (1787). There is little need to wonder whether Nodier or any other member of Maurice's group was sufficiently familiar with the German tongue to have read Heinse's book in the original, since a French translation of *Ardinghello* became available at the turn of the century.

Ardinghello, the hero of Heinse's novel, is a young Florentine painter, a former student of Vasari, who is also endowed with some talent for poetry and music. After many discussions about the nature of art and life, and many adventures— enriched with amorous episodes, political intrigues, wars, and travels—Ardinghello, assisted by his wise and learned Greek friend Demetri, decides to found a new colony on the islands of Paros and Naxos. Demetri recruits the first group of immigrants for these deserted islands, bringing back from Italy "a great number of young Romans, most of them artists, architects, sculptors, painters, all of whom were dissatisfied with their fatherland." Using Parian marble, these artists erected temples and public buildings: "The Athens of Pericles seemed to be reborn from its ashes" (*Ardinghello,* 316–17).

At the same time Demetri formulated a new religion: "His wise and clear dogmas, based on nature, gradually began to spread, and everybody adopted them." The character of this *natural religion* is reflected in the temples that were dedicated to Nature, the Sun, the Air, and the Unknown God. Their high priests, elected by the citizens, composed religious hymns derived from Homer, Plato, and the choruses of the tragic poets, or inspired by their own sublime imagination. In the exercise of their religious functions, they adorned themselves with resplendent costumes of antiquity. The civil constitution of the colony was based on the examples of Rome and Greece, but, in contrast with these models, it proclaimed the absolute equality of all citizens and the common ownership of all property. Total freedom— which extended to sex—was the real foundation of the colony's laws (317–24).

Admittedly life amid the marble temples of a sun-drenched Greek island is hardly comparable to a "retraite" in a half-ruined convent of a Parisian suburb; and the uninhibited, quasi-pagan hedonism of Ardinghello's colony is very far from the atmosphere of cloistered meditation that pervaded Chaillot. Notwithstanding these and many other differences, the two utopian conceptions reveal some major common elements that transcend the comparatively accessory similarities suggested by the costumes or communal living. Above all, in the case of Paros as well as in that of Chaillot, a group of *artists* founded an ideal society aimed at man's regeneration through a return to the beauty, virtues, and ways of life of a remote antiquity. Neither Ardinghello nor Maurice Quay was attempting to start a worldwide revolution: Their respective re-creations of the golden age were open only to a chosen group (much larger, of course, in the case of Heinse's novel), and their utopian experiments were confined to the seclusion of an island, or of a convent. In other words, in both cases the concept of utopia was linked to the suggestion of a deliberate escape and estrangement.

It is true that Heinse is mentioned neither by Nodier nor by Gleizes (or by any other *Barbu*), and that historical perspective can create misleading parallels. However, the chronology of events suggests that the kinship between the utopia of Paros and that of Chaillot represents something more than a mere coincidence. In fact, the sect's removal to the Convent of the Visitation de Sainte Marie almost immediately followed (after approximately one year) the publication of the French translation of *Ardinghello.*

Notwithstanding the possible influence of Heinse's utopia, the Hellenic element of Maurice's primitivism was gradually adulterated in the Convent of the Visitation de Sainte Marie. This evolution was paralleled by the *Barbus'* apparently decreasing enthusiasm for Ossian and their changing attitude toward the Bible. To understand the progressive modification of the sect's ideas, one must realize that, upon leaving David's hospitable abode in the Louvre, Maurice's followers had to face some unavoidable, down-to-earth realities. Despite Gleizes's and Périé's personal wealth, the sect never acquired the means to erect temples, in marble or in any other material, although one might suspect that the renting of a few empty rooms in an abandoned convent was reasonably within the reach of most of the *Barbus* (in fact, the place invited squatters).

The half-ruined convent lent itself no more readily to the re-creation of a Greek golden age than did the studio of David. But from the melancholy grandeur and the mystery of these desolate buildings emanated a far greater emotional aura than from the dusty familiarity of easels, maulsticks, and plaster casts. Kindling a different kind of dream, the ruins of Chaillot possessed the dramatic ability to give new direction to the imagination. Describing the Convent of the Visitation de Sainte Marie, Nodier wrote in his *Une Heure, ou la vision* (1806):

> This dilapidated convent offers one of the saddest impressions which might strike the eyes of man. The only remains of the church are large, desolate pilasters which bear, here or there, a few fragments of a destroyed vault. When the moon shines its light through these columns and the owls are hooting on the cornices; when one then reaches the top of the wild terrace gardens; when one progresses along the high walls, stumbling among the ditches; and when going down the decrepit steps . . . one arrives to almost entirely eroded buildings with nothing but threatening remains of pieces of walls and roofs

supported in an almost miraculous manner; when one arrives by chance to this funereal avenue which, through a rocky slope and under moldy arches, leads to the ancient catacombs; and when, by the light of some dying lamp, one can read on the scattered grave stones the names of these chaste maidens who left their bones there . . . there is no human force which might resist such emotions. (*Les Tristes,* 59–61)

This passage is not the first evocation of the convent by Nodier. After describing the same awesome surroundings in the different and somewhat earlier *Méditations du cloître* (1803), the writer came to reflect on the vanity of man's condition, the illusions and evils of civilization, and the unjust persecutions to which the monastic institution had been subjected through the ages, particularly during the Revolution. Most of this poeticized prose is devoted to a glorification of the ecclesiastical orders. Nodier's description of their earliest phases is particularly interesting:

Their founders were the chosen ones that God had inspired; their reformers, courageous enthusiasts taught by misfortune . . . their ways, their customs, and even their clothes bore witness to the noble and severe character of their mission.

Nearly contemporary to the original faith, their origin went back . . . to the Essenians of Syria, to the Therapeutists of Lake Meoris.

The deserts of Africa and Asia spoke of their grottoes and their hermitages.

They lived in common like the people of Lycurgus and called each other brothers, like the young Theban warriors.

They had remedies like the Indian snake charmers and secrets like the priests of Isis.

Some of them abstained from eating animal flesh and from using speech, like the pupils of Pythagoras. Some of them wore the tunic and the cap of the Phrygians, and others girded their loins, like the men of ancient days. (*Romans,* 83)

Far from being seen as a ghost from the past, monasticism offered an antidote for the curse of Nodier's generation, his own anticipative version of the *mal du siècle*:

Does one know what fatal results so many idle passions and repressed energies can produce? Does one know how close to succumbing to crime is an impetuous heart that is succumbing to boredom? I declare it with bitterness, with fear: Werther's pistol and the executioner's axe have already decimated us!

He cries out: "THIS GENERATION IS RISING AND IS DEMANDING CLOISTERS" (85–86).

In his description of monks, Nodier singled out some of the most unusual attire from their remote past, such as the Phrygian garb, or the costume worn by men of ancient days, rather than the better-known, traditional habit. While multiplying classical parallels and referring to Spartans and Theban warriors, the writer stressed some of the most esoteric aspects of the monks' distant origins, which he traced to the Essenes, Egyptian therapeutists, Indian snake charmers, priests of Isis, and Pythagoreans. The hermetic sacredness of these proto-monastic associations was considered both as the original inspiration for religious orders and the guiding spirit of the group of Chaillot, since Nodier, depicting Maurice's sect in his article of 1832, alluded again to the Essenes, therapeutists, and Pythagoras, as well as to Moravians, Quakers, Plato, and to saints in general (NOD-BAR 440). This inclination for combining religion, philosophy, secret cults, and hermetic esoterica is also reflected in the writings of Gleizes, who, after all, came from Castres, one of the centers of the great medieval Catharist heresy (remembered even today in the region). Among the great vegetarians, he listed the sects of Pythagoras, Epicurus, and Zeno, as well as Buddha, Osiris, Orpheus, Bacchus, and Manco Capac. This mixture of legendary demigods, great philosophers, more or less historical sects, and true religious associations brings to mind the eighteenth-century illuminism of Louis-Claude de Saint-Martin and the much later literary use of hermetic learning, which pervades Flaubert's *Tentation de Saint-Antoine* and Apollinaire's *Alcools*.

These references are not entirely gratuitous, for, in the Convent of the Visitation de Sainte Marie, one senses an increasingly hermetic, illuministic atmosphere in which the utopian idea of a perfect primitive society takes the form of a poetically conceived paramonastic, esoteric group. Appellations such as *illuminés des arts* and *Port-Royal des Méditateurs* are quite revealing in this regard. Thus it is not surprising that Nodier thought he had found in Chaillot the full embodiment of the goals he had hoped to achieve in Besançon with his *Philadelphes*. In one of his first letters to Weiss about the *Barbus,* he declared:

> I have found here another society which has more in common with us [the *Philadelphes*] than all other known societies; but its members have reached their goal so perfectly that we could not show ourselves to them in our lack of purity. (NOD-EST 21)

The aura of loyalty, purity, and sacredness which emanated from this "other society" was so compelling that Nodier confessed a shameful sin to Weiss, in a mode of the Denial of Saint Peter:

> I have not entirely cast off my impurity. . . . This morning, again, I went into a gambling establishment, and I entrusted to chance some silver. . . . Seeing my long beard, my hair hanging over my shoulders, my bare neck, some one thought he recognized me, and said in an undertone: he is an *observateur de l'homme*. I answered aloud: Where is he? and I fled, rushing down the steps, quivering with shame. (NOD-EST 24–25)

This semireligious context must be kept in mind in order to understand the puzzling statements that appeared in Nodier's letters of this period. This is the case, for instance, in the passage in which the writer spoke of the *Barbus'* gathering of herbs for "la Cène"—that is, the Lord's Supper—(NOD-EST 25), or of the assertion that he drank from Maurice's cup, that he smoked his calumet, and that he gave him, in the morning and in the evening, the brotherly kiss (NOD-EST 29). These rituals were colored with exoticism, and the American Indian touch of the calumet—one thinks of Chateaubriand's recently published "American" story *Atala* (1801)—was merely a spice added to a dominant oriental flavor. The Hellenic sun of Heinse and the northern winds of Ossian were left behind. It is evident that the *Barbus'* oriental tobacco, bamboo pipes, collations of milk, honey (NOD-LAR 23), dry figs, and oranges (NOD-EST 25), and, in general, their vegetarianism (NOD-LAR 23) were inspired by the brand of "poetry of the desert" that overflowed from Gleizes's *Les Nuits élyséennes* into the sect's fascination for the lyricism of the Bible. Planning a novel about the biblical Dina (never completed), Nodier wrote:

> I have always loved the Bible; for some time, the Bible has become my book. My imagination, bruised by so many painful failures, is consoled and refreshed by these beautiful scenes of a fortunate age and a romantic climate. Since my youth has been nothing but a bitter cup, I want to cheer my last thoughts under the delightful sky of the Orient, in these beautiful lands which produce nothing but pearls, roses, and perfumes. From time to time, I seem to feel that the atmosphere of Europe is poisoning me and that I have the need to go and breathe the aromatic spices of the Orient. I think that this exquisite honey, these succulent dates, and this fragrant milk will purify my blood and renew my life. (NOD-EST 14)

This trend grew stronger. In the convent of Chaillot the *Barbus* incongruously spoke about the desert (NOD-EST 22), and in writing about Maurice, Nodier quoted the Persian poet Sa'di (NOD-TYP 74). The oriental mode came to influence the sect's dress. Nodier now wrote of its members' Phrygian costume alluding to Middle Eastern monks rather than to Périé's "Paris," and he did not refer to the Grecian garb (NOD-LAR 23). Adulterating his earlier Hellenic dedication, Maurice himself succumbed to this influence. According to Nodier, the Maurice Quay of the Convent of the Visitation de Sainte Marie was now sporting a turban and wearing perfumes. In his description of his friend, the writer, after the usual references to Job, Isaiah, Klopstock, Poussin, Pythagoras, and Jupiter, stated:

> Add to all this the sublime forms of antiquity and romantic accessories like his turban, cloak of crimson [instead of blue], laced boots, and perfumes. . . . You will see that this man is pure magic, a demigod! (NOD-EST 29)

Don Quixote has been completely forgotten, and Agamemnon, the king, has been transformed into a magus, an oriental high priest.

The reading of selected sections of the Old Testament, followed by discussions and Maurice's sermonizing harangues, played an important part in the group's activities. Nodier wrote to Weiss:

I went to see them [the *Barbus*] . . . it was at Peniez'. It was ten o'clock in the evening, and there were only five of us: Peniez, Maurice Quai, Alexandre Hue, Grault and myself. Jenny was there, but she felt sleepy and she went to bed. We sat down in a circle on rugs, and we smoked Oriental tobacco in bamboo pipes; later we ate some oranges and dried figs and we read the Ecclesiastes and the Apocalypse. I do not know if you have recently reread these sublime creations of the most beautiful poetry which has ever been written under the sun, but I was stupefied and was tempted to cry out: men could not have written this! Maurice rose, he unfolded his great crimson cloak and he spoke a language so eloquent and so magnificent that I thought I was still reading the Bible. . . . This voice has the musical sound of a glass harmonica, and his eloquence is like a delicious perfume which sweetly cajoles the senses and penetrates all one's faculties. (NOD-EST 25–26)

When the weather permitted, such meetings were held in the open air, in the gardens of the convent, or, to quote Nodier: "Under the pretty blossoming cherry trees of our terraces of Chaillot." In this bucolic setting the *Barbus* were treated to Maurice's orations on poetry, philosophy, and on the subject of what Nodier called, elusively, "this wholly new science on which," as he was hoping, "was based the regeneration of humanity" (NOD-BAR 445). The deep communal feelings experienced by the sect's members on such occasions were poetically evoked in a Botticelli-like image:

We wore white tunics [like early Christian neophytes] and our hair was floating on our shoulders. We rested on the grass; we spoke of the desert, of friendship, of you [Weiss]; we looked at Paris and we wept. Do not ever come to Paris my poor Charles [Weiss]. . . . But if you ever come there, ask everyone you will encounter if they know the convent of Sainte-Marie and the Méditateurs, and join them in their retreat. (NOD-EST 22)

It is not known whether Weiss ever decided to follow Nodier's advice, but it is obvious that the intent of the *Barbus'* philosophical solitude and of their poetic sessions under blossoming cherry trees could have been misinterpreted by outsiders. Nodier's father, for instance, confused these activities with the eighteenth-century pastel-colored tradition of pastorals *à la Pompadour*. Summoning the familiar cliché of the artist's or the poet's end in the hospital, Judge Nodier wrote to his son (9 February 1802):

Are you composing songs or eclogues? A few passages from your last letter led me to think that you were now yielding to a pastoral bent. . . . This pastoral genre is not worth much more than the others, and all of them lead more certainly to the hospital than to fortune and glory. (Mme Mennessier-Nodier, *Charles Nodier*, 41–42)

A few other outsiders showed a greater understanding, and prominent men of letters like Chateaubriand and Pindare-Lebrun [Ponce-Denis Ecouchard Lebrun], actually found their way to the *Port-Royal des Méditateurs*. Basking in the glow of these famous people's reputation, the group seems to have enjoyed at Chaillot a modest measure of attention from the intellectual elite. Doubtless these visitors were attracted to the convent by Maurice's notoriety, but on occasion they yielded to the inspiration emanating from the sect. Thus, far from being content to observe the *Barbus* as so many *bêtes curieuses,* they sometimes emulated the group's more conventionally creative efforts. According to Nodier:

> This is where Chateaubriand sometimes comes to study the poetry of the desert, that Lebrun tunes his lyre, that Hue sketches his seascapes, and Glaise [Gleizes] his poems. (NOD-LAR 23)

From what has been said previously about the sect's penchant for the oriental, it is perhaps more astonishing to discover that Hue (probably Alexandre-Laurent) could find in the convent some inspiration for painting his seascapes than to learn that Chateaubriand came to the same seventeenth-century ruins to study the poetry of the desert. At any rate, it appears that the life at Chaillot was not entirely confined to contemplation, reading sessions, or collectively experienced emotions.

Nodier's relations with Chateaubriand were somewhat strained by his having written a parody of *Atala* (1802), for which he readily confessed his feeling of shame to his fellow members at Chaillot (NOD-EST 25). Despite Nodier's awkward position, one might suspect that most of the *Barbus* were immensely flattered by Chateaubriand's occasional (and probably very rare, since his name appears only once in Nodier's correspondence) appearance in the Convent of the Visitation de Sainte Marie. Doubtless the great writer aroused considerable interest, especially on the part of Gleizes (whose literary kinship with Chateaubriand has previously been noted). "The poetry of the desert," which Chateaubriand is supposed to have been studying in Chaillot—a possible reference to discussions of *Les Nuits élyséennes*—could plausibly have played some part in the conception of the Middle Eastern trip that he would later describe in *L'Itinéraire de Paris à Jérusalem* (1811).

Pindare-Lebrun seems to have visited Chaillot more frequently than Chateaubriand, and his name recurs in two separate letters of Nodier (NOD-LAR 23 and NOD-EST 25). Almost completely forgotten today, Pindare-Lebrun was a literary celebrity in his time. The fame of this elderly *homme de lettres* (he was born in 1729) rested on a large number of *bouts-rimés,* epigrams, and odes. Most had been written in an earlier phase of his career, but, because of his adaptable talent, he was still very productive, highly successful, and socially prominent at the turn of the century. He cast a striking figure disguised as the Greek poet Pindar at Mme Vigée le Brun's *souper grec* (Chateaubriand, *Mémoires d'outre-tombe,* I, 141). While officially praised and rewarded during the *Directoire* and the *Consulat*—Bonaparte appointed him *Grand Maréchal du Palais*—he remained very much an eighteenth-century galant at heart. In his introduction to Pindare-Lebrun's *Œuvres* (1811), Pierre-Louis Ginguené related that the poet's "lodgings in the Louvre brought him into contact with several young and pretty women." He referred most particularly to "these young artists, or friends of artists" (a few doubtless belonging to Maurice Quay's circle) who "made a game of teasing him," and he added, "it seems that several of them took great pride in receiving some homage from him." Since a number of Pindare-Lebrun's poems at the turn of the century were dedicated to "his beautiful and dreamy Lucile" (*Œuvres*, I, xxxv–xxxvi), one could surmise that, fortified by his literary fame, the old roué had made some attempts at courting Lucile Franque while visiting the convent at Chaillot. Nodier had been in love with Lucile during the very same period:[3] He dedicated his *Pensées de Shakespeare* (1801) to her, and under different names he introduced her in several of his novels, such as *Le Peintre de Saltzbourg* (1803; *Fig. 14*). Nodier is understandably harsh when speaking of Pindare-Lebrun:

> As for Lebrun, he is not a *méditateur,* he is an enthusiast who wanted to attach the wings of Pindar's eagle to the Capitoline goose. He brings his irascible pride among us [the *Barbus*], and the nasty man became angry the other day because while gathering herbs for *la Cène,* we whipped his hands with nettles. That is the naughtiest action I have ever seen done by the *méditateurs.* (NOD-EST 25)

Despite Nodier's personal lack of affinity with Chateaubriand and Pindare-Lebrun, the appearance of these two writers at Chaillot came close to what, with slight exaggeration, might be considered an open recognition of the sect. If the *Barbus* had chosen to exploit such contacts, they could have established Chaillot as one of the most fashionable cultural centers of the capital, a new kind of Salon: the "Salon of the convent of Chaillot." In fact, if Nodier's 1832 account of the meeting between Maurice Quay and Napoleon reflects any degree of truth, it would appear that the *Barbus,* despite their professed angelic innocence, were not entirely immune to the temptation presented by such opportunities. (Pindare-Lebrun, in his function as the *Grand Maréchal du Palais,* was certainly in a position to arrange such interviews.)

Nevertheless, either by chance or by purpose, the sect preserved its essential virtue of self-effacement. The most important reason for this obscurity can perhaps be found in Nodier's characterization of the ultimate aesthetic stance of the *Barbus*:

> The general feeling which for them . . . took the place of religion . . . was, at the beginning, a love, a fanaticism for art. By dint of perfecting it, purifying it in the hearth of their soul, they had arrived to great and sublime nature, and art no longer offered them, in this second phase . . . anything but an object of comparison and the resource of a craft. Nature itself finally shrank in their thoughts, because the sphere of their ideas had widened. They understood that there was something marvelous and incomprehensible behind the last veil of Isis, and they withdrew from the world, for they became mad, that is the word for it, like the therapeutists and saints, mad like Pythagoras and Plato.

> Nevertheless, they continued to visit studios and museums, but they no longer produced any works. Their costumes, their way of life, their sternness,

the solemnity . . . which was natural to them and which was the effortless expression of an untiring habit of contemplation, of an inner life completely spiritualized, imposed on the whole school . . . a sort of respectful pity. (NOD-BAR 442–43)

The *Barbus* faded from the view of the historical spyglass after Nodier's departure for Besançon in the summer of 1802. Upon his return everything was gone. His feelings about the disappearance of his friends are echoed in the police record of his arrest, on 20 December 1803, which was the consequence of his self-denunciation as the author of *La Napoleone.* Nodier, interrogated by the *commissaire* Dubois, stated that his politically incriminating publication had been motivated by the confusion caused by a great sorrow:

D. What are the reasons for the misfortune, which, according to you, you are experiencing at this time?

N. I was an intimate friend here of a young lady by the name of Lucile Franck [Franque], a history painter, and of Maurice Quaï [Quay], also a history painter. They both died shortly before my return to Paris, and this event has been extremely painful for me.[4]

Nodier was very poetic but rather obscure when he evoked the disappearance of the other *Barbus.* In his article of 1832, he wrote:

The soul of these people [the *Barbus*] was quickly consuming its envelope. Consumption or suicide did away with them before they turned twenty-five. Thus, disappeared, in the flower of their age, the strongest and the most tender individuals who had ever honored the human race.

Yet a few pages later in the same article, he said:

One day, they all withdrew and separated in groups into two or three philosophical retreats, but the newspapers said nothing about it. (NOD-BAR 440, 443)

It is impossible to ascertain whether Nodier was implying that his friends had committed suicide or had died of consumption after the sect's fragmentation (after Chaillot?), or whether he was offering two alternative codas to the *Barbus'* chronicle. The reality of course is more prosaic. It is true that Maurice Quay and Lucile Franque died of consumption in their youth, and that some other members of the sect—at any rate, at least one: Delécluze's Augustin D. . . (DEL-DAV 92)[5]— had committed suicide. However, as shown here in Chapter 4, it is equally true that the great majority of the identifiable *Barbus* (the brothers Franque, Broc, Périé, Fabre d'Eglantine *fils,* Alexandre Hue, Gleizes, etc.) simply faded into comparative mediocrity, even though they did survive the disappearance of the group.

Mme Mennessier-Nodier's much later (1867) reference to a revival of Maurice Quay's sect in the Jura region was obviously based on her confusion of the *Barbus* with the *Philadelphes,* a confusion that was compounded by a mistaken notion of their respective chronologies (Mme Mennessier-Nodier, *Charles Nodier,* 44–46). Nodier's correspondence does indeed suggest that during his Chaillot period he nourished eager hopes to link the two movements (NOD-EST 21). However, the writer's later biography fails to reveal anything that could corroborate Mme Mennessier-Nodier's assertion that after the affair provoked by *La Napoleone* her father had made some actual attempts to establish a new branch of the *Barbus* in Besançon.

It appears certain, however, that Maurice Quay's group stimulated some imitators in Paris. Delécluze, for instance, related with some mirth the misadventure of a sub-sect, also composed of students of David, "spending their time in ecstasy in front of Etruscan vases," which was headed by Maurice's "ape," the dancer-actor Monrose. Aroused by their Ossianic beer drinking and some incongruously non-Ossianic guitar music, Monrose's followers, wearing Scandinavian and Grecian rags, decided to leave the city of vices, the "new Babylon," and to live in the forests in imitation of Macpherson's characters. Surprised by the cold and darkness of an autumnal evening in the Bois de Boulogne—the closest available forest near Paris—they tried to follow the example of Ossianic heroes and proceeded to set a tree afire. This adventure (which, according to Delécluze, took place about 1805) ended in a police station, from which the long-haired, bearded young men were released after the humiliation of a shave and a haircut (DEL-DAV 328–30 and DEL-BAR 430–31).

Since Monrose's followers suffered from the historical curse that befalls imitators, it is difficult to say whether they really were so much more ridiculous than the members of Maurice's original sect. At any rate, the episode of the Bois de Boulogne echoed the essential intent of Chaillot: the rejection of modern society. The artist did not accept prevailing clichés, but he was also no longer interested in proselytizing for his projects of utopian reform. He abandoned his hope to change the world around him and channeled his poetic yearning into a concept of separateness, which, in fact, constituted a demonstration of his alienation from society—an alienation dramatized by bizarre behavior. Essentially this point of view parallels the attitude of every nineteenth- and twentieth-century artist who, through the oddity of his clothes and the nonconformity of his deportment, points to the gap that divides him from the rest of the world. This is the very significance of the previously quoted repartee, which was attributed by Nodier to Maurice on the occasion of his alleged meeting with Napoleon: "to separate myself from the world" (NOD-BAR 441).

Thus the *Barbus'* chronicle ended anticlimactically with the tragicomedy of Nodier's arrest and the farce of Monrose's sylvan expedition. The traces of the *Port-Royal des Méditateurs* faded away. The site of the Convent of the Visitation de Sainte Marie became so dangerously eroded by its systematic exploitation as a limestone quarry that the police, concerned with the safety of the projected palace for the Roi de Rome, ordered the owner, Alfred Nettement, to discontinue his commercial excavations (1811).[6] Naturally, the palace for the Roi de Rome was not destined to be built, but eventually the old convent was razed and the hill leveled. It would evidently be futile to search for any mementos of Maurice Quay's group in the records of the building of the much later Palais du Trocadéro (1878) and that of Chaillot (1937). The ashes are cold.

The *Barbus* were always to remain very dear to Nodier, who surrounded their memory with an aura of sacredness. This feeling permeates his letters as well as his previously mentioned publications. It is also echoed, with some melancholy, in his lesser-known *Apothéose de Pythagore* (1808). The preface of this deliberately archaistic *poème en prose* (appearing in print with a monumental, "primitive," typography), described by its author as a "unique and precious moment of primitive society," ends with a moving personal homage to the *Barbus'* leaders:

> What a profound sorrow
> I should feel entering my heart
> When I engrave here
> Like upon the base of the modest funereal stone
> Which I have dedicated
> To their spirits,
> The ever beloved names
> of Maurice
> and
> of Lucile!
>
> (De quelle profonde amertume
> Je me sentirais pénétré
> En gravant ici,
> Comme au bas du cippe modeste
> Que j'ai dédié
> A leurs mânes,
> Les noms toujours aimés
> de Maurice
> et
> de Lucile!)[7]

III: Ideas and Paintings

7

Aesthetic Theories and Inspiration

On the whole, the evolution of the artist's image at the turn of the nineteenth century failed to give birth to any corollary aesthetic evolution—that is, to an identifiable aesthetic trend that could be recognized as independent of the conventional art-historical sequence of the period. Thus in the realm of the popular stage, the painters who were subjected to the new stereotypes always expressed conventional aesthetic attitudes: Fougère appeared as a champion of the Grand Style; Rembrandt admired Dou's *Dropsical Woman*; and Lantara, at first described as a painter of traditional classical subjects and sentimental portraits, later became a landscape specialist. There is no discernible substantive artistic development to parallel the changing cultural definition of the artist's profession. In this regard the *Barbus* represent a most unusual phenomenon: In the course of their early self-assertion as rebellious reformers in David's studio, as well as in their subsequent *retraite* at Chaillot, they seem to have attached themselves to a definite pattern of aesthetically radical points of view.

It has already been seen that some indications of this pattern can be gathered from the statements of Delécluze and Nodier. Because of their firsthand exposure to these points of view, it is possible to surmise that a correlation of the two writers' observations suggests the general orientation of the sect's attitude toward art. These statements imply a process of distillation directed toward a search for sublime beauty and governed by certain concepts: the study of beautiful nature; the observation of antique art; the cult of primitivism; and a contemplative experience that, for the lack of another name, could be called—paraphrasing Poussin—*inner delectation*. This evolution seems to have begun with a comparatively conventional approach— slightly to the "left" of David's *Sabine Women*—advocating harmoniously conceived, very large and lightly shaded forms, and it seems to have ended, far more radically, with the discovery of nature as art, which was eventually followed by a quasi-mystical experience of pure ideation, transcending both nature *and* art.

Understandably, this nirvana of the *Barbus'* search for sublimity—with a transcendental nothingness as its end product—escaped detailed contemporary description as well as modern scholarly study. However, in the hands of some twentieth-century scholars, the earlier phase of the sect's aesthetic thinking was subjected to a measure of "Flaxmanization," in which the *Barbus'* aesthetic aims were approximated to a pictorial ideal of virtually linear, shadowless style.[1] This interpretation appears to find some corroboration in a rationalization of the previously quoted statement about light shadows attributed by Delécluze to Maurice Quay (DEL-DAV 72), as well as in the much later writings of Jacques-Nicolas Paillot de Montabert, an author who was originally associated with the sect. In this regard it should be noted that neither this particular statement ascribed to Maurice (who, in fact, never alludes to line or to linearity), nor any other pronouncement, reference, or surviving work of art, can be summoned to confirm that the idea of abstract linearity, which so emphatically recurs in Paillot de Montabert's later writings, such as the *Traité complet de la peinture* (1829) and most particularly in his *L'Artistaire* (1855), actually expressed the *Barbus'* original credo.

The question requires clarification. Admittedly—even without any specific proof—it is most probable that the sect's aesthetics gave great importance to the concept of line. However, far from reflecting any unusual boldness, the sect's alleged interest in line merely echoed one of the most conspicuously widespread trends at the turn of the century. As such, linearity can hardly be singled out as a revolutionary trait responsible for the reputation of oddity that was affixed to the *Barbus'* aesthetic theories—after all, David himself greatly admired Flaxman's outlines. The same comment evidently applies to two of the sect's other tenets, which refer to the study of beautiful nature and the observation of antique art. The first (a very old idea indeed!) had been incorporated into the tradition of eighteenth-century academic teaching, long before the emergence of the sect; the second of course pertained to the very essence of Neoclassicism. The *Barbus'* cult of primitivism reflected a far less conventional concept, and for this reason it requires special study. This study cannot encompass all the ramifications of the problem, since this book is not devoted to primitivism or primitivistic ideology per se. Far from laying a claim to an exhaustive survey of this complex subject, I aim to explore it only in the framework of the *Barbu* phenomenon.

It is well established that the eighteenth century showed unmistakable signs of a growing interest in primitive art, an interest that is evidenced by sets of engravings containing reproductions of Greek, so-called Etruscan, Roman, and Italian antiquities, the creation of private collections of early classical vases and Italian primitive paintings, and a variety of accounts appearing in travel books. In the course of the eighteenth century, a number of well-known publications, such as Pierre-François-Hugues d'Hancarville's *Collection of Etruscan, Greek, and Roman Antiquities* (1766), devoted to the collection of William Hamilton, began to show an increasing admiration for some forms of Greek and Italian primitive art. The concept of a simple linear outline, acknowledged as a characteristic of painting in its beginnings, was the common denominator that led connoisseurs to bestow equally enthusiastic praise on the works of early Greek and Italian painters.[2]

However, it is important to note that many other statements convey a completely different point of view. The patronizing attitude of some *amateurs* is illustrated by Charles de Brosses's description of the Pisan *Campo santo* (1739):

> All the walls are painted in fresco by the hand of Giotto, Orcagna, Benedetto, Benozzo Gozzoli, etc., who have represented Biblical stories in a very strange, very ridiculous, extremely poor, and most curious manner. (*Lettres familières sur l'Italie*, I, 371)

Debrosses's comments on primitive art cannot be dismissed as appearing too early to be significant since comparable statements kept recurring until the beginning of the nineteenth century. They were not limited to unenlightened *amateurs*. For instance, the erudite Pierre-Charles Levesque, who completed Watelet's *Dictionnaire* (1792), acknowledging the role of Cimabue in the development of Italian painting, wrote: "Mediocre artists would blush today for producing works of art similar to those of Cimabue" (WAT-DIC II, 21). The same Levesque scorned the clumsy productions of "Gothic" artists (II, 429–30), and, speaking about the outlines of the early painters, stated: "At that time, art consisted exclusively of what today we call drawing, and, as long as this phase alone was known, it remained in the utmost state of weakness: these masterpieces looked like the drawings that children create while playing" (IV, 54). In a sense, such disparaging opinions about primitive art found some support in Johann Joachim Winckelmann, the most influential champion of the Neoclassical ideal. The great German art historian believed that Classical art, before reaching its period of decadence, was marked by constant progress. This idea of initial perfectibility allowed him to state that the beginnings of art were "characterized by an extreme simplicity" followed by a steady improvement based on a profound study of rules. For him, primitivism per se warranted no special admiration.[3]

In short, for every adulatory comment about primitive art, one can find a critical one. Thus we may forgo the futile exercise of weighing positive and negative opinions; it is better to admit that the admiration for primitive art was anything but universal. The eighteenth-century publications describing and praising primitive Classical and Italian art have been well-studied.[4] Their importance can be taken for granted, but it is necessary to expand the problem and give it a wider perspective.

Categorizing can be useful. In this regard, for the sake of clarity, it may be first pointed out that until the beginning of the nineteenth century, the idea of primitivism was shaped by three different—but often combined—points of view. They can be loosely described as antiquarian, historical recording, religious identification, and pseudo-scientific and illuministic speculations.

The antiquarian recording of nonclassical primitive art finds its first truly methodical and influential champion in Jean-Baptiste Seroux d'Agincourt (1730–1814).[5] Seroux d'Agincourt enjoyed cordial relations with practically every important scientist and every noteworthy artist of the second half of the eighteenth century. Endowed with a universal curiosity, he developed a great interest in

Romanesque ruins during a geological expedition, and, casting aside his scientific studies, he decided to become the Winckelmann of the barbaric times. In other words, he intended to fill the historical gap that the famous German antiquarian had left open between the classical and modern ages. Consequently, in 1778 Seroux d'Agincourt went to Italy, where he spent the rest of his life studying and drawing all the examples of medieval art he could find. The results of his investigations were posthumously published in the six folios of *L'Histoire de l'art par les monuments, depuis sa décadence au quatrième siècle jusqu'à son renouvellement au seizième* (1823).

Affirming that he failed to discern any primitive phase in Greek art—for which he was nursing a blind admiration (*L'Histoire,* II, 7)—the author was mostly concerned with the evolution of art in Italy between the fourth and the fourteenth centuries. He was struck by the inadequacy of the "sad productions of these unhappy times" (II, 10): For him they represented a phase of utter decadence, and, without yielding to the patronizing irony of de Brosses and Levesque, he was nevertheless equally harsh in his comments. He refers repeatedly to the monotonous and incorrect contours of most of the paintings of this period, their poor composition, and the lack of gradations in color, as well as to the caricature effect of the facial expressions, proportions, and anatomical treatment of figures (II, 91). According to Seroux d'Agincourt, Giotto was the "first reformer of modern art" (II, 39). From this time on the advance of painting, determined by a renewed study of nature, could be measured by the liberation of the successive generations of artists from their former errors and their drawing nearer to the achievements of the High Renaissance (ergo, the classical tradition). The author was never disarmed by any notion of primitive naiveté, and his approach was entirely ruled by a preconceived concern for tracing the slow progress of Italian art from its post-Classical decadence to the Renaissance. In a sense this evolutionary perspective of art in Italy reflected the idea of Winckelmann's perfectibility.

In the French context Seroux d'Agincourt's approach found a parallel in Alexandre Lenoir's *Musée des monuments francais.* Bringing together a large number of works of art confiscated during the Revolution from churches and châteaux, this museum (open in 1793) offered to the Parisian public a unique survey of French art history. Its conception, explained in great detail in the many editions of Lenoir's *Description,* was summarized in the "introductory hall" of the museum. Displaying characteristic samples from all periods, this area was meant to show, in a single glance, the entire development of French art, from the time of the Goths to Joseph-Marie Vien's Neoclassicism. The author clearly states his belief in a cyclic evolution of art history: "The arts are subjected to revolutions just like empires: they successively pass from infancy to barbarism and return, little by little, to their starting point" (*Description,* 1802, 19).

This cycle was the basis of Lenoir's likes and dislikes. Despite his personal Neoclassical leaning as an artist, he was capable of admitting that some thirteenth-century statues of Apostles from the Sainte-Chapelle were "very remarkable by the naiveté of their expression and the simplicity of their execution" (146). But such comments are exceptional, and in general Lenoir expressed little admiration for French medieval art. Thus describing the thirteenth-century room of his museum, he explained:

> The dark lighting of this room, is also imitating the effect of those times; a device through which one perpetually kept in a state of weakness beings whom superstition had stricken with fear; for I have observed that the more one looks back into the centuries which are closest to our own, the more the lighting in public monuments becomes brighter, as though the sight of the sun could only suit the educated man. (122)

Superstition can also explain the shortcomings of the primitive art of much earlier civilizations:

> The Egyptians had only slight notions of painting. . . . [Their] figures are nothing but poorly drawn hieroglyphics. . . . Everything was mystical for this religious people, and superstition impeded the progress of the arts to such a point . . . that their statues are repelling rather than attracting us. (20)

Primitive Greek art was not spared—not because it was a creation of barbarian superstition, but because it reflected the childhood of art. According to Lenoir, before Alexander the Great the painter "dared to draw only monochromatic shapes of an equal tone," and the progress, considered in Seroux d'Agincourt's terms, was brought about by artists "who dared to spread light and shade in their paintings" (21).

The Dark Ages, which followed the disappearance of the Classical world, were marked by barbarism, poor taste, and a monochromatic style. The arts finally returned to their former splendor with the innovations of Cimabue, but in France the restoration of the arts did not begin until the reign of Francis I. Lenoir carefully itemized the imperfections of earlier French works. For instance, the first fourteenth-century oil paintings "only show . . . a representation of nature such as it can be seen with all its defects, in a dry, arid drawing, in a labored work . . . in figures with insipid expressions; that is, representing the Gothic style of the time" (93).

Notwithstanding such comments, Lenoir deplored the destruction of many monuments of this period by the revolutionary iconoclasts, and the professed aim of his museum—to form the taste of art students through "comparisons which can be made between different types of style" (36)—implicitly acknowledged primitive art as aesthetically valid in its own context.

Lenoir was also guided by an intense nationalism: Any primitive art form was interesting insofar as it was French. But this national assertion, typical of this period, was colored by other rather murky emotions. The idea of his museum was originally inspired by the opening of the royal tombs of Saint-Denis (1793), which later formed the nucleus of the exhibition. Lenoir personally witnessed the exhumation of the skeletons and cadavers of the royal families and published an unsettling account of this grisly event in his *Description*. In a bizarre manner this account—one imagines a particularly gruesome version of Edward Young's *Night Thoughts* —brought out the deep-seated French love-hate feelings for their kings, immersed in something bordering on necrophilia. Funeral mementos formed the main staple of the Musée des monuments français, and the art of the past—more particularly primitive art—was stamped in Lenoir's collection with the deep, obscure feelings permeating the memories of the dead.

In the light of this quasi-spiritual atmosphere, it is surprising to observe that the Musée des monuments français failed to spur any religious acknowledgment of French primitive art. About 1800, even before Bonaparte's ratification of the *Concordat* (1802), which reestablished the national legality of Catholicism, the conception of Christian religion as a major source of artistic inspiration was rapidly growing in importance. But in France this idea was seldom extended to an actual recognition of primitive art.

The theocratic philosopher Pierre-Simon Ballanche offered an early illustration of the French religious orientation. In his *Du Sentiment considéré dans ses rapports avec la littérature et les arts* (1801), he considered religion to be "the fertilizing principle of all our success in literature and the arts" (183), and the Catholic religion to have given life "to all the modern masterpieces" (165–66). Yet in this effusive book, which gives as much prominence to Ossian, the troubadours, and the Old Testament as to the great classics of ancient and modern times, the visual arts are treated in a most conservative manner. Ballanche's examples are confined to widely accepted artists, such as Michelangelo, Raphael, and Rubens. Lacking interest in primitivism, the author had no admiration for the Egyptian civilization, "which gave birth to all the arts and which perfected none," or for the Chinese, who created "paintings without perspective" and "grotesque sculptures" (148). For him the legendary invention of Dibutade was interesting only because her tracing of her lover's silhouette on the wall was inspired by love, that is, by "le sentiment," Ballanche's leitmotiv (45). He was totally unconcerned with anything that could be even remotely construed as primitive art.

Chateaubriand's *Génie du Christianisme* (first published in 1802) develops a view that is analogous to that of Ballanche. However, by giving an overwhelming importance to religion per se, it entirely dismisses the role of "le sentiment," and of all other sources of art. Thus according to Chateaubriand, it was not Dibutade's invention of the silhouette—inspired by a "fleeting passion"—but rather God's creation of man that the "Christian school" recognized as the real beginning of art (*Génie*, 1859, 305). To refute the notion of the Church's hostility to the arts, the author stressed the role of Christianity as their protector and patron. After having struggled against countless obstacles, the Christian religion triumphantly brought the arts back on earth during the era torn by the Barbarians' invasions and heresy, following the collapse of the Roman Empire. Beginning with Cimabue in the thirteenth century, and culminating, under the reign of Leo X, with Michelangelo and Raphael, the fine arts progressed, in a manner previously indicated by Seroux d'Agincourt, because of the influence of the Church (305–7).

Chateaubriand attempted to demonstrate the superiority of Christian religion as a source of inspiration, and his bias was limitless. He claimed, for instance, that the true landscape remained unknown to the painters of antiquity, whom he criticized for their ignorance of the rules of perspective and their inability to render depth (624). Paradoxically, he did not speak of the lack of realism in religious primitive painting, but this did not prevent him from criticizing non-Christian primitive art for the same reason. For instance:

> The Egyptians . . . because of their beliefs . . . did not know how to render nature. Some of their paintings, which can still be seen on the walls of their temples, hardly rise, as far as composition, above the *technique* of the Chinese. (624)

Far from identifying Christianity with primitivist naiveté, Chateaubriand suggested that Christianity opened the door through which art escaped from its primitive state.

The most important early intimation of a recognition of primitive art as a unique reflection of divine inspiration appeared in Germany in Wilhelm Heinrich Wackenroder's *Herzensergiessungen eines kunstliebenden Klosterbruders* (1797). Pretending to be a friar writing in the solitude of monastic life, the author was mainly concerned with the mystical character of artistic creation. In his "Raphael's Vision," a short piece devoted to Raphael's inspiration, Wackenroder relates the miraculous experience that inspired Raphael to paint the Virgin Mary. Raphael's vision is due to direct divine assistance, and the author cites a statement he attributes to this famous Italian artist: "I hold myself to a certain mental image, which enters my soul" (*Herzensergiessungen,* 1971 ed., 85).

Raphael, of course, was hardly a primitive. In Wackenroder's other essays, most of the artists who truly deserve this designation—Cimabue, Giotto, Spinello Aretino—receive only a brief and rather perfunctory mention. Nevertheless, some of the merits of the early Italian artists' primitive qualities are not left unnoticed. In the *Chronicle of Artists,* another essay in the same book, Lippo Dalmasio and Fra Angelico are especially singled out because of their "serious and holy mind" and "humble simplicity." The author observes that "they made the art of painting into a faithful servant of religion and knew nothing about the empty display of colors of today's artists" (145).

Wackenroder nursed a particularly enthusiastic affection for early German artists: For him Dürer was the equal of Raphael. In his "Memorial," dedicated to Dürer (in the same book), the writer admiringly notes in his hero's works some of the characteristics usually ascribed to primitive painters: unaffected simplicity, indifference to "glistening external beauty," the absence of cleverness "in the scatter-

ing of light and shadow," and a lack in compositional unity and methodical structure. While admitting that most people considered Dürer's painting stiff and
dull, Wackenroder implicitly discovered in these very shortcomings a reflection
of the honesty, seriousness, and expressiveness of the early German character. He
exclaims: "True art sprouts forth not only under Italian sky, under majestic domes
and Corinthian columns,—but also under pointed arches, intricately ornamented
buildings, and Gothic towers" (114–17).

This idea, free from religious and nationalistic connotations, is expounded with
even greater daring in Louis-Guillaume-René Cordier de Launay's *Théorie Circonsphérique des deux genres du beau* (1806). Cordier de Launay's theory rests on
the assertion that all works of art borrow forms from nature. Consequently, the
artist can either use these forms in the particular combination given to him by
nature, or, conversely, he can recombine them at will into a new, imaginary whole.
This choice, influenced by the action of temperature on the nervous fibers, determines two contrasting but equally valid types of beauty: The first, characteristic of
temperate climates, corresponds to *exact imitation;* while the second, prevailing in
regions of extreme cold or extreme heat, is based on *composite recombination.*
Cordier de Launay, who is particularly interested in the second type, defines its
nature by applying systematically—but *in reverse*—the rules of Aristotle's *Poetics*
and Quintilian's *Institutiones oratoriae* (implausible subject; lack of unity of action,
time, and place; lack of organization and ordered proportions, etc.) (*Théorie*,
29–33).

To illustrate his ideas in literature, the author contrasted Homer's *Iliad* (*exact
imitation*—temperate climate) with Milton's *Paradise Lost* (*composite recombination*—extreme cold) and Saint John's *Apocalypse* (*composite recombination*—extreme heat) (34). He experienced greater difficulties with the visual arts when he
attempted to contrast Gothic stained-glass windows, Indian painted textiles, arabesques, and lacquered Chinese folding-screens (visual equivalents of *Paradise
Lost* and *Apocalypse*) with Phidias, Apelles, the Belvedere Apollo, Raphael, and
Claude Lorrain (visually corresponding to the category of the *Iliad*) (235–37).

Some of Cordier de Launay's comments are nevertheless very significant. Discussing medieval stained-glass windows, for instance, he wrote:

> These paintings on glass which one can still see in our old Gothic churches
> . . . are composite. The images are pressed against each other and superim-
> posed without chiaroscuro, without aerial perspective, without harmony, in-
> deed without anything which distinguishes and characterizes the style of exact
> imitation. (237)

The author admired this type of primitive art for aesthetic reasons, independently
of Wackenroder's notions of Christian inspiration and nationalism. In fact, Cordier
de Launay's rehabilitation of primitivism also included exotic non-Christian categories, such as the frequently disparaged Chinese art, as well as other oriental
productions:

One is free to choose between these two types of Beauty, but one should not exclude the one which is alien to you. Friends, one should not accuse of barbarism masterpieces in which everything reveals genius. . . . There are some lacquer screens, some arabesques which I value as much as our most beautiful paintings. (238)

Cordier de Launay's plea in favor of a different kind of beauty reflected the ambiguities surrounding all the "unusual" types of art—such as the manifestations of primitivism—that could not be neatly pigeonholed in the approved categories of the time. Here the aesthetic understanding of primitivism was especially confused by speculations—mixing pseudo-science and illuminism—about what was referred to as the Primitive World.

The concept was based on the belief in the existence of an incredibly ancient and superior Atlantean-like human race, which thrived before the time of the great flood. According to this myth, the humanity of this antediluvian Golden Age, the age that preceded the Egyptian and all other known cultures, was the perfect humanity—characterized by giant stature and longevity—of true philosophers, inventors, and creators.

The eighteenth-century interest in the Primitive World was not limited to any one group. Although rooted in French thinking, according to Le Flamanc, it had an international character, including Swedenborg (in Sweden); Pallas (in Russia); Herder and Novalis (in Germany); Burnet and Warburton (in England); and Deluc and Mallet (in Switzerland). In France this idea preoccupied countless people: Fleury, Banier, Ramsay, Dupuy, Martin, Pezron, Terrasson, de Brosses, de Maillet, Robinet, d'Holbach, de la Metterie, Bailly, Delisle de Sales, Savary, Dupuis, Pluche, Court de Gébelin, Buffon, etc.[6] This incomplete listing is sufficient to show that the dream of the Primitive World attracted men from every level of European thinking, ranging from pure scientists to the most ethereal illuminati.

The idea of the Primitive World stimulated a search for the surviving monuments of the great Primitive civilization. It was thought that a few remains of these monuments—most of which had been destroyed by the great flood—had inspired all subsequent cultures. The question also spurred a search for the distant descendants of those members of the great Primitive race who, at the time of the flood, could have survived by taking refuge on the mountain peaks or plateaus above the water. One assumed that these remote descendants could be identified among some later ethnic groups, most particularly in northern Europe (Scandinavians, Scots, Germans), and that their original language was closest to Celtic. The possibility of direct offsprings was not discarded, and the extent of the eighteenth-century enthusiasm for such science-fiction speculations is best illustrated by an expedition of the French royal navy in 1771, which was sent to the austral regions with the mission to rediscover the lost continent of the primitive Atlantis.[7]

Primitive art was seen in terms of a dual perspective: as the sublimely barbaric art of possible primitive survivors and as the highly sophisticated art of the original

Atlantean race. This twofold contradictory context clouded anything that could be defined as primitive at the turn of the nineteenth century.

Because of the lack of evidence, the character of the artistic productions of the Primitive World was surmised on the strength of pure imagination. Thus the famous Antoine Court de Gébelin—often celebrated in his own time as the most learned scholar of the century—wrote in his monumental *Monde primitif* (1777) that the Greek invention of the silhouette was preceded, in the Primitive World, by a different kind of art: "the Hieroglyphic Paintings, those which are Symbolical of the Gods and the Marvels of Nature; Paintings created by gratitude for the happiness of society long before friendship had inspired men to immortalize their figures" (Court de Gébelin, I, 27–28).

But for the author, remembering the Horatian *Ut pictura poesis,* the art of the Primitive World was above all characterized by didactic and poetic allegory:

> Thus it is from Allegory, born for the instruction of the human race that . . . all these Arts: Poetry, Painting, Sculpture, etc., borrowed their colors, their images, their comparisons, their power, their sublimity. It is from Allegory that the genius of the Poet, that of the Painter, etc., have blossomed. . . . Even when they have to imitate physical objects in a most servile manner, they always add, in order to render them more attractive, some traits or allegorical connotations which uplift them and soften this servile imitation which was not made for Art. (28)

In chastising the pedestrian logic of the contemporary critic, Court de Gébelin stressed the expressiveness and the semi-abstract quality of this allegorical art:

> [The critic] . . . cannot appreciate a genius who has continuous lapses, who constantly hides his course, who sacrifices correctness to harmony, severity to grace, accuracy to elegance and to color . . . who wants to appeal to the mind through the senses and the imagination, for he is convinced that it is necessary to move the soul by all possible means. (29)

In his *Histoire philosophique du monde primitif* (1795–96), Jean-Claude-Izouard Delisle de Sales, like Court de Gébelin, traced the origin of the art of the Primitive World to hieroglyphics: ". . . it is known that the first writing was hieroglyphic, and hieroglyphics are nothing but painting" (*Histoire philosophique,* VII, 176).

But Delisle de Sales gave a somewhat lesser importance to allegory, and he attached no significance to abstraction. According to him, painting rapidly reached a great degree of sophistication, most particularly with Hermes—a mythological disguise for one of the great sages of the Primitive World—who had learned this art on the Tatar plateau, the original site of this early civilization. He achieved such an impressive skill, demonstrated by the likeness of his portraits of Saturn's family, that he became the Van Dyck of his century. Unfortunately this gallery of portraits disappeared, but, according to the author, it was comparatively simple to recognize some surviving echoes of other examples of the great art of the Primitive World:

> I always suspected that one had to ascribe to this period the originals of the Paintings of Centaurs, marine Panthers, and other objects of Nature, no longer in existence today, which helped to develop Zeuxis' talent, and which have been found, in our time, in the ruins of Pompeii and Herculaneum. (176–77)

This hypothesis is verified for two reasons. First:

> It is certain that, when Nature was closer to its period of adolescence and had a stronger generating power, it gave birth to a legion of creations which were destroyed by the frosts of its old age. We consider these creations as monsters only because our limited understanding cannot comprehend the works of Nature at the time when it was all powerful. (177)

Second:

> The man of taste easily distinguishes several periods in paintings such as the frescoes of the *Aldobrandine Wedding,* the decorations of the Thermae of Titus and those of Livia, and the mutilated paintings which the lava of the Vesuvius has preserved for us in Herculaneum. Three quarters of these monuments of art, without any accuracy of drawing, without any boldness of composition, and without the finish which can redeem these primary defects, evidently originate from the decadence of taste, which began to manifest itself under the first emperors.
>
> The paintings, daringly drawn, representing beings which have vanished in the history of Nature, which our arrogant ignorance calls imaginary beings, are obviously copies, carefully made, from originals executed in primitive times. (95–96)

Thus singling out a "beautiful painting" from Herculaneum, one that depicts a bacchante offering a golden cup to a sea panther, the author observed that this conception does not reflect "the disordered imagination of a delirious artist," and that it contained nothing "which might be contrary to the known laws of Physics; nothing which Philosophy might have the right to call a mistake of Nature" (178).

Consequently, according to Delisle de Sales, the art of the great civilization of the Tatar plateau was eminently realistic, and it could be compared favorably to anything produced in modern times: "It is probable that they already had there Leonardo da Vincis and perhaps Raphaels." Far from being limited to painting, the art of the Primitive World probably also involved sculptors equaling François Girardon and Jean-Baptiste Pigalle, and architects comparable to Michelangelo (180–82). Bringing the Primitive tradition closer to Greece, the author maintained that the art of the century of Pericles corresponded to one of the "intermediary ages," which, after a period of decadence (Egypt?), brought man's genius to his original height (96–97).

Toward 1800, perhaps because of the cumulative pressure of these ideas, the independent validity of primitive art—in the context of the relative historical moment of its appearance—began to be acknowledged even in some publications that were basically hostile to primitivism. For instance, the Italian architect Francesco Milizia, in his *L'Art de voir dans les beaux-arts,* a work translated into French by General Pommereul (1797–98), stated that "during at least a dozen centuries, from Constantine to Raphael, the human race was barbarian and saw everything with a barbarian eye." Then he interprets this state of things by a succession of historical "generation gaps." In his imagination he hears the protest of a multitude of early Tuscan artists, such as Cimabue, Gaddi, and Giotto, saying "we saw well." They are followed by a later group of painters, Orcagna, Starnina, etc., who raise their voices, repeating "we saw better." Even later, some artists, such as Masaccio, Uccello, Castagno, Botticelli, Pollaiuolo, Verrocchio, and Signorelli, loudly shout that "they have seen better yet." Michelangelo appears after them, and his voice, muffling all the earlier voices, proclaims: "I am divine." Raphael "smiles," and, finally, Raphael Mengs "roars with laughter" (*L'Art de voir,* 60–61).

In time the image of the primitive artists' confinement in the historical prison of some dark century inspired additional justifications for their shortcomings. For instance, in his *Discours historique sur la peinture moderne* (1812), Toussaint-Bernard Eméric-David wrote: ". . . [painting] did not emerge from the state of deterioration into which it had fallen, because in spite of this decadence, it did not cease to produce all the good which was expected from its works, that of inspiring religious feelings" (200).

Most, if not all, of these theories and points of view were undoubtedly known to the members of Maurice Quay's group, as were the publications devoted to classical antiquities. It is certain that Seroux d'Agincourt's ideas were propagated among the pupils of David by Paillot de Montabert, who, before enrolling in 1796 in the famous studio, had been one of the most fervent disciples of the famous antiquarian. There is little doubt that the *Barbus* were familiar with Lenoir's concepts, since his Musée des monuments français was during their time one of the most conspicuous *curiosités* of Paris. Similarly, it is known that Ballanche's early writings were greatly admired by Nodier (NOD-LAR 22), and, as mentioned earlier, Chateaubriand exchanged literary ideas with the members of the sect at Chaillot. The question of Wackenroder is not quite as clear. But it is plausible to think that his essays (which had not yet been translated) were discussed in David's studio by the sculptor Christian Friedrich Tieck, one of the great painter's German pupils (he was the brother of Ludwig Tieck, a celebrated poet and Wackenroder's intimate collaborator). In regard to Court de Gébelin's *Monde primitif,* Delisle de Sales's *Histoire philosophique du monde primitif,* and the numerous similar publications, one might recall that about 1800 the subject of the Primitive World permeated the air, and that it was familiar to the cultured people of the time. Admittedly, it is impossible to ascertain whether Cordier de Launay's ideas ever caught the attention of the *Barbus,* but his book (published almost immediately after the sect's disappearance) typifies the growth of the various points of view that asserted the importance of primitive art. Finally, the repeated expressions of tolerance (however reluctant!), such as those of Milizia and Eméric-David, had a reassuring ring, which could only have strengthened the *Barbus'* faith in their credo.

It is significant that the often confusing and contradictory kaleidoscope of ideas on primitivism which prevailed during the sect's heyday fails to reveal any publication that matched Maurice Quay's audacity. While it is evident that Maurice's thinking was influenced by earlier ideas, not a single author of his time ever dared to proclaim that primitive art was not merely valid, interesting, or exciting, but actually uniquely superior to all the other kinds of art.

The question of Maurice Quay's approach to primitivism directly brings up the examination of the writings of Paillot de Montabert. Speaking of this former disciple of Seroux d'Agincourt, Delécluze states that Paillot de Montabert was irresistibly impressed by Maurice: "Although he was the first one to laugh at the extravagant form that Maurice gave to his doctrine, fundamentally, it was impossible for him not to recognize the power of the ideas and sometimes of the reasoning of the young madman" (DEL-DAV 96–97). Paillot de Montabert entered David's studio at a comparatively ripe age (in 1796 he was twenty-five years old). Having fallen in love with art theory, he soon began his *Traité complet de la peinture* (first published in 1829). According to Delécluze: "This wisely composed work, with each of its parts treated with such thoughtfulness, maturity, and wisdom, essentially presents the core of Maurice's doctrine, but organized by a calm and methodical mind" (DEL-DAV 97). The nine volumes of this treatise appeared long after the disappearance of the *Barbus.* However, some sections of this book—showing considerable differences from the final version—came to light much earlier in the form of an article in the *Magasin Encyclopédique* (March 1812), which was republished separately that year, with the title *Dissertation sur les peintures du moyen âge, et sur celles qu'on a appelé gothiques.* It is certain that Paillot de Montabert's ideas were no longer those of Seroux d'Agincourt, but it is impossible to ascertain how faithfully he subscribed to the sect's creed. Nevertheless, the comment by Delécluze, as well as the date of this *Dissertation*—approximately eight years after Maurice's death—suggests a great closeness.

This kinship is of course colored by a number of ideas that have previously been considered in this chapter. Thus Paillot de Montabert's *Dissertation* begins with an implicit homage to the bygone artists of the Primitive World, a homage that he later deleted in the corresponding section of the *Traité complet* (III, 1–38). At the very opening of the *Dissertation,* the author expresses his dismay at the scorn and forgetfulness that the newly civilized nations displayed toward "the true initiators of their arts and their first masters" (8). Egypt is singled out, rather surprisingly, as an illustration of these cultural nouveaux riches, for the ancient Egyptians claimed that their nation was the original cradle of their revered mysteries, arts, and sciences. He dismisses this pretension with a reference to the ideas of Court de Gébelin and Delisle de Sales:

> If our imagination . . . turns back for a moment towards the ancient times and envisions again the faraway periods of the first ages of the world; if it tries to recapture the remnants of human knowledge which had escaped this great catastrophe, known under the name of Flood, it will find again, beyond the traditional chronology, more ancient propagators of artistic endeavor; and the pride of the so-called inventors disposes us to mistrust their vanity. (8)[8]

Thus, according to Paillot de Montabert, "the Egyptians [as well as other ancient cultures such as that of the Indians] owed the benefit of their arts to more ancient peoples," that is, to the people of the Primitive World. While the Egyptians succeeded, in a limited measure, in exploiting this inheritance, their complacency and pride prevented them from returning to the older doctrines, which could have inspired true masterpieces (9).

Despite the documents that were transmitted by the Egyptian civilization (presumably the echoes of the Primitive World), the Greeks denied the significance of "these primitive sources of the perfection of their arts" (9). Equaling the Egyptian pride, they claimed to have invented everything, from Dibutade's silhouette to Apelles' masterpieces. In turn, the Romans' vanity and corruption led them to forget their Greek masters: "Ostentatious taste triumphed over the naiveté of nature, and the style of the schools of antiquity began to disappear. . . . Art, in spite of some remaining greatness, began to show deterioration" (12–13).

According to Paillot de Montabert, the art of the Middle Ages, despite the barbarous aspects of the times, did not suffer from the same false pride: "In those unhappy times, one was more concerned with gathering the surviving remnants of the arts than in pretending to perfect them" (14). He finds in this veneration of the past sufficient justification for ascribing to medieval art some of the points of view usually associated with the Renaissance:

> This respectful humility . . . brought back the age of simplicity and prepared the glory of the Leonardos and the Raphaels. One saw, in these times already so far away from us, the rebirth of a need to honor again beautiful antiquity; the need to appreciate it was unanimously acknowledged, and simple nature was loved and cherished once again. One tried to extract its ingenuousness, its expressions, its calm, and its liveliness. The influence of events was the only obstacle. It is true that the sciences were not studied, but hearts were more wholesome; minds were less cultured, but common sense had that much more strength because of it: in one word, this state of the arts left everything to hope for and nothing to fear in regard to their progress. (14–15)

These ideas, which seem to reinterpret Wackenroder's holy humility in a Classical vein, are buttressed with an invocation of Christian religion—as the protector of the arts, and their source of inspiration—which recalls Ballanche and Chateaubriand. Paillot de Montabert submits that one finds here the true foundations of Raphael's art:

And what right do we have to ridicule these first expressions of a naive gratitude and of a dawning religion? How inconsistent and false would be the
moderns' criticism which, although claiming Raphael as the prince of painters,
would refuse to recognize as useful and valuable these very models which have
guided and illuminated the first steps of this great man, models which, themselves, were derived from the priceless sources of antiquity! (16)

Parenthetically, Raphael's debt to his primitive predecessors had already been
pointed out by Alexis-François Artaud de Montor, another disciple of Seroux
d'Agincourt. In his *Considérations sur l'état de la peinture en Italie, dans les quatre
siècles qui ont précédé celui de Raphaël* (1808), Artaud de Montor wrote that
these early artists

were responsible for spurring Raphael's emulation, ennobling his soul and
elevating his enthusiasm. . . . Thus, let us pay some homage to rivals who
have been left far behind, but to whom we perhaps owe the masterpieces of
the immortal founder of the Roman school. (*Considérations,* 10)

At any rate, for Paillot de Montabert the conclusion is clear: "Our duty is not to
create a new art, but . . . to rediscover the art of the ancients" (*Dissertation,* 16).

However, Paillot de Montabert, who was not satisfied to stress the importance
of primitive art, launched an assault against the art that followed Raphael, despite
the fact that, according to him, art during this period enjoyed a consideration that
reestablished its activity and vigor:

In the paintings, drawing acquired accuracy of perspective and lost its naiveté;
it gained boldness and energy and lost truth and propriety; the study of
anatomy became ostentatious; magnificence of forms became artificial; the
artist appeared greater than his work and fame became confused with perfection. Composition was abandoned to the capriciousness and the whims of
artists, and it was assuaged only when the reminiscences of the order and the
symmetry of antiquity came, per chance, to affect the solution of artistic problems. . . . Finally, what was inevitable happened, that is, the fame of the
most skillful artists compelled and drove the others. Instead of trying to rediscover the knowledge of men like Phidias, Praxiteles, and Protogenes, one
had to imitate the proud ardor of Michelangelo; instead of borrowing and re-
newing ideas from Nature, one derived them from the Academies already
celebrated in those times. . . . It was given to our century and to our schools
to reject and to erase prejudices which had been fought for so long in vain.
. . . in France, one celebrated man [David] astounded and enlightened even
those who had been in deepest darkness. (23–26)

Paillot de Montabert vigorously and repeatedly attacked the Renaissance:

One is far too convinced that the sixteenth century saw the rebirth of painting
and, very improperly, one gives the name of *renaissance* to the period when,

on the contrary, this art perhaps began to be subjected to the last symptoms of deterioration. . . . If the far too famous Michelangelo's pompous works have attracted everyone's attention, it is nonetheless true that he is responsible for the loss of the antique naiveté in art. (41)

If Paillot de Montabert's ideas reflected those of the *Barbus,* his general dislike of the Renaissance, Baroque, and Rococo periods had some bearing upon the sect's conception of the artist in society:

Thus, the times when art becomes corrupted are not those during which it loses its public consideration and its honors, but rather those in which it no longer rests upon the greatest principles which are its only true foundation; and such is the eternal order of things that all the display of men like Cortona and Bernini, all the notoriety of the Van Loos and the Bouchers, all the luxury of the charlatans have never been able to disguise the debased state of painting. (41)

This passage has significant implications. When Maurice Quay asked the artist to become an active reformer and, later, invited him to withdraw from society to the convent at Chaillot, the leader of the *Barbus* was undoubtedly distressed by the public's lack of understanding and the degrading vaudevillian conception of his profession. But he was not attempting to replace one type of debasement by another: For him, the humiliations of the artist's popular image were not to be counteracted by a striving for social consideration and honors, but rather by a social estrangement, an escape into a total commitment to ideal principles.

For Paillot de Montabert, the rediscovery of the great principles was a difficult undertaking, for

since the rebirth of sciences and letters, starting with the century of Leo X, the moderns have always been too dazzled and infatuated with all this mass of new and growing knowledge. From this time on, the arrogance of schools erected a barrier which isolated us from antiquity. (46)

Because of the resulting confusion, a reevaluation of medieval painting—which was, after all, closer to the nineteenth century than the art of antiquity—could constitute a first step toward the understanding of the fundamental principles (48).

The author stressed the nobility, the simplicity, the *oneness,* and the classical inspiration of the medieval compositions. This inspiration is reflected in the "expression" of medieval paintings, despite their faults of perspective and other technical weaknesses. Paillot de Montabert particularly admired the severe gravity that added force and unity to their "expression." Gravity is "natural to man," and the author observed it among the "savages of America, Africa, and even of Italy" (52). Unavoidably, one is reminded of Nodier's comments about the "severity" and the "solemnity" of the *Barbus* (NOD-TEM 442).

One should not think that Paillot de Montabert suggested that medieval primitive painting must be admired because of some linear, two-dimensional, Neoclassic, monochromatic quality. It is true that such an attitude could perhaps be suggested because of his dislike of the fastidious realism of the late-medieval northern schools and his hatred for oil painting (he was trying to perfect the technique of encaustic). Thus he stated that the influence of Dürer and Van Eyck contributed to the decadence of taste (35) and that Van Eyck's invention of oil painting "had made art lose its naïveté of color" (58). However, Paillot de Montabert had little to say about Etruscan vases, and he was very far from dismissing color as an important factor. Minimizing the apparent harshness of the medieval color scheme, he remarked:

> The harshness and discordance of colors is much less shocking when the entire color scheme is bright and luminous, such as the one which was used in those times [medieval period], than when the colors are as muted as those which are used in oil painting. (57)

But medieval colors can be beautiful, and their effect was sometimes enhanced with chiaroscuro and contrasts of values. Thus, according to the author, the early Venetians,

> like the Orientals, looked for brilliance of color, even going so far as to use devices which could increase this brilliance. . . . Well before Giorgione, there were painters who were concerned with the relative proportions of light and dark areas and studied the effect of value contrasts. Consequently, this school could not help but to become the cradle of the modern conception of color. (32)

Such comments on color and chiaroscuro suggest that, if Paillot de Montabert is to be trusted to any serious degree as the sect's theoretician, one must conclude that the aesthetic statements attributed by Delécluze to Maurice Quay give a highly simplified and somewhat distorted idea of his thinking.

Paillot de Montabert concluded by stressing that medieval paintings—especially those of the Italian primitives (he still remembers Seroux d'Agincourt)—present, despite their technical shortcomings, the "sublime and naïve qualities which constitute the character and the dignity of art." Consequently he submitted that "the cognoscenti must consider them and study them without prejudice . . . as easily understandable translations, which can provide the explanation of the secret idioms of a language difficult to know well" (59–61).

These "secret idioms" point to the author's quasi-mystical belief in an art-historical evolution based on the transmission of sacred seeds that originated in the great Primitive World: Primitive art is considered a hallowed repository, almost a reliquary, of the original candor, simplicity, and greatness, freed from technical artifice and human vanity and reaching far back into the most exalted periods of man's genius. It is significant that Paillot de Montabert chose for early publication in his *Dissertation* the theme of primitivism rather than that of drawing or any of the other many subjects that would be discussed in his later writings.

It is true that he would give great importance to line in his *Théorie du geste* (1813, 165–200). However, the qualities of line he stressed in this work, most particularly unity and simplicity, are not related to the concept of abstract outline or primitivism. Paillot de Montabert did not establish this relationship until his *Traité complet de la peinture* (1829–51 edition, VI, 175–79)—and then only marginally. His most extreme position in this matter was expressed only in the solemnly sacerdotal prose of *L'Artistaire* (published posthumously in 1855). A passage in this book gives the measure of the exalted significance he now attached to primitive linearity, which was never expressed before in his other writings:

> The greatness and infallibility of *l'opticographie linéaire* (which we call linear drawing or line) have been the reason for its having been considered, from the time of the earliest stages of the world, as a sacred language, which must be taught and used only by priests and the initiates. (111)

The author adds the notion that "the primitive simplicity which we observe in works of art is not the result of ignorance but rather that of knowledge" (112). Thus curiously bringing to mind Paul Signac and Jan Verkade, he maintains that in addition to being a priest the artist must also act as a scientist, establishing the geometric truth of his lines and the chromatic grammar of his colors (194).

Doubtless this is a distorting mummification of the *Barbus'* theories. The date of publication of the book (1855) clearly indicates that above all it is directed against the new nineteenth-century schools; this explains Paillot de Montabert's barbs ridiculing the Romantics' Gothicomania and their search for spirituality. Ironically, the serpent is biting its tail!

Among the former friends of the *Barbus,* not a single theoretician chose to uphold the banner of Maurice Quay. In his *Nouvelles études du coeur et de l'esprit humain* (1840), Paul Duqueylar—the controversial painter of 1800 whose work had been exalted at that time by the members of the sect—dogmatically expounded old ideas about art, tradition, and Christianity. He expressed his admiration for "these wonderful remnants of the art of the Egyptians" (*Nouvelles études,* 435), and he gave perfunctory praise to some early Italian artists, such as Cimabue, Masaccio, Ghirlandaio, and Perugino (437–38). However, on the whole his attitude is very conservative. He opposed the nineteenth-century Romantics' sacrifice of beauty for the sake of expressiveness, and he deplored the "pronounced mark of gothicism, ugliness, and bad taste" of the productions of Western art from the sixth to the fourteenth century (437–39).

These late publications confuse, distort, or radically contradict the conception of primitivism as it was known at the turn of the nineteenth century. But even if one confines oneself to the writings that could have been known to the *Barbus,* or to those that plausibly reflect their thinking, one can summon up only a most elusively fluid idea about the meaning, or meanings, of the primitivism of 1800. This very lack of definition prevailed of course during the *Barbus'* own time, and it offered to the sect's artists a wide spectrum of possible stylistic avenues, all of which were seen as types of primitive art. Undoubtedly, for the *Barbus,* Heinse's utopia could have provided a model for the first step toward the reconquest of man's sublime Atlantean past, Nodier's "golden age" (NOD-LAR 23). However, as artists they were limited neither to the mythical notions of antediluvian models nor to a Flaxmanized interpretation of "Etruscan" vase painting. In fact, they could legitimately help themselves to practically anything, from archaic Greek and early Italian art to French and German medieval productions, or possibly to even later European examples. All in all, the *Barbus* could channel their sense of originality through their own individual conception of primitivism.

8

The Works

The spectrum of possible primitivist attitudes of 1800 must be taken into account to understand the diversity of the *Barbus'* productions. In discussing these works, it must first be pointed out that the well-established notion of idleness, and even laziness, which clung to the sect was not entirely justified (most probably this reputation had originally been inspired by the *Barbus'* meditative stance). A number of contemporary references and some surviving examples of the *Barbus'* works suggest that their alleged lack of industry was not typical of every period of the sect, and that it certainly was not a characteristic that stamped each follower of Maurice.

Delécluze himself is in part responsible for the perpetuation of this image: "How sad but useful it is to ask oneself: what is left from so many efforts of the imagination, from so many bizarre, even original conversations? Nothing; not even a single painting" (DEL-BAR 429). Nevertheless, in the same article, speaking of his friendship with the *Barbus'* leader, he described some aspects of Maurice's artistic productivity:

> I only saw him once in his studio. It was an enormous room in which a canvas, thirty feet long, was placed diagonally. In the black triangle, behind the canvas, one could see some straw, used as a bed, and some household utensils. The other triangle was the actual studio. That is where I saw my friend Agamemnon preparing his palette, which was four feet wide, in front of his canvas on which one could see, still in a state of drawing, the subject of Patrocles sending Briseis back to Agamemnon. (DEL-BAR 420–24)

According to Delécluze, Maurice never even began to paint this composition (one may wonder why he was "preparing his palette"); but the writer admits that, in contrast with other *Barbus,* he was quite industrious as a painter:

> In the school of David, he produced a rather large quantity of studies, stamped with truth, grandeur, and beauty, which impressed everyone. Since that time, after my judgment grew in maturity through the comparison of a great number of paintings, I had the opportunity to see once more the productions of this

young man; and it is certain that they were foretelling a painter. (DEL-BAR 424)

The same sense of unfulfilled promise is suggested in the case of Lucile Franque. Thus Mme Mennessier-Nodier wrote that Lucile (her aunt) left after her death "many incomplete works" that "bear the mark of a poetic and superior talent" (*Charles Nodier,* 92). Nodier's daughter can be trusted for the first of these two statements, since she doubtless had the opportunity to see many of Lucile's works in the Messageot-Charve homestead at Quintigny (near Lons-le-Saunier, Jura), where she was born and raised. However, Mme Mennessier-Nodier was not a knowing art critic, and some of the other comments about Lucile's works are perhaps more revealing. For instance, in an article in the *Biographie universelle & historique des femmes célèbres mortes ou vivantes* (1830), an anonymous contributor who mentions Lucile's literary works (*Essai sur les harmonies de la mélancolie et des arts* and *Le Tombeau d'Eléonore*) wrote:

> Madame Franque's talents showed the greatest promise from her most tender age. Several paintings full of touching melancholy received from her teachers a very flattering acknowledgment. They thought that, one day, she would become the Ossian of painting. (II, 426)

One wonders whether the last statement is historically true, or whether it was inspired by Nodier's earlier adulatory suggestion that Lucile could have become, if she had wished it, "the Michelangelo of poetry or the Ossian of painting" (NOD-TYP 76).

However poeticized, Nodier's opinion cannot be easily bypassed, for it is more than certain that he was familiar with Lucile's art. From this point of view, Charles Weiss's article in the Michaud *Biographie universelle,* a piece that was expressly written to satisfy Nodier's undying devotion to Lucile, has particular significance. In fact, in including her name in the list of the biographies assigned to Weiss, one of the editors of the celebrated *Biographie* noted: "Nodier wants you to write the article."[1] Weiss personally knew the Messageot-Charve family, and he was well known for his precision. It is true that his article gives an inaccurate date of Lucile's death (1802 instead of 1803). However, besides mentioning her unpublished literary works it offers a general characterization of her paintings, which, according to the author, were based on subjects "always derived from an intermediate world and an intermediate nature" (Michaud, *Biographie,* XV, 43). It is not too far from "the Ossian of painting," and some information about the work that Lucile was hoping to show at the Salon of 1802 would be welcome indeed. Her intent to enter the official exhibition of that year is known from the appearance of her name, "Melle franque (Lucile) Peintre," in the handwritten *Enregistrement des notices par ordre alphabétique* of the Salon of 1802 (Archives of the Louvre). This document contains no further clarification, and Lucile's planned entry, as well as her name, are left unmentioned in the printed *Explication* of the Salon of 1802.[2] Such references yield scanty information about the lost productions of Maurice and Lucile, but they are certainly sufficient to demonstrate their professional productivity.

Far more details are known about some of the other *Barbus*. For instance, the brothers Franque entered two paintings in the Salon of 1806: Jean-Pierre's *Dream of Love, Inspired by the Power of Harmony* (No. 208) and Joseph-Boniface's *Hercules Rescuing Alcestis from Hades* (No. 207). The first of these works found its way into the Museum of Valence, where it perished in the fire of 1972. The second, first exhibited in the *Chambre des Pairs,* was later sent to Meudon and vanished without a trace. Neither of the two pictures had been photographed or engraved. Jean-Pierre's *Dream of Love* remained largely unnoticed, and, according to an oral description by the director of the Museum of Valence, it is supposed to have been a dull Neoclassical painting. But Joseph-Boniface's *Hercules* attracted some attention, and Pierre-Jean-Baptiste Chaussard devoted a relatively lengthy passage to this work in *Le Pausanias français* (1806):

> This painting, executed with great energy, is the product of an exalted imagination. . . . Alcestis is pretty, but perhaps too small for Hercules, who is gigantic and whose forms are mannered. . . . As to the reflections of the flames and of the daylight, they are rather odd, for Hercules appears to be lighted by the infernal flames . . . in a way which confuses the play of light and dark as well as the fantastic shapes projected by the shadows, which are difficult to distinguish.
>
> This painting, which is not without merit . . . does not produce a pleasant effect; as a matter of fact, it is not sufficiently finished. Why torture one's imagination to create things which are bizarre rather than pleasing and true? . . . After M. Franque studies his subjects with greater care and tames his imagination, he will produce very good works. (*Le Pausanias français,* 448–49)

Unfortunately, as in the case of Jean-Pierre's *Dream of Love,* many of the *Barbus'* productions failed to inspire critical comments. This was the fate of two drawings exhibited by Périé: *The Bark of Charon* (Salon of 1810, No. 637) and *The Dream of Ossian* (Salon of 1812, No. 709). At least the first is known from an engraving (*Fig. 43*), while some idea about the other can be gathered from the official description of the Salon: "Seated near the tomb of Fingal, Ossian is falling asleep at the sound of Malvina's harp; the shades of his parents appear to him" (*Explication* . . . 1812, 77). It is apparent that while many of the works of the best-known members of the sect are totally lost, several of their paintings were recorded and dated, and in a few cases described.

It is possible, of course, that the *Barbus'* earliest efforts could have reflected an abstract linear style. However, there are no surviving paintings or drawings of this kind, and the available evidence points to the fact that Maurice's followers did not pursue any sectarian "party line," that they were attracted to a great diversity of subjects and felt free to explore a variety of styles. Even if one grants that these observations refer to a considerable length of time, during which the sect's members were beginning to shed their *Barbu* characteristics, it is still possible to submit that the variegated quality of their production must have inescapably echoed the multiplicity of individual paths that could have been followed, at the turn of the century, under the banner of primitivism. One can only conclude that in this regard it is hazardous to "predict" what particular type of subject, or style, could be legitimately expected from the members of the group.

The question of the *Barbus'* surviving works can be broached by first considering the Ossianic composition (*Fig. 23*), which was entered in the Salon of 1800 by Paul Duqueylar, one of the sect's most enthusiastic sympathizers. Failing to attract serious attention as a primitivist manifesto, this painting nevertheless incited enough notoriety to create something very close to a primitivist scandal.[3] It is not known whether Duqueylar ever became a full-fledged, properly costumed member of the sect, but it is certain that he came to share many of Maurice's ideas. According to Delécluze, Duqueylar, born in Digne (Basses-Alpes) in 1771, joined the studio of David at a relatively late date:

> Duqueylar was not young, he was at least twenty-five years old, and he always felt the effect of his late start. . . . Duqueylar, belonging to a noble family, had received an excellent education. . . . However, despite the polish of his manners, one always felt in him a core of native roughness which was echoed in the turn of his ideas and in his talent as an artist. (DEL-DAV 95)

Perhaps because of this inherent "roughness," he was particularly responsive to the call of primitivism: "Maurice's opinions and an assiduous reading of Ossian . . . left so deep an impression on Duqueylar's imagination, that this influence left a permanent mark on his mind and his talent" (DEL-DAV 95).

Delécluze described Duqueylar's Ossianic painting of 1800 as a work "which, doubtless, was not devoid of energy, but which had such a wild and bizarre effect that it was appreciated only by a few of his friends" (DEL-DAV 95). It is not always easy, of course, to agree on the validity of terms such as "wild" and "bizarre," and a twentieth-century critic observes: "Delécluze does not need much to be impressed: today, Duqueylar's *Ossian* does not seem particularly 'wild'; a little 'bizarre' at most" (Ternois, "Ossian et les peintres," 187).

Duqueylar's painting shows a rather conservative bow-and-arrow composition, which recalls the formal structure of seventeenth-century works such as Massimo Stanzioni's *Sacrifice to Bacchus* and Poussin's *Triumph of David* (both in the Prado). It also shows well-defined planes, conceived in a bas-relief Neoclassical manner, and includes several familiar, vaguely classicizing types. Nevertheless Duqueylar's huge canvas (273 x 347 cm) displays a number of less conventional aspects. The astonishingly dissonant color scheme of this composition—with its vermilion and white accents and violet shadows—found no parallel in the Salon of 1800. This feeling of strangeness is further stressed by a few Quattrocentesque figures, some of which—like the woman with windblown hair, on the left—are hauntingly reminiscent of Botticelli. On a different level, this archaistic flavor is also felt in the awkwardness of some of the attitudes—as in the figure with a raised arm, on the far right—and in the almost clumsy delineation of some of the details, such as the dog that seems to be howling below the weapons hanging to the left of the central figure.

Either deliberately or unconsciously, Duqueylar's use of a primitive mode reflects the "primitive" subject of his painting. Identified by Delécluze as *Ossian Chanting His Poems* (DEL-DAV 95), this subject was probably inspired by one of the poems of the Ossianic cycle—"primitive" par excellence, according to Maurice Quay—entitled *Berrathon*. In this painting, the *Homer of the north,* watched by his son Oscar and other Ossianic heroes, sings the funeral hymn of Malvina, his daughter-in-law, who lifelessly reclines at his feet (*Ossian,* II, 207–14). Appearing before the well-known Ossianic compositions of Girodet and Gérard (Salon of 1803), Duqueylar's work is the very first illustration of an Ossianic literary theme to be exhibited in the official Paris Salon.[4]

There is little doubt that this question of novelty—underlined by the unusual size of Duqueylar's painting—played a major role in stimulating the curiosity of the visitors in the Salon, and that the very conspicuousness of this composition increased its vulnerability to the critics' barbs. The hostility of these writers was particularly spurred by two closely related factors: the primitivistic strangeness of Duqueylar's style, and the primitivistic eccentricity of the vociferous defenders of his painting.

The anonymous critic of the *Mercure de France* wrote:

> One could see in the Salon this year a painting which is said to represent a scene of the life of Ossian. This very ambitious and very ridiculous production offers nothing but a crude image of art in its infancy, which if it had suddenly appeared in the middle of the thirteenth century, would not have even deserved the just praise bestowed upon the first attempts of Giotto and Cimabue. For, in these shapeless fragments that, gratefully, curious artists come to visit in the Campo Santo of Pisa, "la bella vergognosa" [Benozzo Gozzoli] at least brings to mind an image of painting adorned with the naive grace of childhood. One does not see in Pisa, as in the case of these figures identified as Ossian's companions, a dog which one tends to confuse with a tree trunk. It is asserted that the supporters of this bizarre canvas (for I do not want to offend the art of painting by considering this work as one of its creations) call themselves *Penseurs* [thinkers]. Personally, I must confess that among the painters who bear this glorious title, I am rather satisfied with Poussin, and I find it difficult to believe that innovators can improve on him. Despite the beautiful enthusiasm of its supporters, it is doubtful that this work will stimulate many imitators. But it might be useful to reiterate to the young artists, rightly forewarned against the false style which prevailed forty years ago, that one should not replace it by another approach which, although quite different, is no less erroneous; that in order to avoid being vague, soft, and mannered, one should

not become cold, hard, and harsh; that even the purest and the most stern simplicity has limits; and that paintings are not sculpture reliefs. (*Mercure de France,* 22 December 1800, 33)

In the same vein, Charles-Paul Landon observed in the *Journal des Arts* (Salon of 1800) that in seeking "naive and virginal simplicity," Duqueylar risked finding only "sterility," "aridity," and "insignificance." The critic developed this idea in a lengthy but revealing passage:

> Mr. Queylar [Duqueylar], intent to exercise the powers of his imagination and to give visible form to his poetic thoughts, scorns . . . everything which contributes to the charm and essence of painting, that is, color, harmony, effect, aereal perspective, reasonable arrangement of groups and masses, and finally the seductiveness of brushwork. I should like to tell him that, without any doubt, he should not claim that he is actually practicing painting, and I urge him, from now on, to undertake preferably either the study of sculpture reliefs or to revive the use of monochromatic paintings, which were the first attempts of the artists of antiquity.
>
> If a young writer, in order to avoid the glitter, which is the defect of several of our poets, pretending to ignore the masterpieces of men like Corneille, Racine, and Voltaire, would choose as models these young, antiquated, gothic poets, who are in many ways comparable to what, in painting, we call the old masters, one wonders what scolding he would receive from men of taste. Such, however, is the position that M. Queylar [Duqueylar] seems to have adopted.
>
> . . . I would have given much less attention to this artist, if I were not so tired of the exaggerated praises bestowed on the painting of Ossian by several young students.[5]

Speaking of Duqueylar's painting, Landon and the *Mercure* critic mentioned sculptural reliefs and monochromatic painting of antiquity, but they referred much more often to the medieval and Quattrocento aspects of primitive art (Giotto, Cimabue, Benozzo Gozzoli, "Gothic" poetry, etc.). Neither the *Mercure de France* nor the *Journal des Arts* recognized in Duqueylar's painting anything related to linear style or to Etruscan vases.

The *Barbus'* enthusiastic support of Duqueylar's composition underlined their well-known admiration for Ossianic literature: It is indeed fitting that the very first Salon painting inspired by Ossianic lore was the work of one of the sect's sympathizers! But the *Barbus'* fervent acceptance of this painting has an additional significance, for it confirms the previously discussed hypothesis that the members of their group felt by no means compelled to conceive primitive style solely as a variation of John Flaxman's famed linearity.

Far from being limited to theory, this observation can be extended to actual productions by the sect's members. In fact, the Salon of 1800 provided concrete proof of this with Jean Broc's huge (350 x 450 cm) *School of Apelles*[6] (*Figs. 24 and*

25), which appeared practically next to Duqueylar's somewhat smaller canvas on the same wall of the Salon (*Fig. 21*). Of course Broc was not a mere sympathizer but a true follower of Maurice Quay; for this reason his *School of Apelles,* despite its failure to stimulate as much curiosity as Duqueylar's *Ossian,* commands a special interest as the first work of a full-fledged *Barbu* ever entered in an official exhibition.

The critics' tepid comments about the *School of Apelles* can be easily related to its unmistakable effect of *déjà vu.* Immediately recalling Raphael's *School of Athens,* Broc's composition multiplies echoes from the masterpiece of the Camera della Segnatura, from some aspects of its spatial concept and the architectural staging to the attitudes and the facial characteristics of the figures. This eclectic fervor was duly exposed by the Salon writers, and some of them went so far as to accuse the painter of plagiarism. The critics adopted a patronizing tone and often noted that, after all, the author was "a young artist" and the *School of Apelles* his "first work." In the same vein, they paid Broc some lukewarm compliments, congratulating him for having followed "the excellent principles one derives from David's lessons" and observing that, despite its lack of depth, his painting was fairly well drawn.[7]

But the truly revealing criticisms went beyond what might be considered Broc's beginner's faults. For instance, Landon wrote in the *Journal des Arts* (1800): "Affecting a monotonous color scheme and a certain dryness of brushwork, the artist reveals his intention to imitate some old masters in the very aspects in which they are the least praiseworthy."[8] The same idea was developed in *Le Coup-d'oeil sur le Salon de l'an VIII* (1800):

> One can criticize the painting of citizen Broc for a lack of vigor and a pallid color which recalls old frescoes or worn cartoons. This is the way color was used at the time of the rebirth of Art, and one can find some examples in the paintings of Perugino or in those of the early Raphael. The magic of chiaroscuro is not sufficiently studied, and one perceives a feeling of dryness. It seems that, when the early painters elevated their art to a beauty of drawing which probably amazed them, they very timidly dared to apply color on the lines they had drawn. They feared to mar the purity of their contours and painted poorly in order to draw better. Have we come back to the same point? And has their experience been lost?[9]

Thus the *School of Apelles* was essentially castigated as a pastiche—a pastiche in which the artist's borrowings from Raphael, "aged" through a process of artificial fading, were expected to evoke the appearance of old Quattrocento pictures. Today it is difficult to subscribe to this judgment: Far from being pallid, Broc's colors, contrasted against a grayish, neutral architectural background, give the impression of lightness and intensity. In fact, the color scheme seems to have been thought out in view of oppositions (the rose pink and the orange tonalities of Apelles' cloak contrasting with the blue of his tunic), or for the sake of chromatic sequences (the draperies of his pupils, approaching their master from the left, evolve from blue-green to yellow, from yellow to yellowish green, and from yellowish green to red).

Broc's feeling for color—which, according to Delécluze, had already been noted by David (DEL-DAV 55)—is revealed even in the various hues of the hair of his figures, in one case a fiery red.

The Salon criticisms can perhaps be understood in terms of the visual context of the period. Broc used few dark shadows (they tend toward a light grayish brown), and his tonalities, devoid of reflections and translucences, are confined to closely delimited areas. As a result, his colors give an immediate impression of distinctness and freshness, qualities that probably appeared unusually simplistic and antiquated to the critics of 1800, accustomed as they were to the murky color mélanges of the Davidian school. Taken aback by the apparent "primitivism" of Broc's color scheme, these critics translated their experience into terms such as "worn cartoons" and "old frescoes," which transposed into the color effect of the *School of Apelles* the antiquated quality recognized in its style.

It is tempting to continue the exploration of Broc's primitivism by considering other possible signs of the Quattrocento influence. Aside from the color scheme, this influence seems to be echoed in the awkward affectation, stiffness, and emphatic angularity of the attitudes and pantomimes of several of Apelles' students. In particular, two of them, in the foreground on the far left, bring to mind some of the figures of Signorelli's fresco of the *General Resurrection* (Cathedral of Orvieto): the first, in a standing position with his arms folded, arches his chest and juts his buttocks; the other, his head turned toward his standing fellow student, half-reclines on the floor, leaning on one arm. Such search for resemblances and derivation—which could be pursued almost indefinitely—can become misleading, for one might plausibly suspect that Broc did not have to try very hard to appear a little gauche and dry.

Independently from Broc's stylistic Quattrocento primitivism, a study of the subject of his painting casts some light upon another important concept pertaining to the *Barbus*. In this regard, it should be noted that the "official" title of this work, *The School of Apelles,* which appears in the *Explication* of the Salon of 1800, gives a very incomplete idea of its true meaning. Broc's composition, far from representing Apelles' "school," specifically depicts the Greek master at the moment he begins to describe to his students the theme of his still-unfinished painting *Calumny*. Predictably, Broc did not rely entirely on his imagination to "reconstruct" the long-lost Greek masterpiece: The supposed sketch of Apelles' celebrated painting, visible on the large panel placed on an easel on the right of the composition (*Fig. 25*), is directly derived from the drawing *Calumny* (Louvre, Cabinet des dessins), which in 1800 was attributed to Raphael (*Fig. 26*).

To understand Broc's idea, one must recall that according to Lucian (*De Calumnia,* 2–5) Apelles executed his allegory of Calumny as a protest against the false accusation that he had plotted a rebellion against King Ptolemy. In Broc's painting the Greek artist, standing before his easel, explains the outlines of his projected composition to his students. The young people appear to be astonished and indignant. Some, interrupting their normal studio work, attentively listen to

Apelles' words; others gesture to impose silence on their schoolfellows, who are still unaware of the great painter's speech; others eagerly rush up to their master.

The theme of Apelles' *Calumny* had of course been depicted by a number of earlier artists (Botticelli, Federico Zuccaro, Giovanni Battista Moroni, etc.). But these painters, having limited themselves to Lucian's allegorical description—conceived in vitro—gave a very general significance to their interpretations, which was applicable to any individual and any situation. Broc, challenging a well-established tradition, was the first artist to project the old subject of Apelles' *Calumny,* as a picture within a picture, within the context of the great Greek master's personal life, amid his enthusiastic pupils in his studio (or "school"). Thus restoring to the subject its original meaning, the French *Barbu* endowed his painting with a definite reference to the artist's condition:[10] He shows a great painter daringly protesting against injustice with the powerful weapons of his own profession. It is curious to observe that the injustice that befell Apelles did not originate with the art critics—a familiar leitmotiv—but from the men in power. It is difficult to decide whether the *School of Apelles* contains a specific political allusion (for instance, a reference to David's imprisonment of 1794), but it is certain that this painting projects, for the first time, the image of a noble and maligned artist, isolated from society and confined to his own professional class. Such a heroic image of protest—also the first of its kind—can be acknowledged as a reflection of the *Barbus'* attitude toward society, as well as their proud answer to the scornful vaudevillian caricatures of the creative man's predicament, which was exemplified by Fougère and Lantara.

Perhaps because of the unfavorable position of the *School of Apelles* in the Salon—exhibited unusually high on the wall—the critics, unable to recognize Apelles' "sketch of Calumny," failed to comprehend Broc's dramatic intent and felt that his painting lacked emotional appeal. Apparently the artist understood the implications of these comments, and the following year (1801) he exhibited two new paintings, which were acknowledged by the Salon critics to possess the "touching" character missing in the *School of Apelles*.[11] He chose to interpret two pathetic death themes: the *Death of Hyacinth (Fig. 27)* and the *Shipwreck of Virginie.*

The subject of the first of these two paintings[12] is based on a classical myth, best known from Ovid's *Metamorphoses* (X, 165–215). Both Apollo and Zephyr fell in love with the young Hyacinth; one day, while Apollo and Hyacinth were enjoying a game of discus throwing, the jealous Zephyr, the wind god, changed the course of the missile hurled by Apollo, thus causing Hyacinth's death. It is unnecessary to magnify the importance of the "homoerotic" or, to borrow a term used at the turn of 1800, the *"antiphysique"* implications of this theme. Broc's depiction of the story of Hyacinth is in no way more revealing of any sexual proclivity than, for instance, Le Sueur's depiction of the myth of Ganymede; and the effeminacy of Broc's figures is no more symptomatic than the effeminacy of Girodet's *Endymion,* David's *Bara,* or Guérin's *Aurora and Cephalus.* Whatever the nature of the private relationships that prevailed among the members of Maurice Quay's sect, Broc's conception most plausibly alludes to the myth of friendship and love, viewed in their purest and chastest form, which was consecrated by the respectability of classical humanism. It might be pointed out that many letters of the period show that the concept of an idealized friendship could be expressed with an intensity of feelings—recalling the two schoolboys in the opening pages of Roger Martin du Gard's *Les Thibault*—which today can be misunderstood.

The question of the effeminate appearance of Broc's figures can perhaps also be considered in relation to their probable sources: While the *School of Apelles* recalls the early Raphael and Signorelli, the *Death of Hyacinth* brings to mind Botticelli and Perugino. Despite its references to archaic Greek vase painting—particularly noticeable in the geometrized striation of Apollo's drapery—Broc's composition is dominated by soft Quattrocento echoes. But it also reveals traces of far more recent influences; for instance, Broc's grouping recalls Pierre-Paul Prud'hon's *Phrosine and Mélidore* (*Fig. 28*), and the melting chiaroscuro of his figures, surrounded by a luminous outline, shows some kinship to Girodet's *New Danaë* (*Fig. 29*). Nevertheless, the two amber-colored, willowy, languid heroes of the *Death of Hyacinth*, silhouetted against a greenish-blue sky, which grows increasingly lighter toward the horizon, are more evocative of the Quattrocento. This aspect explains once more the Salon critics' renewed observations about the faded quality of Broc's painting. In fact, these comments were somewhat more justified in 1801 than they had been in 1800, and it seems that the painter deliberately chose to give them additional validity.

Despite the award of an official honorable mention, *The Death of Hyacinth* enjoyed little more than a *succès d'estime* in the Salon. The viewers were clearly unsettled by Broc's primitivism, and the critic for the *Moniteur Universel* observed that his painting was "more bizarre than original" (1 November 1801).

Inspired by Bernardin de Saint-Pierre's celebrated *Paul et Virginie* (1787), *The Shipwreck of Virginie*, Broc's second work in the exhibition, abandoned the golden nostalgia of classical myths for the pathos of a popular "modern" novel. Unfortunately the painting has been lost, but its general appearance can be gathered from a drawing and engraving executed by Antoine Maxime Monsaldy for his panoramic view of the Salon of 1801 (*Figs. 30 and 31*).

The Shipwreck of Virginie, perhaps because it did not suggest any conspicuous primitivist oddity, fared considerably better with the critics than *The Death of Hyacinth*. For example, an anonymous article in the *Moniteur Universel*, notwithstanding the observation that Broc's two productions shared "the same qualities and the same faults," offered a sympathetically sensitive, poetic description of *The Shipwreck of Virginie*:

> The storm has ended, but the sky is still heavy with clouds, pierced by the pale rays of the moon. . . . Seated on a lonely, narrow rock, which barely rises above the surface of the immense sea, Paul is holding in his lap the body of Virginie, whom he has just pulled from the water. She is dead, and her lover, numbed by sorrow, has joined his hands and has placed them on the heart of

the young virgin, as though he wanted to give her warmth. . . . He is looking at her without seeing her. He is the unhappiest of men without quite realizing the full extent of his suffering. (*Moniteur Universel,* 1 November 1801)

Yet according to the same critic, Broc's "simple and touching" composition contains a serious shortcoming. This flaw, which seems to be related to the tendency of the painter's early works, can be seen in the ultimate fading of the colors:

> The color scheme is monotonous; its blackish-grey tone and its heaviness destroy the entire effect. Virginie has the greyish color of the water, and Paul shows the dead tonality of Virginie. Broc does not seem to have learned yet the great art of contrast.

The criticisms of Duqueylar's *Ossian* showed that the monochromatic color scheme was associated with primitive art. Thus one may wonder whether the *grisaille* effect of *The Shipwreck of Virginie* represents a further deliberate effort at primitivism on Broc's part, rather than a mere attempt to imitate the somewhat monochromatic appearance of some contemporary paintings, such as Gros's *Sappho at Leucadia,* which was exhibited in the same Salon.

Whatever Broc's intentions may have been, he chose to depict a nocturnal drama. This choice, as well as the nature of the subject matter, unavoidably impelled the anonymous critic for the *Moniteur Universel* to liken *The Shipwreck of Virginie* to Jean-François Hue's obviously similar *Shipwrecked Family* (*Fig. 32*), which faced Broc's painting at the same Salon:

> Hue has interpreted almost the same subject, with a more assured and experienced brush; it is also a nocturnal shipwreck. An unfortunate father has taken refuge on an isolated rock, with his wife and his child who seem to be dead.

The two compositions are indeed so similar that one is led to the conclusion that Broc's idea had been directly derived from Hue. Since Jean-François Hue's two sons, Horace (Horace-Joseph?) and Alexandre-Laurent, belonged to the *Barbus* sect, it is highly probable that Broc had the opportunity to study their father's *Shipwrecked Family* in his studio before its completion. The work of a highly competent and respected artist, this painting could explain why Broc decided not to follow closely Bernardin de Saint-Pierre's account of the death of Virginie. Freely interpreting the text of the novel, the painter chose instead to dramatize his subject by anchoring it—as Jean-François Hue had done in his *Shipwrecked Family*—to the characteristic staging of shipwrecks and floods (with a few large sculptural figures placed in the foreground), which was in great vogue at the time.

Lucile Franque presents a more difficult question than Broc: She never exhibited in the Salon (her hope to enter the Salon of 1802 was not fulfilled), and her most characteristic works, which, one might recall, depicted subjects taken from "an intermediate world and an intermediate nature," have been lost. However, the problem is not entirely hopeless, for I had the good fortune to rediscover and study two of her paintings—both portraits—in the homestead of the Messageot-Charve family at Quintigny.

The larger of the two pictures (150 x 119 cm) is a group portrait of six members of the Messageot-Charve family (*Figs. 33 and 34*). In the background, from left to right, is Lucile herself, her half-brother, Louis-Maximin Charve, and her stepfather, Judge Claude-Antoine Charve. In the foreground is Mme Charve, Lucile's mother, with two of her daughters: on the left, Liberté-Constitution-Désirée Charve (born in 1792!), Lucile's half-sister, and, on the right, Françoise-Cécile Messageot (nicknamed Fanny), Lucile's sister. Three important members of Lucile's family are not represented in the painting: her brother, François-Xavier Messageot, her husband, Jean-Pierre Franque, and her daughter, Isis-Mélanie-Chrisotémie-Laodamie. The absence of Lucile's brother can be easily explained by the fact that at the turn of the century he was serving as a midshipman and became a prisoner of war during the ill-fated expedition of Santo Domingo (1800–1801). The omissions of Lucile's husband (or husband-to-be) and daughter are perhaps more significant, for they seem to reflect Lucile's uncertain marital status. On this basis one may hypothesize that the painting was executed sometime before Lucile's marriage (10 January 1802)—probably about 1801—since in this group portrait Louis-Maximin, who was born in 1786, looks at least fifteen or sixteen years old.

The artist visibly tried to convey the idea of the links of affection interlocking the two branches of her family around the impressively matriarchal figure of Mme Charve. Lucile rests her hands on the shoulder of Louis-Maximin; the young man, leaning toward his mother, holds Fanny's hand over the shoulder of Liberté; and this little girl, held by her mother around her waist, has placed one hand on Fanny's arm and the other on her lap. Lucile's grouping, with its chain of holding hands, creates an effect recalling the iconography of the ultimate family farewell in classical funerary stelae, as well as that of the Mystical Marriage of Saint Catherine, or that of the Holy Family (in his isolation Judge Charve is given the role of some kind of latter-day Saint Joseph). The keystone of the composition, the powerful Mme Charve, of course summons other parallels that involve comparably dominant figures. One thinks, for instance, of two paintings in the Louvre: Dumont le Romain's *Mme Mercier Surrounded by Her Family* and *The Three Ladies of Ghent* (for a long time attributed to David); or, even more directly, of the anonymous *Family of the Clock-Maker Michel* (?) in the Musée de Tessé, Le Mans.

Mme Charve's ruddy, earthy, almost peasantlike face (she wears a typical coif of the Jura) is contrasted with the ethereal, mournfully enigmatic representation of Lucile. Dressed in black and wreathed with *soucis* (calendula belonging to the sunflower family), possibly an allusion to Clytia, one of Apollo's tragic lovers, or a reference to Van Dyck's self-portrait with a sunflower, she stands, like a melancholy incorporeal guardian angel, watching over her family's destiny. The painting is engagingly awkward and mysteriously touching. Notwithstanding their physical closeness, their pensive tenderness, and the links established by their gestures, the figures fail to suggest an active psychological interaction, and their glances do not meet. In fact, their compression against one another and against the picture plane seems to accentuate their individual loneliness. The primitivist connotation of this effect is stressed by the quasi-Gothic verticality of the composition, with its repetition of triangles, and by the isolation of light and warm color areas (silvery white, vermilion, lemon yellow, yellow ocher, flesh tonalities) against a very dark, purplish-brown, neutral background. The figures, which appear to be suspended in space, convey a strangely apparitional feeling.

It is true, of course, that the type of idealization seen in some of Lucile's figures and their emphatic modeling, underlined with reflections, create a classical frame of reference, somewhat akin to the style of Mme Constance Charpentier. Nevertheless, the spirit of the picture is distinctly non-Davidian. While it is impossible to determine the degree of primitivism Lucile intended, her painting gives an overwhelming impression of youthful gaucherie, sincerity, and sensitivity. Yet undeniably, an archaic flavor can be felt; and my immediate impression of this portrait, upon viewing it in Quintigny, brought to mind reminiscences of Holbein and of some German sixteenth-century paintings.

The smaller picture in the same private collection at Quintigny (60 x 49 cm) is a portrait of Jean-Antoine Gleizes (*Fig. 35*). The round, handsome face and the puffy eyes of the vegetarian philosopher are recognizable from his other representations;[13] and, dissipating all doubts about the sitter's identity, on the back of the canvas appears the inscription: *Auguste Gleizes par Lucile Franque* (Gleizes was known as Auguste among the *Barbus*).

The painting is technically more advanced than the Messageot-Charve portrait. The brushwork is freer and the outline more flowing; the background is less uniform, growing lighter near the figure of the sitter so as to add to its relief. Gleizes's fluid glance and half-smile give a delicately pensive expression to his face, further poeticized by a pervadingly vaporous chiaroscuro: Lucile's sincerity is not lost, but the effect here is much softer and more subtly transient than her depiction of the members of the Messageot-Charve family. Although the painting is not quite finished (the area of the shirt still shows the brown underpainting), it is certain that it is anything but primitivistic in any sense of this term. This work brings to mind certain portraits of Prud'hon (for instance, the portrait of Vallet, in the Louvre), and one derives a strong impression that Lucile came under this master's influence at some point in her short career. Since Gleizes left Paris in 1802, it is probable that Lucile executed his portrait sometime between 1801 and 1802, after the Messageot-Charve group.

These paintings of Duqueylar, Broc, and Lucile Franque—all of them unquestionably executed before 1803—reflect the known ramifications of the *Barbus'* style, or styles, that had evolved at the apex of the sect's activity. To pursue the consideration of this question further within the same chronological borders, it is necessary to leave the realm of documented works to explore the less firm region of speculations. To minimize the danger of subjective opinions, this discussion is limited to two examples: *The Portrait of Bonaparte as First Consul*, by Joseph-Boniface Franque, in the Musée Marmottan, Paris, and *The Study of an Unknown Youth,* attributed to Maurice Quay, in the Musée Granet, Aix-en-Provence.

Joseph-Boniface Franque's portrait (*Fig. 36*) depicts Napoleon in his early thirties (he was born in 1769 and became First Consul in 1799), wearing the official red velvet costume adorned with the gold embroidery of his rank. Its authenticity and attribution to Joseph-Boniface are vouched for by its provenance: It is traceable to the heirs of Napoleon's sister, Elisa Bacciochi, Princess of Lucca and Piombino.[14] This portrait, however, raises a question as to its date. On the basis of its iconography—a representation of the First Consul—it is naturally tempting to assume that the painting was executed between 1799 and 1804 (the period of the *Consulat,* which generally corresponds to that of the *Barbus*). But it is known that the brothers Franque (certainly Jean-Pierre and probably Joseph-Boniface) painted many posthumous portraits of famous men, and one cannot dismiss, a priori, the possibility that the Marmottan portrait might have been executed not only after the *Consulat* but even after the end of the Empire (that is, after 1815).

The problem is further complicated by a question of style. The figure has an almost cardboardlike character: the outline is harshly linear, the modeling perfunctory, and the drawing (for instance, the sitter's ear) somewhat amateurish. The vermilion uniform lends a fresh decorative note to the picture, but psychologically the artist falls short of capturing any of the qualities ascribed to Bonaparte—qualities that seldom escaped even the least-gifted daubers of the time. Since the brothers Franque had acquired a solid reputation for professional skill in David's studio, the awkwardness of the portrait could hardly be considered a result of the artist's incompetence. One is forced to choose between two hypotheses: negligence or deliberate primitivism.

With regard to the former possibility, one must note that Joseph-Boniface Franque's *Bonaparte* seems to follow a prototype established by Gros's full-length depiction of the First Consul in the Musée de la Légion d'Honneur (*Fig. 37,* an X [1801–2]; engraved by William Dickinson). Even if the picture of the Musée Marmottan was part of a multiple commission forcing the artist to a hasty manufacturing, it would be difficult to believe that he would have displayed such slackness in depicting Bonaparte's features for a member of the Imperial family, even after Waterloo.

The more attractive theory of deliberate primitivism appears to be supported by the obvious fact that the picture in the Musée Marmottan is undoubtedly far more primitive-looking than any other known portrait painted by Joseph-Boniface (see, for instance, the portrait of Elisa Bacciochi in the Bibliothèque Marmottan, or that of Marie-Louise at Versailles). One wonders, however, whether Maurice Quay's primitivist gospel could really have inspired a type of naiveté bringing to mind the yet to come *images d'Epinal*.

All in all, because of some unmistakable traces of a rather austere brand of Neoclassical idealism—evoking the early 1800s rather than the period following 1815—the theory of deliberate primitivism seems to be more plausible. This hypothesis is reinforced by the historical context. Napoleon was very concerned with his imperial status, and during the Empire his representations as First Consul show him in active political or military roles rather than in official state portraits. It is simply inconceivable to think that Princess Elisa, who was repeatedly scolded by the Emperor for seeking personal publicity, would have committed the *faux pas* to exhibit the portrait of her brother, as a First Consul, in one of her palaces during her reign in Italy (1805–14). Moreover, it is known that she broke completely with Napoleon after 1814. Most probably the Marmottan portrait was executed between 1802 and 1804, before her departure for Italy (1805), either for her *hôtel* on rue de la Chaise in Paris, or for her country house, Folie Sainte-James at Neuilly.[15] Finally, it can be noted that the routinely skillful portraits of the Bacciochi family, executed by Joseph-Boniface Franque in Italy, after 1812,[16] bear no resemblance whatsoever to the style of Bonaparte's portrait.

The *Study of an Unknown Youth* (*Fig. 38*) is associated with Maurice Quay's name on the strength of an old but unverified tradition of the Musée Granet, and, in the absence of any other painting attributed to the *Barbus'* leader, one is reduced to an analysis in vitro. In this study the gentle inclination and cast of the young man's head, the inquisitive expectancy of the expression, the arrangement of the folds of the drapery, and even the source of light with its resulting pattern of shadows recall one of the figures of Eustache Le Sueur's *St. Bruno Receiving a Message From the Pope* (Louvre). The uncombed, ruffled hair of the young man suggests that its author, possibly attracted by Le Sueur's papal messenger, decided to transpose this figure into a study from nature, probably using a student as a model.

It is hardly surprising, of course, to discover that a painting by Le Sueur, the "French Raphael," possibly provided a source of inspiration for a later picture, but it is astonishing to observe that a work that might have been derived from this seventeenth-century master could display such a strong feeling of originality and commanding energy. Technically, the modeling of the study is characterized by three-dimensional vigor and logic. The brushwork forms a clearly visible web, which adds tactile emphasis to the three-dimensional definition of the facial configuration, and the contrasts of light and dark are kept very strong without marring the precision and purity of the contours. While the general aspect of the painting remains unmistakably classical, the artist nevertheless succeeds in conveying his sitter's individuality. This noble, sensitive image is totally free from either the glacial psychological vacuum or the maudlin sentimentality that so often dominates the human representation at the turn of the century.

The traditional attribution by the Musée Granet is not implausible. At the risk of using an old art-historical formula, it is possible to suggest that it would be difficult to understand why anyone would have ascribed—probably sometime in the nineteenth century—without justification, such an impressive and engaging work to a completely unknown painter like Maurice Quay, rather than attributing it to some historically recognized artist. If one is willing to entertain the validity of this traditional attribution, one is forced to admit that the *Study of an Unknown Youth* seems to confirm David's opinion about Maurice: "He loves nature and has a good under-standing of the antique" (DEL-DAV 63). In fact, the painting is not Davidian, but it possesses something of David's strength, and it is possible to hypothesize that this is one of Maurice's early studies done in his master's studio before 1800. As previously mentioned, Delécluze, describing some of the early works of the *Barbus'* leader, stated that they were stamped with truth, grandeur, and beauty, and that they promised a true painter (DEL-BAR 424). Of course the attribution by the Musée Granet is far from conclusive, but this work does not contradict Delécluze's impression.

After the deaths of Maurice and Lucile, the *Barbus'* art unavoidably became the art of the former *Barbus*. While such later material is less pertinent to the subject of this book, it still retains a measure of usefulness: It can confirm what is already known about the group's early stylistic tendencies before 1804, and it can also pro-vide some valuable insight, however slight and indirect, into what is irretrievably lost. Since the validity of such a study diminishes as the turn of the century recedes from the former *Barbus'* productions, a consideration of the group must be focused on a period that is reasonably close to its heyday. In this category one must give a special place to Broc and the brothers Franque.

Despite the critics' ambivalent comments about his early Salon entries, Broc's work soon began to attract the Imperial patronage. In 1805 he is mentioned, along with some highly successful artists (Gérard, Gros, etc.), as one of the painters who were commissioned to do the full-length portraits of the eighteen *maréchaux de France,* intended for the *salle de concert* of the Tuileries (*Gazette de France,* 30 June 1805). His contribution, the portrait of Maréchal Soult, is known from a copy by Louis-Henri de Rudder at Versailles (the original was destroyed during the upheaval that followed the Franco-Prussian war). Very probably in the same year, he also painted *The Death of General Desaix (Fig. 39),* the most pathetic episode of Napoleon's victory at Marengo (1800), which he exhibited in the Salon of 1806.

Such a patriotic theme did not remain unnoticed, and the artist was praised for his well-ordered composition and, most particularly, for the psychologically eloquent nuances with which he expressed the sorrow of Desaix's companions-in-arms, which was less restrained in common soldiers than in officers. Yet notwithstanding these complimentary comments, the critics felt that Broc's brushwork was heavy, the color scheme lacking in harmony, the drawing showing some faults, and the sense of depth unconvincingly rendered. To quote Chaussard's *Le Pausanias français* (1806): "The only thing this painting needs . . . is to be better painted" (264–66).

This mixture of commendation and condemnation is easy to understand. In *The Death of General Desaix,* Broc encountered the very difficulty that David faced that same year in the *Coronation of Napoleon*: Because of the overwhelming pressure of circumstances, aesthetic ideals had to be subjugated to historical explicitness. The "national" character of Broc's painting—which required a discernibly traditional staging (possibly inspired by Benjamin West's *Death of General Wolfe,* 1771) and a clearly recognizable depiction of modern heroes (Napoleon, Desaix, etc.), military uniforms, banners, and weapons—offered little room for independent stylistic experimentation. In *The Death of General Desaix* and apparently in the portrait of Maréchal Soult, the character of the artist's earlier works is still echoed in a generally grayish color scheme—a vestigial "faded fresco" effect—and in the somewhat wooden character of the figures. In fact, the group with the moribund Desaix, who is held by his faithful hussar, seems to have been deliberately conceived to bring to mind the frequently admired grouping of *The Shipwreck of Virginie*. *The Death of General Desaix* retains something of Broc's earlier disarming awkwardness and charm. But Maurice's ideals have now been severely corroded, and Broc, the former *Barbu*, seems to have been ready to stumble into the pedestrian literalism and eclecticism of the minor practitioners of Napoleonic battle scenes.

In terms of the *Barbus'* primitivism, Broc's subsequent works are even less significant. He continued to enter his productions in the Salon: some were new conceptions, such as *Rinaldo and Armida* (1810, whereabouts unknown) and *The Fortune-Teller* (1819, Musée Baron-Gérard, Bayeux), while others were merely "repeats," such as both *The Death of Hyacinth* and *The Shipwreck of Virginie*, re-exhibited in 1814 and 1819, respectively. *The Death of Hyacinth* seems to have enjoyed a modest degree of success (it was engraved by Normand and by Dusart), but on the whole Broc's works were bypassed by the critics, and he seems to have faded into obscurity.

During this period Broc contributed designs, inspired by Bernardin de Saint-Pierre's *Paul et Virginie,* for a series of *tableaux-tentures* (wallpaper printed in distemper colors from wood blocks), produced by Mader and Dufour (1820).[17] These designs (*Fig. 40*), executed in *grisaille,* are somewhat remarkable because of Broc's imitation of Joseph Vernet or Jean-François Hue and, especially, because of his early use of motifs derived from Chinese or Japanese landscapes. Independently from such potboilers, in at least one of his late paintings, *The Fortune-Teller,* Broc unexpectedly reveals a coloristic-naturalistic style, rooted in a typical seventeenth-century theme, that combines Venetian and Caravaggiesque elements. It seems that in his mature years Broc was not averse to following the advice given to him much earlier by David:

> Broc, you have some talent . . . especially for color . . . pay attention: for color. Thus, don't put it in your head that you are a Raphael. Look, study the masters who are good for you, suitable for you: Titian, Tintoretto, Giorgione. (DEL-DAV 55)

The case of the brothers Franque is far more complex. None of their productions prior to 1806 has ever been described, or even mentioned. Furthermore, with the exception of the previously discussed portrait of Bonaparte, none of their works prior to 1808 has been preserved. One must also keep in mind that the two brothers collaborated on many occasions, and it is often difficult to distinguish their respective styles. Notwithstanding these vexing questions, the post-*Barbu* works of the brothers

Franque invite investigation, for it is plausible to think that they may contain some surviving traces of the two artists' earlier trends.

The Allegory of the Condition of France Before the Return from Egypt (1810; *Fig. 41*) is the earliest—preserved and dated—unquestionable example of the brothers Franque's production. This very large painting (261 x 326 cm) was recently attributed to Jean-Pierre, but this convincing attribution does not quite erase all the problems. Thus one must point out that the very first, truly firm illustration of the brothers Franque's work already raises the question of authorship: The painting is signed *Franque,* but the initial is illegible, and contemporary sources alternately identify the author as either Jean-Pierre or Joseph-Boniface.[18]

The theme of the *Allegory* is the dream, or vision, of Bonaparte at the end of the Egyptian campaign, before the coup d'état of the *18 Brumaire*. The allegorical personification of France, threatened by evil emblematic deities (Crime, Fanaticism, the British leopard, etc.), implores the victorious general to return from the land of the pyramids to save the nation from the disastrous government of the *Directoire*. To quote Landon, the allegorical figures that appear in the midst of the cloudy area, on the left of the painting, have an "aerial" character, and only the figure of the French hero, on the right, is remarkable by its "vigorous sense of relief." According to the same author, this contrasting treatment of the figures suggests that Napoleon, awakened by this vision of France's misfortunes, "rises to rush to her help" (Landon, *Salon de 1810,* 74–75).

The relation of the apparitional, vaporous, and cloudy composition to contemporary depictions of Ossianic subjects was noted almost from the beginning.[19] The idea of mixing Ossianic and political themes, and the character of some specific details—such as the head with windblown hair and fiercely rolling eyes emerging from the clouds under the figure of France—are reminiscent of Girodet's famous Ossianic *Apotheosis,* which glorifies Napoleon and the dead generals of the Republic (1802, Malmaison).[20] But above all it is evident that the painter responsible for *The Allegory of the Condition of France Before the Return from Egypt* was particularly influenced by the composition of François Gérard's *Ossian Evoking Ghosts* (*Fig. 42*).[21] Bonaparte is given the place of the bard Ossian, while the personification of France and the other allegories replace the ghosts of the members of Ossian's family.

The stylistic treatment of this *Allegory* seems to fall within an evolution that is suggested by the available descriptions of some earlier, lost works of the Franque brothers. The hypothesis of such a filiation is made especially plausible by Joseph-Boniface's *Hercules Rescuing Alcestis from Hades* (1806), which, as previously mentioned (*Le Pausanias français,* 448–49), was noted for its "exalted imagination" and its "odd" play of lights and darks. Based on the implications of a dream theme, it is quite possible that a comparable chiaroscuro effect also had characterized Jean-Pierre's *Dream of Love, Inspired by the Power of Harmony* (also exhibited in 1806). According to the *Registre* of the Louvre, this composition—bearing a title that recalls Lucile's *Essai sur les harmonies de la mélancolie et des arts*—depicted "a young man playing a harp near a sleeping woman."

The *Barbus'* fanatic admiration for Ossian and their general inclination for mystery could of course find a much more likely expression in a darkly vaporous pictorial rendering, akin to Girodet, Gérard, and Prud'hon, rather than in a shadowless, linear style. It is most tempting to surmise that long before the works of the brothers Franque this "Ossianic" treatment appeared in Lucile's paintings depicting subjects "derived from an intermediate world and an intermediate nature." Her magnetic personality and her reputation as "the Ossian of painting" suggest that she could have been the initiator of this trend in the *Barbus'* circle, a role that is partly confirmed by the strong chiaroscuro tendency evidenced in her portraits of the Messageot-Charve family and Gleizes.

In a certain measure, this trend is echoed in Périé's most Neoclassical but very dark *Bark of Charon* (*Fig. 43*) and, most probably, in his *Dream of Ossian* (1812), which, from its description in the *Explication* of the Salon of 1812, directly brings to mind Gérard's *Ossian Evoking Ghosts*. It is possible to suggest that, to a lesser degree, the tendency is still present in the lithographs executed by Périé for a volume devoted to the Château of Chambord (*Fig. 44*),[22] which show insistent oppositions of lights and darks. One must observe, however, that in the late works of the brothers Franque, this stylistic disposition is absorbed into a development that might be considered a form of the nineteenth-century Rubenist revival. Joseph-Boniface's spectacular *Eruption of the Vesuvius* (*Fig. 45*), for instance, displays strong chiaroscuro contrasts and warm tonalities, as well as violent pantomimes, which are integrated in an animated Baroque composition. The painting brings to mind Charles Le Brun, François-Gabriel Doyen, and, to a certain degree, Gros. These qualities are also apparent in Jean-Pierre's dramatically Baroque *Conversion of Saint-Paul* (1819, Dijon).

One should not yield too hastily to oversimplification. As in the case of the two distinct stylistic approaches simultaneously exemplified in Broc's *Death of Hyacinth* and *Shipwreck of Virginie,* in the works of the brothers Franque, the avatars of the "Ossianic" chiaroscuro are paralleled by other trends. Proof of this duality can be found in Joseph-Boniface's *Daphnis and Chloe* (1808, La Réunion), as well as in Jean-Pierre's *Angelica and Medor* (*Fig. 46*), *Jupiter Asleep in the Arms of Juno* (1822, Montauban), and his very late *Madonna and Child* (*Fig. 47*). All these productions, lacking any emphatic chiaroscuro effect, reveal a less dramatic, softer, lighter, and far more classicizing style (openly Raphaelesque in the case of the *Madonna and Child*). One could conjecture that this approach, distantly related to Joseph-Boniface's *Bonaparte* (if one is willing to accept an early date for this portrait), represents a very late and highly adulterated application of Maurice Quay's preaching. But at this point, speculations become highly hazardous, since these classicizing works—with borrowings ranging from the idyllic compositions of Gérard to the Madonnas of Raphael—are free from any kind of primitivism or unusual experimentation, and since they can be much more simply understood as a late reflection of conventional Neoclassicism.

In this regard, one must stress the artistic adaptability of the brothers Franque. Without speaking of Jean-Pierre's rather mediocre and obviously eclectic historical portraits executed for Versailles, the two brothers' *Battle of Zurich* (1812; *Fig. 48*), Joseph-Boniface's *Portrait of the Empress Marie-Louise and the King of Rome* (1812, Versailles), Jean-Pierre's *Monument of Queen Clotilde* (before 1818, Mâcon), and the same brother's *Saint John the Baptist Admonishing Herod for His Adultery* (1828, Saint-Jean-Saint-François, Paris) echo a multitude of contemporary stylistic attitudes. *The Battle of Zurich* recalls the productions of minor battle specialists, such as General Le Jeune (with the added influence of Gros); *Marie-Louise* recalls secondary portraitists, such as Robert-Jacques Lefèvre; the *Monument of Queen Clotilde* brings to mind the interior scenes of Granet; and *Saint John the Baptist* represents a competent if not inspiring combination of elements derived from Guérin and Delacroix.

Mediocrity triumphs at the end. Free from the Olympian influence of Maurice Quay and Lucile Franque, the brothers Franque, like Broc, Périé, and doubtless other former *Barbus,* seem to have explored all the available conventional or successfully innovative channels that could have brought them recognition and livelihood.

Conclusion

The greyness of the former *Barbus'* later careers and the conventional character of their later productions can give a distorted idea of the role of the sect. A different measure of its influence is suggested by the *Rapport sur les Beaux-Arts,* which was submitted to Napoleon in 1808 by a deputation of the Fine Arts section of the *Institut de France.* This official account, written by Joachim Le Breton, attempted to trace the progress of French art during the preceding twenty years. Toward the end of his survey of painting, the author, the Perpetual Secretary of the highly respected *Institut,* humorlessly remarked:

> One could have thought at one time that a sort of delirium had overtaken some young painters who had formed a sect in order to establish a system of painting; and, since nothing is as contagious as madness in the Fine Arts, especially during periods of general effervescence, we really had reason to fear that this example might influence the youth of the school. (113)

Without being explicit, this passage unmistakably refers to Maurice Quay's sect and Le Breton's observation about its excesses was confirmed by Delécluze, who noted that Maurice's "more or less brilliant and witty extravagances" created "real havoc" in the imagination of the beginning art students (DEL-DAV 92).

In Le Breton's *Rapport* the discussion of the contagious madness of the sect's members is immediately followed by a consideration of the primitivist folly of other young artists:

> This danger [that of the *Barbus'* sect] was succeeded by an even more serious one, because it was not as open to ridicule and, for this reason, it caused us more concern. Again, some other young painters, but endowed with more talent . . . have tried to introduce a skimpy and cold manner of drawing by exaggerating what is referred to as *the finish,* a style full of rigidity and pretension at originality but which was bordering on the bizarre: by wanting to introduce naiveté in their manner of painting, they were regressing to the infancy of art. In fact, they thought that they were distinguishing themselves by new progress, but they only succeeded in achieving oddity. (113)

It is difficult to identify these "other young painters." In castigating their regression toward the infancy of art, Le Breton could have been referring to the naive meticulousness of the "troubadour" School of Lyons, to the archaizing distortions of Ingres and his imitators, to other primitivist tendencies—or generically, to the ensemble of such manifestations.

Whatever the specific meaning of these allusions, the author closed his comments on a reassuring note: "Happily these fears have been dispelled: it appears, judging from the latest public exhibitions and from the directions taken by the schools, that this mistaken ambition is now being rejected" (113–14).

In reality Le Breton's complacency corresponded to little more than wishful thinking, for official condemnations of the same heresy continued to recur several years after the publication of his *Rapport* (at least until 1815, according to François Benoit, 315). These repeated expressions of alarm on the part of the establishment prove that the primitivist credo had been diffused among young artists well beyond the confines of Maurice Quay's circles and that the primitivist idea remained alive after the disappearance of the sect. Based on Le Breton's *Rapport,* one can conclude that the *Barbus* had not been easily forgotten by the authorities. The sect's contagious madness had implicitly been held responsible for the initiation and diffusion of primitivist ideas, and it was officially considered to be a serious threat to the young school of painting.

Paradoxically, the diffusion of primitivism seems to have been unwittingly supported by David himself. According to Delécluze:

> While meditating upon his subject of Leonidas [*Leonidas at Thermopylae* (1800, completed in 1814)] and immersing himself entirely in the study of the principles of Greek art, David was nourishing his mind and his eyes with the most severe and the most beautiful statues of antiquity. Struck, at the same time, by the analogous beauty which he thought he could recognize in the modern old masters, such as Giotto, Fra Angelico da Fiesole, and especially Perugino [in other passages, Delécluze also mentions Signorelli and Masaccio], David took his inspiration alternatively from the famous compositions of these two periods. (DEL-DAV 219)

David's interest in primitive art had very possibly been stimulated by the fanaticism of his rebellious students (troublemakers' excesses can be very eloquent!). Delécluze related that Jean-Pierre Franque proudly claimed that his teacher had followed Maurice's advice in composing *The Sabine Women* (the introduction of nude figures) (DEL-DAV 188), and one cannot discount the possibility that a variety of the *Barbus'* other ideas came to permeate David's thinking.

Yet as early as 1790—long before *The Sabines* and before the sect's appearance—Girodet reported that the painter of *The Oath of the Horatii* had been telling his students that "a skillful man can find profit in copying *Etruscan pitchers*" (Gérard, I, 133). Thus David's interest in classical archaic art would seem to have antedated the advent of the *Barbus,* whose influence—beside their contagious enthusiasm—would have been chiefly expressed in the master's use of nude figures and his discovery of the Quattrocento.

It appears certain, however, that David considered Quattrocento art primarily as a source of principles (isolation of the figures, one-plane composition, etc.) rather than as a fountainhead of refreshing naiveté and grandiose sublimity, or as a mine for direct borrowings (DEL-DAV 219–20). From this point of view David's attitude diverged from that of some of his non-*Barbu* followers who came very close to the actual imitation of primitive style.

Ingres, who offers the best-known illustration of this approach, had often been chastised for this very reason. In 1806 Chaussard wrote: "Here, in another manner, not less hateful since it is Gothic, M. Ingres strives to nothing less than to push art backward by four centuries, to bring us back to its infancy, and to resurrect the style of Jean de Bruges [Van Eyck]" (178). Ingres was subjected periodically to this kind of attack throughout the first quarter of the century. For instance, in 1819 Gustave Jal, in words directly recalling the phraseology and tone of the criticisms incited in 1800 by Duqueylar and Broc, ironically observed in *L'Ombre de Diderot*:

> A man [Ingres] who could have been worthy of praise because of his talent, haunted by a mania for originality, has searched for new paths. He has strayed, and it is the fruits of his ridiculous errors that are before our eyes. M. Ingres thought that the painting of the twelfth and thirteenth centuries was still fashionable today or that it could become fashionable again. (149)

Ingres's primitivism shows a great variety of types, ranging from the hieratic, Byzantine-like *Napoleon* (1806, Musée de l'Armée), the target of Chaussard's diatribe, to the Botticelli-like *Angelica* (1819, Musée de Montauban), which inspired the acid remarks of Jal. The painter's incredible primitivist boldness is exemplified in the extreme character of the Uccello-like distortions of *Paolo and Francesca da Rimini (Fig. 49)*.[1]

The fact is that in its search for antique purity, Neoclassicism naturally lent itself to a variety of primitivist tendencies, and, beside the clear-cut illustrations given by Ingres, primitivist signs appeared on many levels within the Davidian mainstream. They were often quite conspicuous, as in some early drawings of Girodet that clearly imitate the stylistic mannerisms of early Greek vase painting (for example, *The Return of the Warrior, Fig. 50*). But, more often than not, primitivist suggestions had a more subtle, pervading character. In a work by a leading member of the "troubadour" School of Lyons, Pierre-Henri Revoil's *Childhood of Giotto (Fig. 51)*, it is limited to the borrowing of Cimabue's figure from a fresco in the Spanish Chapel of S. Maria Novella in Florence. In a painting by another of David's pupils, Jacques-Louis-Michel Grandin's more Neoclassically "pure" *Blinding of Daphnis (Fig. 52)*, the primitivist Quattrocento quality is revealed in the elongation and angularity of the figure of the main character.[2] The tendency is not confined to the school of David, however. A hitherto unpublished small historical composition *(Fig. 53)*, which can be identified as a work of one of Jean-Baptiste Regnault's students—Pierre-Edmé-Louis Pellier's *Victory of Odysseus at the Paeces' Games* (exhibited in 1814)—recalls somewhat the combination of Neoclassic and primitivist elements of Broc's *School of Apelles*.[3] Pellier's delicately precise Quattrocento-like style demonstrates that some followers of David's chief competitor had been exploiting the same vein as the students of the painter of *The Sabine Women*.

Doubtless the *Barbus'* theories, and perhaps some of their works, played an important part in these developments. However, notwithstanding Le Breton's observation on the madness transmitted by the members of the sect to other young artists, and Delécluze's description of the havoc brought about by Maurice's ideas in David's studio, one hesitates to ascribe to the *Barbus* the exclusive responsibility for the occurrences of such primitivist episodes. The theories of Seroux d'Agincourt, Lenoir, Wackenroder, Cordier de Launay, Court de Gébelin, Delisle de Sales, and Paillot de Montabert point out the magnitude and elusiveness of the problem. One cannot easily dismiss the possibility that the very elements that originally shaped the *Barbus'* ideas, acting independently, could also have shaped the ideas of their contemporaries, as well as those of the succeeding, primitivistically oriented artists. Thus one must acknowledge that the sect played a central role that was considerably more important than that of a mere catalyst; but it would be misleading to view this role as a unique source of primitivist influence.

The question of influence is particularly difficult to judge when it is considered in the context of the Nazarenes, a German sect that chronologically followed the *Barbus*.[4] The problem is especially compelling because of the external resemblance between the two groups. After all, the Nazarenes decided to lead a communal, semi-monastic life in the Roman monastery of S. Isidoro (1809). They wore strange wide cloaks, had long hair, and tried to recapture the simplicity and purity of the medieval age. Despite the somewhat superficial character of the similarities linking the *fratelli di S. Isidoro* with the *méditateurs* of the convent at Chaillot—the former cultivated a resolutely Catholic religiosity and nationalistically German primitivist ideals—it is difficult to resist the hypothesis of filiation.

While it is not known whether any full-fledged *fratello* ever befriended a member of the *Barbus'* group, it is certain that a few young German artists worked in David's studio, and some of them were indirectly connected with the Nazarene movement. The waves of influence may have flowed in both directions. It is quite possible, for instance, that the painter Gottlieb Schick (1776–1812) derived some of his primitivist traits from contact with the sect of Maurice Quay: His *Sacrifice of Noah* (1805, Staatsgalerie, Stuttgart) suggests an interest in Masaccio, which could have been stimulated during the German artist's stay in David's studio (1798–1802) during the *Barbus'* heyday. Conversely, one of Schick's German friends, the sculptor Christian Friedrich Tieck (1776–1851), who studied under David during the same period (1798–1801), could have brought to Maurice Quay's sect some of the ideas that later came to spur the Nazarenes. Although Tieck never joined the Nazarene brotherhood and his sculpture shows no primitivist qualities, he had early contacts with the Romantic circles of Berlin, and he was the brother of the poet Ludwig Tieck, the intimate collaborator of Wackenroder. The young German sculptor, who actually designed the monument to Wackenroder (1798, Potsdam Marmor palais), achieved some prominence in David's studio: He received the second prize at the *concours de l'an VIII,* and his relief *Priam at the Feet of Achilles,* carved for this competition, was honored by being reproduced in the first volume of Landon's *Annales du Musée* (1800, pl. 9). These facts suggest that it is not at all implausible to think that Tieck held conversations with the members of the *Barbus'* group and that he shared his knowledge of his brother's and Wackenroder's ideas and writings with them.

Such speculations are as inconclusive as they are intriguing. Without either accepting or rejecting the theory of the derivation of the Nazarene movement from the *Barbus,* one must simply admit that available documentation is insufficient for reaching a conclusion.[5] Instead of further rationalizations, one may attempt to view the subject, in different terms, against the backdrop of the aesthetic crisis that was germinating in the late eighteenth and early nineteenth centuries. The meaning of this crisis has been generally overlooked. I have attempted to demonstrate elsewhere[6] that primitivism is a highly fluid phenomenon that, all in all, can be understood as an aesthetically spiritual, aristocratic, and escapist reaction against the contemporary striving for scientifically defined facts and a scientifically produced optical truth. This last tendency, linked with the beginning of the Industrial Revolution, represented an essentially popular, commonsensical attitude that found its justification in the proliferation of scientific theories and inventions. It was conspicuously reflected in the immense popularity of *transparents, silhouette machines, physionotraces, panoramas, dioramas,* and, in general, in the multiplication of *trompe-l'oeil* and other illusionistic devices that eventually led to the "perfect visual lie" of photography. The aesthetics of this new scientific vulgarization of optical verisimilitude were directly confronting the pseudo-philosophical, illuministic, and utopian points of view that prevailed in the late eighteenth century and which were ingrained in the primitivist faith. Thus without discarding the hypothesis of filiation, it is possible to visualize the *Barbus* and the Nazarenes as two similar but distinct reactions against the increasingly oppressive cult of popular science and the pedestrian tendency to equate the "correct" recording of visual experience with art.

The historical significance of the *Barbus* should not be weighed solely on the scale of aesthetic doctrines. Whether or not one is to visualize Maurice Quay's sect as the prime fountainhead of primitivism, as a catalyst, or as the first truly conspicuous manifestation of the approaching primitivist wave of the nineteenth century, which was to culminate with the pre-Raphaelites and Gaugin's Pont-Aven group, it deserves to be remembered as a deeply moving, collectively shared, most unusual human experience, and a unique youthful adventure. The *Barbus'* chronicle is the earliest recorded instance of a sect of young artists deciding not only to oppose the prevailing aesthetic points of view of their times but also to change their times, and eventually to "secede" from their own historical era. These aspects of their thinking can of course be best understood when viewed against the changing image of the artist, modeled by unfulfilled heroic dreams, humiliating popular clichés, and vaudeville stereotypes.

It might be instructive to take a parting look at the question of the artist's image and his position in society by reading Jal's *Les Soirées d'artistes.* This article, published in *Le Livre des cent-et-un* (1831, I), unravels the problem (which was acquiring the status of a permanent crisis) seen in the perspective of the generation that immediately followed the *Barbus*. The article opens with an indignant exposé of the humiliating position of the artist in eighteenth-century society, followed by a discussion that contrasts this deplorable state with the new situation of 1831:

> Today, everything is changed. . . . An artist now respects the host who receives him to dinner as much as he is respected by him. He is an ornament for society where he is admitted on an equal footing; he is not society's toy. One derives benefit from his conversation, from his knowledge; perhaps one takes advantage of his renown, but the roles have been changed, and it is no longer the artist who commonly plays the part of the flatterer. (112–13)

It can be seen that each succeeding generation was prone to claim that they had finally given to the artists—an appellation now extended to poets and musicians, as well as painters—a proper place and true recognition in society. Admittedly we are very far from the time when Watelet reminded the artists of their obligation to fight their naturally low inclinations. However, the new status should not be confused with total integration. Thus Jal added, after having exalted the artists' recently won social equality:

> The artists, since the Restoration, have felt that they were important, and that in society they formed a world of their own, a world of kindred intellects. I do not believe that they ever thought that some day their world would dominate and legislate the other. The vanity, for which they are so much blamed, when one does not think to criticize the vanity of so many other people who have nothing to justify it or to at least excuse it, has not blinded the artists to this point. They have seen that they were not understood, and that, although they were received with favor, even with distinction into society, they were looked upon with curiosity, like foreigners whose language could not be comprehended. They were afraid to fall back into the situation from which the revolution of 89 had extracted them and they have grouped themselves and closed ranks, in the fear that the order of things which had begun in 1815 would reinstate them, in the Parisian salons, into the degrading position from which they had escaped thirty years ago. (113)

This pride of belonging to a special group of kindred intellects, or a class apart, the certitude of not being understood by the other members of society, and the suspicion, insecurity, and need to close ranks indicate that during the Restoration artists were still haunted by the same old demons. The psychological makeup of the creative personality—whatever it might be—presumably had a part in the coalescence of these anxieties. However, beyond this element, which is always elusive, and beyond the insufficiently known economic factors, social and cultural gears meshed in the shaping of the artist's image at the end of the eighteenth century and certainly played a crucial role in his increasing sense of alienation.

Vincent van Gogh most probably never heard of the *Barbus*, but his dream of the yellow *maison des amis* at Arles had essentially been inspired by the same curse of secret loneliness and by the same eager need for understanding as Maurice Quay's dream of the *retraite* at Chaillot. Every artist would openly agree with Vigny's *Stello* that, in the creative process, "Solitude is sacred" (XL, 751). But, while most artists would probably also agree that "all associations have all the shortcomings of convents" (XL, 751), in their hearts they often feel the urge to flock with kindred souls. The point is that artists are unique, paradoxical, and vulnerable. To borrow once again from Vigny (XL, 753), who compares artists to swallows: "They say to men: *Protect us, but do not touch us.*"

Abbreviations

AUL: François-Victor-Alphonse Aulard, *Paris sous le premier empire: Recueil de documents pour l'histoire de l'esprit public à Paris* (Paris: Cerf, Noblet, Quantin, 1914).

CAR-PRO: Louis Carrogis Carmontelle, *Proverbes dramatiques,* C. de Mery, ed. (Paris: Delongchamps, 1822).

COL: *Collection des Théâtres français, suite du répertoire* (Senlis: Tremblay, 1829).

DEL-BAR: Etienne-Jean Delécluze, "Les Barbus d'à présent et les barbus de 1800," *Le Livre des cent-et-un,* 1832, published in the appendix of Delécluze, *Louis David, son école et son temps, souvenirs* (Paris: Didier, 1855).

DEL-DAV: The main portion of Etienne-Jean Delécluze, *Louis David, son école et son temps, souvenirs,* actually written in 1855.

JD: *Journal des Débats.*

LEV-GRI: George Levitine. "The Eighteenth-Century Rediscovery of Alexis Grimou and the Emergence of the Proto-Bohemian Image of the French Artist," *Eighteenth-Century Studies,* vol. 2, no. 1 (Fall 1968).

MAR: Jean-François Marmontel, *Mémoires,* Maurice Tourneux, ed. 3 vols. (Paris: Bibliothèque des bibliophiles, 1891).

NOD-EST: Charles Nodier, *Correspondance inédite,* Alexandre Estignard, ed. (Paris: Librairie du Moniteur universel, 1876).

NOD-LAR: Charles Nodier's letter in Jean Larat, *La Tradition de l'exotisme dans Charles Nodier* (Paris, 1923).

NOD-SAL: Charles Nodier, *Le Peintre de Saltzbourg, journal des émotions d'un cœur souffrant* (Paris: Charpentier, 1850).

NOD-TEM: Charles Nodier, "Les Barbus," *Le Temps,* 5 October 1832, published in the appendix of Delécluze, *Louis David, son école et son temps, souvenirs* (Paris: Didier, 1855).

NOD-TYP: Charles Nodier, "Deux beaux types de la plus parfaite organisation humaine" (first published in *Essai d'un jeune barde,* 1804), published in Delécluze, *Louis David, son école et son temps, souvenirs* (Paris: Didier, 1855), 75–76.

REP: *Répertoire général du théâtre français* (Paris: Nicole, 1818).

WAT-DIC: Claude-Henri Watelet, *Dictionnaire des arts de peinture, sculpture et gravure,* 5 vols. (Paris: Prault, 1792).

Notes*

Chapter 1

1. In Goncourt, *L'Art du XVIIIe siècle,* I, 42. The idea recurs throughout the nineteenth century. Thus in defining "La Bohème," Murger writes: "c'est la préface de l'Académie, de l'Hôtel-Dieu ou de la Morgue" (*Scènes de la vie de Bohème,* Paris, n.d., vi).

2. See Levitine, *"Vernet Tied to a Mast in a Storm."*

Chapter 2

1. Carmontelle, *Proverbes et Comédies posthumes,* Mme de Genlis, ed., I, 394–414.

2. See Levitine, "Les Origines du mythe de l'artiste bohème en France: Lantara."

3. See Renouvier, *Histoire de l'Art pendant la Révolution,* 178, n. 1.

Chapter 3

1. For other early Italian examples, see Chastel, "La Légende médicéenne," *Art et Humanisme à Florence au temps de Laurent le Magnifique,* 11–28; see also Rudolf Wittkower and Margot Wittkower, *The Divine Michelangelo,* London, 1964, 163 ff.

2. An interesting discussion of this type of theme can be found in Haskell, "The Old Masters in Nineteenth-Century French Painting."

3. The term is coined by Monglond, *Le Préromantisme français,* I, *Le héros préromantique.*

4. In *Lettres adressées au baron François Gérard,* I, 127–28.

5. Lucas-Dubreton, *Le Culte de Napoléon, 1815–48,* 59.

6. For instance, see [Chaussard], *Le Pausanias français,* 337–48, or Landon, *Annales du musée,* I, 57–58.

7. Archives nationales, AF IV, 1498, in Aulard, *Paris sous le premier empire,* II, 703–4.

Chapter 4

1. Nodier, "Deux beaux types de la plus parfaite organisation humaine" (first published in *Essai d'un jeune barde,* 1804), in Delécluze, *Louis David,* 74–76.

2. Delécluze, "Les Barbus d'à présent et les barbus de 1800" (first published in *Livre des Cent-et-un,* VII, 1832), in Delécluze, *Louis David,* 423.

* The original spelling and punctuation of all French texts and documents have been preserved. Complete references can be found in the Bibliography.

3. Archives nationales. MS F⁷ 6457.BP9691–9740, 30 Frimaire, an XII (22 December 1803).

4. Archives of the mairie de Puteaux (Département de la Seine), MS, Registre N 1737 à 1757. Among several pieces related to the Quay family, these archives contain the baptismal certificate of Jean-Maurice Quay, the future *Barbu*'s father:

> Ce huit auost mil sept cent quarante six a été baptisé nous soussigné Jean Maurice né d'hier sur cette Paroisse Fils de François Maurice Quay Jardinier chez Monsieur le Président Mesle demeurant à Paris rue des Capucines Paroisse Saint-Roch et de Louise Marguerite Colibert sa légitime épouse. Le Parain Jean Sauvage Jardinier de Monseigneur le Duc de Grammont en sa maison de Plaisance à Puteaux. La Maraine Jeanne Marguerite Stouder femme de Gérard Colibert, Tailleur demeurant sur cette Paroisse, tous on signé avec nous excepté le Parain qui a déclaré ne le savoir, de ce interpellé suivant l'Ordonnance. F.

The father of François-Maurice, Antoine cay [Quay] came from the province of Genevois, in Savoie. He married Louise Marguerite Colibert on 15 November 1745. Her father, Gérard Colibert, was a tailor, born in Verdun, Lorraine, who died on 24 June 1749. Gérard Colibert's son-in-law was Benoist Stouder, "soldat au régiment des gardes suisses" (ibid., 1749).

5. Archives de la Seine, MS, 1ᵉʳ arrondissement, 1819. These archives contain the death certificate of Jean-Maurice Quay:

> Quay, Jean Maurice
> Date du décès 6 Janvier 1819
> Ancien jardinier né à Puteaux, Dpt de la Seine—73 ans—
> 13 rue Joubert (Vendôme) Nom de l'épouse pas connu

6. Archives nationales, the Minutier central des Notaires. This collection contains a number of legal manuscript pieces concerning the Quay family, most of which refer to Jean-Maurice Quay's borrowing of money or sale of land (XXI, 55 bis, 108, 126, 219, 601, 621; XXXI, 291). The most informative of these documents (XXXI, 280) is the "Inventaire fait après décès de Margueritte Simon femme Maurice Quay" (8 Frimaire, an V [28 November 1796]).

It must be noted that in the eighteenth century the same Christian name was traditionally repeated from father to son. Quay, a comparatively uncommon name, recurs only in the Dauphiné-Savoie region. The recurrence of the "Maurice Quay" combination in the same family is unique, and in my opinion this factor is a serious basis for thinking that the painter Maurice Quay was the son of the gardner Jean-Maurice Quay.

7. This date can be inferred by cross-checking the text of Delécluze's *Louis David*. All of Delécluze's statements on the chronology of his experience in the famous studio imply that at the time of his enrollment (late 1796–early 1797) Maurice was already one of the most influential students of David (DEL-DAV 48–49, 188). Needless to say, the Maurice Quay biography is far from complete. Some earlier errors must be dispelled: For instance, Nodier, referring to Napoleon's interview of Maurice Quay (1803 ?), speaks of the First Consul's nieces and states that they were the daughters of Joseph Bonaparte (NOD-TEM 441). This information could not be correct, for Joseph's children were not of the age and sex that would have justified Nodier's assertion. If Nodier is at

all trustworthy about the interview, the two nieces can most probably be identified as the two daughters of Lucien Bonaparte, from his first marriage to Christine Boyer: Charlotte (born in 1795) and Christine-Egypte (born in 1798). These two girls were, respectively, eight and five years old in 1803.

8. The baptismal certificate of Marguerite-Françoise-Lucie [Lucile] Messageot in the Mairie of Lons-le-Saunier, MS:

> Le treize septembre mil sept cent quatre vingt est née et a été baptisée Marguerite Françoise Lucie Fille de Monsieur Jean Joseph Messageot, ancien Officier de Cavalerie, chevalier de l'ordre Royal et Militaire de Saint-Louis, demeurant en cette ville et de Dame Marie Françoise Clerc, mariés, laquelle a eu pour parrain Monsieur Claude François Jovin, Lieutenant Général criminel aux Baillages et résidant de Lons-le-Saunier et pour Marraine Mademoiselle Claudine Marguerite Vuillermoz aussi de cette ville, les deux soussignés.

9. The most accurate description of Lucile's family can be found in an article by Marius Dargaud: "Autour d'un centenaire, Charles Nodier, jurassien." See also Magnin, "Charles Nodier naturaliste," 483; and Monnier, *Souvenirs d'un octogénaire de province,* 201–3.

10. Lucile's biographies are very vague as to her master's identity. Mme Mennessier-Nodier refers to Pierre-Narcisse Guérin and to David (*Charles Nodier: Episodes et souvenirs de sa vie,* 92). Lucile's name does not appear in the listing of David's students and nothing is known about her possible relationship with Guérin.

11. Archives de la Seine, 1799, 1er arrondissement. The original dating of the Republican calendar is 29 Fructidor, an VII. Lucile's daughter died on 4 February 1870 [MS death certificate of the Commune de Quintigny (Jura) copied on 12 August 1969].

12. 20 Nivôse, an X (copy of the marriage certificate of the Commune de Quintigny, 12 August 1969).

13. 3 Prairial, an XI. Archives de la Seine MS DQ^8 16– vol. 13. The address given in this document is 59 rue de Chaillot, Champs-Elysées.

14. MS Baptismal certificate in the Mairie of Buis-les-Baronnies (Drôme):

> Jean Pierre et Joseph Boniface Francou jumeaux de jean et de marguerite signouret nés le onze d'aoust mille sept cent soixante quatorze ont été baptisés le même jour par nous secondaire soussignés, le parrain du premier enfant a été etienne pierre tisserand signé avec nous, la marraine marie francou sa tante illitérée [sic] enquise et requise. le parrain du second appellé joseph boniface a été joseph louis boniface brusset lequel a prêté la main Sr. joseph brusset[?] notaire son grand père, la marraine marie anne rose brusset signée avec nous mr Joseph brusset qui a prêté la main au parrain
> armand secondaire
> pierre

15. See Bernard, *Histoire de Buis-les-Baronnies,* 232–33.

16. Their names appear in the *Tableau des élèves de l'Ecole gratuite de dessin* (May 1786–August 1787) and in the *Catalogue des Elèves de l'Ecole gratuite de Dessin de la ville de Grenoble* (since 10 November 1788). Both documents belong to the Bibliothèque municipale de la ville de Grenoble (MS 66.241 and 66.240).

17. *Département de la Drôme, Compte de la Gestion,* 1792, 33–34.

18. Letter of 7 February 1792 quoted in David, *Le Peintre Louis David, 1748–1825, Souvenirs et Documents inédits,* 98.

19. Delécluze, *Louis David,* 69, 71, 187.

20. "rue de Maillot au couvent des dames sainte Marie division des champs élisée premier arrondissement." This address is given (on 16 Nivôse, an X [6 January 1802]) in a manuscript letter written by Judge Charve (Lucile's stepfather) to the mayor of Quintigny requesting the publication of the banns on the occasion of Lucile's marriage to Jean-Pierre Franque (Mairie de Quintigny).

21. For the last years of Joseph-Boniface's career, see Marmottan, *Les Arts en Toscane sous Napoléon, La Princesse Elisa,* 81–82, 181, n. 2, and Lorenzetti, *L'Accademia di Belli Arti di Napoli,* 86–87, 211–12.

22. Inès d'Esmenard, "Peintre d'histoire et de portraits," is mentioned as one of his students (Gabet, *Dictionnaire des artistes de l'école française au XIXᵉ siècle,* 255).

23. On 28 March. See Dargaud, "Autour d'un centenaire." For additional information about the brothers Franque's biography, see Rochas, *Biographie du Dauphiné,* I, 401; also see Brun-Durand, *Dictionnaire biographique et Biblio-iconographique de la Drôme,* 339.

24. See the painter's birth certificate in Levitine, " 'L'Ecole d'Apelle' de Jean Broc," 286, 293 n. 3.

25. David, *Le Peintre Louis David,* 326. See also DEL-DAV 50.

26. In 1800 his address is given as "chez C. David, au Palais national des Sciences et des Arts" (*Explication des ouvrages de peinture . . . des Artistes vivans, Exposés au Muséum central des arts le 15 Fructidor, an VIII,* 11).

27. Thus in 1801 his address is "rue de l'Observance, No 7" (*Explication . . . le 15 Fructidor, an IX–2 September 1801,* 8).

28. See Tilander, "Tapet med romantiskt litterärt motiv." A beautiful copy of this wallpaper can be seen in the Musée des Arts Décoratifs in Paris. I am grateful to Mme Nouvel for the information she kindly gave to me on this matter.

29. The exact date of Broc's death is not known. Polish sources mention both Lopatov and Topatyn (Galicia, Poland) as the location of Dwernicki's homestead. See *Polski Slownik Biograficzny,* VI, 22; and also *Herbaz Polski,* Part I, V.

30. The most reliable information on Périé can be found in Nayral, *Biographie castraise,* 117–29. See also Estadieu, *Annales du pays castrais,* 416; and Nicolas, *Histoire des artistes . . . nés dans le département du Gard,* 13–14.

31. Yet he is honored with an entry in Firmin-Didot's *Nouvelle Biographie générale,* XI, 306. See also Gabet, *Dictionnaire des artistes,* 156–57, and Benoit, *L'Art français sous la Révolution et l'Empire,* 312.

32. The few data on Jean-François Hue's sons can be found in Gabet, *Dictionnaire des artistes,* 359. See also Nodier's letter published in Larat, *La Tradition et l'exotisme dans l'œuvre de Charles Nodier,* 23.

33. Yet the handwritten *Registre pour l'inscription* of the Salon of 1802 mentions a landscape (No. 207) by "Hue fils, Joseph," possibly Horace-Joseph (Archives du Louvre).

34. For available biographical and biliographic data, see Lyonnet, *Dictionnaire des Comédiens français,* II, 20. One can also consult general biographies such as the *Biographie nouvelle des contemporains,* VII, 3. See also NOD-LAR 23.

35. Nodier, *Correspondance inédite,* Estignard, ed., 25.

36. Marcel Prault-Saint-Germain was a hydraulics engineer who tried several times to exhibit in the Salon the drawings on his projected plan for a canal uniting the Rhine to the Seine. See the *Registre pour l'inscription* of the Salons of 1802 (No. 239) and 1804 (No. 372). Prault-Saint-Germain possibly belonged to a group of young, rather visionary scientists, such as Fabre d'Eglantine *fils,* who joined the *Barbus* through the intermediary of Charles Nodier. For Prault-Saint-Germain's project see: *Projet de la seule navigation naturelle et commerciale qui existeroit en Europe, et joindroit le Rhin à la Seine jusqu' à Paris, sous la dénomination de: Navigation Bonaparte.*

37. A good biography of Gleizes can be found in *Biographie Universelle,* Michaud ed., XVI, 626–33. See also Nayral, *Biographie castraise,* III, 566–69.

38. One of the best recent studies of this period is Oliver, *Charles Nodier: Pilot of Romanticism.*

Chapter 5

1. See Van Tieghem, *Ossian en France.*

2. Landon, "Exposition du Salon du Musée," 124–26.

3. 15 Floréal 1800, MS belonging to M. René Angliviel, originating from the Château de la Nogarède, graciously brought to my attention by M. Jean Carle.

4. Quoted in Labouisse-Rochefort, *Variétés littéraires et biographiques,* 274. The question of the *Barbus'* false beards is also mentioned by Delécluze (DEL-BAR 428–29).

5. Labouisse-Rochefort, 273. A note states that Périé began to wear the *Barbu* costume in 1798, (273).

6. *Police Générale—Rapports de la Préfecture de police an VIII–an IX, 3 Frimaire, an IX* (Préfecture de Police, MS, F⁷ 3829).

7. *Le Petit Arlequin au Muséum ou les tableaux d'Italie en vaudeville,* MS 83–85 (fully quoted in Levitine, "The *Primitifs* and Their Critics in the Year 1800," 211). Similar feelings are echoed in the two anonymous letters published in the *Journal des Arts* (16 October and 15 December 1799) reproduced in James Henry Rubin's very interesting "New Documents on the Méditateurs: Baron Gérard, Mantegna, and French Romanticism circa 1800," 786–87.

8. On the basis of the two previously mentioned letters (see n. 7), Rubin suggests that the scission between David and the *Barbus* had to have occurred before 16 October 1799 (op. cit., 787). He is undoubtedly correct if one equates scission with expulsion. However, it is possible to point out some qualifying factors: (1) the letter of 16 October states that David expelled only *"quelques-uns"* of the *Barbus;* (2) Nodier visited the Franques' apartment in or after December 1800; (3) Broc was still living "chez C. David" in the Louvre in 1800 (see chapter 4, n. 26). Thus one is led to think that the expulsion of 1799 did not produce David's immediate and total break with all the members of the sect.

9. Bibliothèque de l'Arsenal, Paris, MS 15.030/16.

10. Henry-Rosier, *La Vie de Charles Nodier,* 49.

11. 18 Messidor 1800, MS belonging to M. René Angliviel, originating from the Château de la Nogarède, graciously brought to my attention by M. Jean Carle.

12. Gleizes's theories are succinctly but clearly presented in *Biographie Universelle,* Michaud ed., XVI, 626–33.

13. Larat, *La Tradition et l'exotisme dans l'œuvre de Charles Nodier,* 20–21.

Chapter 6

1. Archives de la Préfecture, MS A 130, an IX, 15 Germinal, an IX.

2. Archives de la Préfecture, MS A 126, an IX.

3. See Mme Mennessier-Nodier, *Charles Nodier,* 90.

4. Archives nationales, MS F⁷ 6457 BP 9691–9740.

5. According to this passage of Delécluze, Augustin D . . . jumped from the towers of Notre-Dame. In her notes Madame Gleizes relates a similar (and probably the same) incident:

> Il y a quelques mois qu'un élève de l'Ecole de David se précipita du haut des tours de N. Dame ayant laissé chez lui un dessin représentant ce moment.

Madame Gleizes's note is dated 15 Floréal 1800, a fact which suggests that this suicide took place three years before the sect's disappearance (MS belonging to M. René Angliviel, originally from the Château de la Nogarède).

6. Paul Marmottan, "Les Achats de terrains pour le Palais du Roi de Rome," *Bull. de la Soc. historique d'Auteuil et de Passy,* 7ème année, 1910, 1911, 1912, 178.

7. Nodier, *Apothéoses et imprécations de Pythagore.* Oliver, in his *Charles Nodier,* erroneously points out Lucile's and Maurice's absence from this table of honor, 57.

Chapter 7

1. See, for instance, Friedlaender, *David to Delacroix,* 49–50.

2. See Rosenblum, *Transformations in Late Eighteenth-Century Art,* 163 ff.

3. Winckelmann, *L'Histoire de l'art de l'antiquité,* I, 5, 15. Speaking of Sicilian medals of the earliest style, Winckelmann states that they provide an unchallengeable proof "que l'idée de la beauté, ou proprement l'exécution du beau, n'était pas une qualité innée et donnée avec l'Art aux Artistes grecs: il est certain que celles des tems suivans sont infiniment supérieures aux premières" (II, 224). The most ancient Greek style was "droit et dur," comparable to that of the artists of the early modern school (described as "sec et roide"), before the restoration of art effected by Michelangelo and Raphael (II, 269).

4. A thorough study of the subject can be found in Previtali, *La Fortuna dei primitivi dal Vasari ai neoclassici;* see also Rosenblum, *Transformations,* 163 ff.

5. See Lamy, "La Découverte des primitifs italiens au XIXᵉ siècle, Seroux d'Agincourt. . . ."

6. Le Flamanc, *Les Utopies prérévolutionnaires,* 94 ff. I should like to thank Mr. S. Whitney for bringing this book to my attention.

7. Ibid., 143–52.

8. For this question, see Levitine, "Trompe-l'oeil Versus Utopia."

Chapter 8

1. Bibliothèque de Besançon, MS 1890, folio 81, 9 Juin 1815.

2. It is possible, of course, that Lucile's entry was rejected by the jury. However, since her name is recorded without the information that usually accompanies the listing of the participants, one is inclined to think that she had a change of mind at the last moment, perhaps because of her illness.

3. See Levitine, "The *Primitifs* and Their Critics in the Year 1800," 212–19; see also Levitine, " 'L'Ecole d'Apelle' de Jean Broc." I would like to express my most sincere thanks to Professor James Henry Rubin for generously providing me with an almost unobtainable photograph of Duqueylar's painting.

4. A detailed bibliography of the Ossianic influence in painting can be found in the catalogue of the exhibition *Ossian,* held in the Grand Palais, Paris, in 1974, 113–17. See also Levitine "L' *Ossian* de Girodet et l'actualité politique sous le Consulat"; and Levitine, "L'Aigle épouvanté de l' 'Ossian' de Girodet."

5. Landon, "Exposition du Salon du Musée," 122–26.

6. See Levitine, " 'L'Ecole d'Apelle' de Jean Broc."

7. Landon, "Exposition du Salon du Musée," 72, 75, 78; *Journal du Bulletin universel des sciences, des lettres et des arts* (Coll. Deloynes XXIII, 634, 14–15); *Le Verre cassé de Boilly, 7; Mercure de France* (Coll. Deloynes, XXII, 633, 725); *Coup-d'œil sur le Salon de l'an VIII,* 11–12; *Arlequin au Muséum, les tableaux en vaudeville,* 11–12.

8. Landon, "Exposition du Salon du Musée," 73–74.

9. *Coup-d'œil sur le Salon de l'an VIII,* 12.

10. Professor Horst W. Janson has kindly brought to my attention an unpublished composition by Nicolai Abraham Abilgaard, engraved by Johan-Frederick Clemens (1785), entitled *Le Sort des artistes,* which reflects an attempt to adapt the allegory of Calumny to the theme of the artist subjected to ignorant criticism.

11. *Le Moniteur Universel,* 10 Brumaire, an IX (1 November 1800), XXIV, 40.

12. See Levitine, " 'L'Ecole d'Apelle' de Jean Broc," 292; and Robert Rosenblum's entry to the catalogue of the exhibition *De David à Delacroix: La peinture française de 1774 à 1830,* 340–41.

13. In particular a lithograph by Grégoire and Deneux, kindly brought to my attention by M. Jean Carle. It is clear that this lithograph represents Gleizes later in his life.

14. See Lefuel, *Catalogue du Musée Marmottan,* 106.

15. For Elisa's biography see Fleuriot de Langle, *Elisa, soeur de Napoléon I.*

16. For instance, the portraits of Félix Bacciochi, Prince of Lucca; Elisa Bacciochi; and Frédéric Napoléon Bacciochi. These three paintings belong to the collection of the Bibliothèque Paul Marmottan (see Fleuriot de Langle, *Bibliothèque Paul Marmottan, Guide Analytique,* 6–7).

17. See Chapter 4. This type of wallpaper is also known as *panoramique.* In such works the artist played a most subservient part and his drawings were very seldom pre-

served. I should like to express my thanks to Mme Nouvel, Curator of the Wallpaper Collection of the Musée des Arts Décoratifs, Paris, for kindly providing me with important information in this matter.

18. For the latest discussion of this problem see Jacques Foucart in *French Painting 1774–1830: The Age of Revolution,* 421–22.

19. Ibid.

20. See Levitine, "L'*Ossian* de Girodet et l'actualité politique sous le Consulat."

21. See Hélène Toussaint, "Ossian en France," in the catalogue of the exhibition *Ossian,* 78–82.

22. Merle and Périé, *Description historique et pittoresque du Château de Chambord.*

Conclusion

1. For Ingres, see, for instance, Rosenblum, *Transformations,* 187–88; Rosenblum, *Jean-Auguste-Dominique Ingres;* and Schlenoff, *Ingres, ses sources littéraires,* 61–90. The character of Ingres's absorption of Quattrocentesque qualities brings to mind the much later (1845) primitivism of William Haussoullier's *Fountain of Youth,* in which Baudelaire noted the influence of Giovanni Bellini (*Salon de 1845,* 819–22).

2. See Levitine, "Trompe-l'œil Versus Utopia," 22–23.

3. This attribution is based on two factors: (1) the particular subject of this painting is very seldom exemplified in art, and it is definitely known that Pellier interpreted this very subject in a work entered in the Salon of 1814; (2) a comparison of the painting, in the Musée Magnin, with a known painting of Pellier, *Oedipus Cursing His Son* (Musée d'Angers), which is signed and dated (1809) and which was exhibited with the *Victory of Odysseus at the Paeces' Games,* also in the Salon of 1814: Despite a difference of scale, this comparison reveals a very definite stylistic kinship.

In reference to the question of combinations of Neoclassic and primitivist elements, J. H. Rubin (op. cit.) states that Gérard's *Cupid and Psyche* (1798), because of its "lack of colour complexity," is related to "the quattrocentesque experiments of the Méditateurs," such as Broc's *Death of Hyacinth.* Giving a great role to Mantegna's influence, Rubin takes the position that "it would appear that for the Méditateurs, the *Cupid and Psyche* represented an assimilation of certain possible Mantegnesque qualities" (787–88).

4. For a recent study of the Nazarenes, see Andrews, *The Nazarenes.*

5. It is far easier to show the influence of the Nazarenes on some later developments of French painting (see Charles Lenormant, *Beaux-Arts—1851—Orsel et Overbeck,* Paris, 1851). These developments were amusingly evoked by Théophile Gautier in his "Feuillets de l'album d'un jeune rapin" where he describes how he became a primitive, "a painter of the angelic school," considering Perugino already a bit "Van Loo" and, following the examples of Johann Friedrich Overbeck and Peter Cornelius, taking his inspiration from German and Flemish primitive art, 311–22.

6. See Levitine, "Trompe-l'œil Versus Utopia," 9–26.

Bibliography

Unpublished Manuscript Sources

Besançon (Jura), Bibliothèque
    Letters of Pillet to Charles Weiss, MS 1890: fol. 40v. (6 October 1814); fol. 56r. (30 September 1814); fol. 81r. and v. (9 June 1815).
    Correspondence of Charles Nodier, MS 1417; fol. 25r. and v. (11 Ventôse, an IX [2 March 1801]); fol. 26r.

Buis-les-Baronnies (Drôme), Mairie
    Baptismal Certificate of the Franque brothers (11 August 1774).

Castres (Tarn), Mairie
    Birth Certificate of Antoine-Hilaire-Henri Périé (30 May 1780).

Grenoble (Isère), Archives municipales, Bibliothèque municipale
    Registration of the Franque brothers at the Ecole gratuite de dessin: GG No. 241 (1763–, October 1786–August 1787); GG No. 240 (15 November 1786).

Lons-le-Saunier (Jura), Mairie
    Baptismal Certificate of Lucile Messageot (13 December 1780).

Nogarède, château de la (Mazère, Ariège)
    MS notes of Mme Gleizes, originating from the château de la Nogarède, communicated by M. Jean Carle (entries: 15 Floréal [5 May] 1800; 18 Messidor [17 July] 1800).

Paris, Archives du Louvre
    Salon of 1800 (an VIII): *Registre d'inscription des productions des artistes.* . . .
    Salon of 1801 (an IX): *Registre pour l'inscription des ouvrages de peinture.* . . .
    Salon of 1802 (an X): (1) *Enregistrement des notices par ordre alphabétique,* (2) *Registre pour l'inscription des ouvrages de peinture.* . . .
    Salon of 1804: *Registre pour l'inscription des ouvrages de peinture.* . . .
    Salon of 1808: *Registre d'inscription des productions des artistes.* . . .
    Salon of 1810: *Registre d'inscription des productions des artistes.* . . .
    Salon of 1812: *Registre d'inscription des productions des artistes.* . . .
    Salon of 1814: *Registre d'inscription des productions des artistes.* . . .

Paris, Archives nationales
    Charles Nodier's police interrogation: F7 6457 BP 9691–9740 (30 Frimaire, an XII [22 December 1803]).
    Documents concerning the financial transactions of Jean-Maurice Quay: Minutier central des notaires XXI, 55 bis (16 Messidor, an III [4 July 1795]), 108 (29 Floréal, an III [18 May 1795]), 126 (9 Fructidor, an V [26 August 1797]), 219 (5 Vendémiaire, an VII [26 September 1798]), 601 (Juillet 1793), 621 (Floréal, an III [1795]); XXXI, 291 (11 Brumaire, an X [2 November 1801]).
    Inventaire fait après décès de Margueritte Simon femme Maurice Quay: Minutier central des notaires XXXI, 280 (8 Frimaire, an V [28 November 1796]).

Paris, Archives de la Préfecture de Police

    Police description of unusual characters in Paris: MS F⁷ 3829 (3 Frimaire, an IX [24 November 1800]).

    Police description of the couvent de la Visitation de Sainte Marie: MS A 130 (15 Germinal, an IX [5 April 1801]); MS A 126 (an IX).

Paris, Archives de la Seine

    Birth of Isis-Mélanie-Chrisotémie-Laodamie Franque, copy of the original certificate provided by M. Dargaud (1ᵉʳ arr., 29 Fructidor, an VII [15 September 1799]).

    Death of Lucile Franque: DQ⁸ 16, vol. 13 (3 Prairial, an XI [23 May 1803]).

    Death of Jean-Maurice Quay, copy of the original police report (6 January 1819).

Paris, Bibliothèque de l'Arsenal

    Charles Nodier's Réglement d'une société de Philadelphes, MS 15. 030/16.

Paris, Bibliothèque de l'Ecole des Beaux-Arts

    Valory, Chevalier de, *S'il est plus avantageux aux artistes de vivre dans la retraite ou dans le commerce du monde*, MS 202–1 (read at the Académie royale on 8 January 1763 and 5 May 1764).

Puteaux (Seine), Mairie

    Documents concerning the members of the Quay family at Puteaux, Section d'Etat civil, MS, Registre N 1737–1757.

Quintigny (Jura), Mairie, Documents originating from the Mairie of Quintigny, communicated by M. Alexandre Clavier.

    Judge Charve's request for the publication of banns for the marriage of Jean-Pierre Franque and Marguerite-Françoise-Lucile Messageot (16 Nivôse, an X [6 January 1802]).

    Copy of the wedding certificate of Jean-Pierre Franque and Marguerite-Françoise-Lucile Messageot (20 Nivôse, an X [10 January 1802]).

    Copy of the death certificate of Isis-Mélanie-Chrisotémie-Laodamie Franque (4 February 1870).

Published Sources*

Abrantès, la duchesse de. *Mémoires de la duchesse d'Abrantès, ou souvenirs historiques sur Napoléon, la Révolution, le Directoire, le Consulat, l'Empire et la Restauration.* Paris, 1831–35, 18 vols.

The Age of Neo-Classicism. Exhibition held at the Royal Academy and the Victoria and Albert Museum, London, 9 September—19 November 1972. The Arts Council of Great Britain, London and Harlow, 1972.

Andrews, Keith. *The Nazarenes: A Brotherhood of German Painters in Rome.* Oxford: Clarendon Press, 1964.

Anon. *Arlequin au Muséum, les tableaux en vaudeville.* Coll. Deloynes, XXII, 629.

Anon. *Coup-d'oeil sur le Salon de l'an VIII.* Paris, n.d.

*All mentions of Coll. Deloynes refer to the great collection of printed and manuscript documents in the Cabinet des Estampes, Bibliothèque nationale, Paris: *Collection de pièces sur les beaux-arts imprimées et manuscrits recueillis par Pierre-Jean Mariette, Charles-Nicolas Cochin et M. Deloynes.*

Anon. "Exposition des ouvrages de peinture, sculpture, gravure, architecture, composés par les artistes vivans," *Journal du bulletin universel des sciences, des lettres et des arts*. MS, Coll. Deloynes, XXIII, 634.

Anon. "Exposition de peinture, sculpture, architecture et gravure," *Mercure de France*. MS, Coll. Deloynes XXII, 633.

Anseaume, Louis. *Le Peintre amoureux de son modèle*. Paris, 1759.

Arnault, A. V. *Souvenirs d'un sexagénaire*. Paris, 1833, 4 vols.

Artaud de Montor, Alexis-François. *Considérations sur l'état de la peinture en Italie, dans les quatre siècles qui ont précédé celui de Raphaël*. Paris, 1808.

Aulard, François-Victor-Alphonse. *Paris sous le Consulat*. Paris, 1903–9, 4 vols.

————. *Paris sous le premier empire: Recueil de documents pour l'histoire de l'esprit public à Paris*. Paris, 1912–23, 3 vols. AUL.

Autreau, Jacques. *Œuvres*. Paris, 1749.

Bachaumont (Louis Petit de Bachaumont). *Mémoires secrets pour servir à l'histoire de la République des Lettres depuis 1762 jusqu'à nos jours*. London, 1777–89.

Ballanche, Pierre-Simon. *Du Sentiment considéré dans ses rapports avec la littérature et les arts*. Lyon, 1801.

Barré, Pierre-Yon, Picard, Louis-Benoît, Radet, Jean-Baptiste, and Desfontaines, François-Georges. *Lantara, ou le peintre au cabaret*. Paris, 1809 (also in COL 73, *Vaudevilles*, II).

Barré, Pierre-Yon, Radet, Jean-Baptiste, and Desfontaines, François-Georges. *Le Château et la chaumière, ou les arts et la reconnaissance*. Paris, 1814.

————. *Le Peintre français en Espagne, ou le dernier soupir de l'inquisition*. Paris, 1809.

————, and Bourgueil. *Le Peintre français à Londres*. Paris, 1802 (an X).

Baudelaire, Charles. *Salon de 1845*, in *Œuvres complètes*, La Pléiade, ed. Bruges, 1964.

Bawr, Mme de. *Mes Souvenirs*. 2d ed., Paris, 1853.

Beaunoir, Mme de (Pseudonym for Robineau, Alexandre-Louis-Bertrand). *Le Sculpteur ou la femme comme il y en a peu*. [Paris], 1784.

Beckford, William. *Bibliographical Memoirs of Extraordinary Painters* [1780]. Robert J. Gemmett, ed. Rutherford, N.J.: Fairleigh Dickinson University Press, 1969.

Benoit, François. *L'Art français sous la Révolution et l'Empire*. Paris, 1897.

Bernard, Dr. Claude. *Histoire de Buis-les-Baronnies*. Vaison-la-Romaine, 1971.

Biographie nouvelle des contemporains ou dictionnaire historique et raisonné de tous les hommes qui, depuis la révolution française ont acquis de la célébrité . . . Paris, 1822.

Biographie Universelle, Joseph-François Michaud, ed., 1856.

Biographie Universelle & Historique des femmes célèbres mortes ou vivantes. L. Prudhomme, ed. Paris, 1830.

Blanc, Charles. *Histoire des peintres de toutes les écoles: Ecole française*. Paris, 1862.

Blanvillain, J. François C. *Le Pariséum, ou Tableau actuel de Paris*. 2d ed. Paris, 1809.

Borenius, Tancred. "The Rediscovery of the Primitives," *Quarterly Review* 239 (April 1923): 258–70.

Bouilly, Jean-Nicolas. *Une Folie*, COL 64, *Opéras-com. en prose*, VII, 71–186.

———— and Pain, Joseph. *Fanchon la vielleuse*, COL 73, *Vaudevilles*, II, 172–319.

————. *Teniers*. Paris, an IX.

Brosses, Charles de. *Lettres familières sur l'Italie*, Yvonne Bezard, ed. Paris, 1931.

Broutet, F. "Charles Nodier et sa vie jurassienne," *La Nouvelle revue Franc-Comptoise,* vol. 11, no. 41, fasc. 1, 1970.

Brun-Durand, Justin. *Dictionnaire biographique et Biblio-iconographique de la Drôme.* Grenoble, 1900.

Buix, Aimé. *Quelques grands hommes des Baronnies.* Vaison-la-Romaine, 1953.

Caillot, Antoine. *Mémoires pour servir à l'histoire des mœurs et usages des français.* Paris, 1827.

Carmontelle (Louis Carrogis). *Proverbes dramatiques,* C. de Mery, ed. Paris, 1822. CAR-PRO.

————. *Proverbes et Comédies posthumes,* Mme de Genlis, ed. Paris, 1825.

Caylus, Comte de. *Recueil d'antiquités égyptiennes, étrusques, grecques et romaines.* Paris, 1752–67.

———— and Mariette, Pierre-Jean. *Recueil des peintures antiques.* Paris, 1757.

Chastel, André. *Art et Humanisme à Florence au temps de Laurent le Magnifique.* Paris, 1959.

Chateaubriand, François-René de. *Génie du Christianisme.* Paris, 1859.

————. *Mémoires d'outre-tombe,* La Pléïade ed. Paris, 1966, 2 vols.

[Chaussard, Pierre-Jean-Baptiste.] *Le Pausanias français; état des arts du dessin en France, à l'ouverture du XIXe siècle: Salon de 1806.* Paris, 1806.

Chronique scandaleuse de l'an 1800, pour l'an 1801, Recueil d'Anecdotes, jugemens, Méchancetés et Vérités, sur les hommes du jour, les Artistes, Auteurs, Acteurs, Entrepreneurs. . . . Paris, 1801 (an IX).

Cochin, Charles-Nicolas. *Les Misotechnites aux enfers.* Amsterdam, 1763.

Collection des Théâtres français, suite du répertoire. Senlis, 1829. COL.

Cordier de Launay, Louis-Guillaume-René. *Théorie Circonsphérique des deux genres du beau.* Berlin, 1806.

Court de Gébelin, Antoine. *Monde primitif analysé et comparé avec le monde moderne.* . . . Paris, 1774–96.

Curtis, Melinda. "The Pursuit of Primal Purity in the 19th Century," *Search for Innocence: Primitive and Primitivistic Art of the 19th Century.* Exhibition held at the Art Department Gallery, University of Maryland, 23 October–10 December 1975, College Park, 27–69.

Dargaud, Marius. "Autour d'un centenaire, Charles Nodier, jurassien," *Le Nouvelliste,* Lyon, 7 January 1944.

David, Jacques-Louis-Jules. *Le Peintre Louis David, 1748–1825, Souvenirs et Documents inédits.* Paris, 1880.

De David à Delacroix, La peinture française de 1774 à 1830. Exhibition held at the Grand Palais, Paris, 16 November 1974–3 February, 1975, Paris, 1974.

Delécluze, Etienne-Jean. "Les Barbus d'à présent et les barbus de MDCCC," *Le Livre des cent-et-un,* Paris, 1832, VII, 61–86. Also reproduced in Delécluze, *Louis David, son école et son temps, souvenirs.* Paris, 1855, 420–38. DEL-BAR.

————. *Louis David, son école et son temps, souvenirs.* Paris, 1855. DEL-DAV, DEL-BAR, NOD-TYP, NOD-TEM.

[Delisle de Sales, Jean-Claude-Izouard.] *Histoire philosophique du monde primitif.* 4th ed. Paris, 1794–95 (an III).

Département de la Drôme, Compte de la Gestion, 1792.

Descamps, Jean-Baptiste. *La Vie des peintres flamands, allemands et hollandais.* Paris, 1753–63, 4 vols.

[Dézallier d'Argenville, Antoine-Joseph.] *Abrégé de la vie des plus fameux peintres.* Paris, 1745–52, 3 vols.

Dieulafoy, Michel. *Le Portrait de Michel Cervantès,* COL 48, *Comédies en prose,* IX, 369–495.

Diderot, Denis. *Salon de 1765,* in *Diderot Salons,* Jean Seznec and Jean Adhémar, eds. Oxford: Oxford University Press, 1960, 4 vols.

Dumersan, Théophile-Marion. *Chants et chansons populaires de la France.* Paris, 1843.

———. *Chansons nationales et populaires de France.* Paris, 1851.

Dumolin, Maurice. *Etudes de topographie parisienne.* Paris, 1930.

Duqueylar, Paul. *Nouvelles études du cœur et de l'esprit humain. . . .* Paris, 1840.

Eméric-David, Toussaint-Bernard. *Discours historique sur la peinture moderne.* Paris, 1812.

Encyclopédie, Denis Diderot, ed. Geneva, 1777.

Estadieu, M. *Annales du pays castrais.* Castres, 1893.

Etienne, Charles-Guillaume, Morel, Servières, Joseph, and Moras, P. *Rembrandt ou la Vente après décès.* Paris, an IX.

Explication des ouvrages de peinture et dessins, sculpture, architecture et gravure, des artistes vivans, exposés au Muséum central des arts. Paris, an VIII.

Explication des ouvrages de peinture et dessins, sculpture, architecture et gravure, des artistes vivans, exposés au Muséum central des arts. Paris, an IX.

Explication des ouvrages de peinture, sculpture, architecture et gravure, des artistes vivans, exposés au Musée Napoléon. Paris, 1806.

Explication des ouvrages de peinture, sculpture, architecture et gravure, des artistes vivans, exposés au Musée Napoléon. Paris, 1808.

Explication des ouvrages de peinture, sculpture, architecture et gravure, des artistes vivans, exposés au Musée Napoléon. Paris, 1812.

Falconet, Etienne-Maurice. *Œuvres diverses concernant les arts.* Paris, 1787.

Fauriel, Claude-Charles. *Les Derniers jours du Consulat.* Paris, 1886.

Fleuriot de Langle, Paul. *Bibliothèque Paul Marmottan, Guide analytique.* Boulogne-sur-Seine, 1938.

———. *Elisa, sœur de Napoléon I.* Paris, 1947.

Fontaine, André. *Les Doctrines d'art en France.* Paris, 1909.

French Painting 1774–1830: The Age of Revolution. Exhibition held at the Grand Palais, Paris, 16 November 1974–3 February 1975; The Detroit Institute of Arts, 5 March–4 May 1975; The Metropolitan Museum of Art, New York, 12 June–7 September 1975. Detroit, 1975.

Friedlaender, Walter. "Eine Sekte der 'Primitiven' um 1800 in Frankreich und die Wandlung des Klassizismus bei Ingres," *Kunst und Künstler* 28 (1930): 281–86, 320–26.

———. *David to Delacroix.* Cambridge, Mass.: Harvard University Press, 1963.

Fuseli, Henry. *Geschichte der besten Künstler in der Schweitz.* Zurich, 1769–74, 4 vols.

Gabet, Charles. *Dictionnaire des artistes de l'école française au XIXe siècle.* Paris, 1831.

Gautier, Théophile. "Feuillets de l'album d'un jeune rapin," *Le Tiroir du Diable. Paris et les Parisiens.* Paris, [1844?].

Gérard, Henri Alexandre, Baron, ed. *Lettres adressées au Baron François Gérard,* 2d ed. Paris, 1886.

Giorgi, Francesco. *La Villa Baciocchi.* Bologna, 1910.

[Girodet, Anne-Louis]. *La Critique des critiques du Salon de 1806.* Paris, 1806.

Gleizes, Jean-Antoine. *Le Christianisme expliqué, ou l'unité de croyance pour tous les chrétiens.* Paris, 1830.

―――. *Les Nuits élyséennes.* Paris, an IX [1800].

―――. *Thalysie, ou système physique et intellectuel de la nature.* Paris, 1821.

Goncourt, Edmond and Jules de. *L'Art du XVIIIe siècle.* Paris, 1912.

―――. *Les Portraits intimes du dix-huitième siècle, ed. définitive.* Paris, n.d.

Grimm, Friedrich Melchior, and Diderot, Denis. *Correspondance littéraire, philosophique et critique,* Maurice Tourneux, ed. Paris, 1877–82, 16 vols.

Guizot, François-Pierre-Guillaume. "De l'état des beaux-arts en France, et du salon de 1810," in *Etudes sur les beaux-arts en général.* Paris [1851], 3–100.

Haskell, Francis. "The Old Masters in Nineteenth-Century French Painting," *Art Quarterly* 34, no. 1 (Spring 1971): 55–85.

Heinse, Wilhelm. *Ardinghello und die glückseligen Inseln.* Lemgo, 1787.

―――. *Ardinghello et les îles de la félicité, histoire italienne du seizième siècle,* Weltzien and Faye trans. Paris, an VIII.

Henry-Rosier, Marguerite. *La Vie de Charles Nodier.* Paris, 1931.

Herbaz Polski, Boniecki, ed. Warsaw, 1902.

Hofmann, Werner. "D'une aliénation à l'autre; l'artiste allemand et son public au XIXe siècle," *Gazette des Beaux-Arts* (October 1977): 124–36.

Jacquelin, Jacques-André and Lafortelle, A. M. *Le Peintre dans son ménage.* Paris, an VIII.

Jal, Gustave (Pseudonym for Auguste Jal). "Les Soirées d'artistes," in *Le Livre des cent-et-un.* Paris, 1831, I, 109–45.

―――. *L'Ombre de Diderot et le bossu du Marais; dialogue critique sur le Salon de 1819.* Paris, 1819.

Jouy, Victor-Joseph-Etienne de, Lonchamps, Charles de, and Dieulafoy, Michel. *Le Tableau des Sabines,* COL 74, *Vaudevilles,* III, 209–85.

Klenze, Camillo von. "The Growth of Interest in the Early Italian Masters, from Tischbein to Ruskin," *Modern Philology* 4 (October 1906): 207–68.

Kris, Ernst. *Psychoanalytic Explorations in Art.* New York: Schocken, 1967.

Labouisse-Rochefort, Jean-Pierre-Jacques-Auguste de. *Variétés littéraires et biographiques extraites du journal intitulé L'Echo judiciaire.* Toulouse, 1851.

Lacombe, Jacques. *Dictionnaire portatif des Beaux-arts.* Paris, 1766.

[La Font de Saint-Yenne,] *Réflexions sur quelques causes de l'état présent de la Peinture en France,* 1752.

Lagrange, Léon. *Joseph Vernet, sa vie, sa famille, son siècle, d'après des documents inédits.* Brussels, 1858.

Lamy, M. "La Découverte des primitifs italiens au XIXe siècle, Seroux d'Agincourt (1730–1814) et son influence sur les collectionneurs, critiques et artistes français," *La Revue de l'art ancien et moderne* 39, no. 22 (January 1921): 169–81 and 40, no. 227 (June 1921): 182–90.

Landon, Charles-Paul. *Annales du musée et de l'école moderne des beaux-arts.* Paris, an
IX–1801–10, 9 vols.

———. "Exposition du Salon du Musée," *Journal des Arts,* 1800. MS, Coll. Deloynes,
XXIII, 635.

———. *Salon de 1808.* Paris, 1808.

———. *Salon de 1810.* Paris, 1829.

———. *Salon de 1812.* Paris, 1812.

Larat, Jean. *Bibliographie critique des oeuvres de Charles Nodier.* Paris, 1923.

———. *La Tradition et l'exotisme dans l'œuvre de Charles Nodier.* Paris, 1923.

Laugier, Abbé. *Manière de bien juger des ouvrages de peinture.* Paris, 1771.

Le Breton, Joachim. *Rapport sur les Beaux-Arts.* Paris, 1808.

Le Brun, Ponce Denis [Ecouchard]. *Œuvres.* Paris, 1811, 4 vols.

Le Flamanc, Auguste. *Les Utopies prérévolutionnaires et la philosophie du 18e siècle.*
Paris: J. Vrin, 1934.

Lefuel, Hector. *Catalogue du Musée Marmottan.* Paris: Morancé, 1934.

Lenoir, Alexandre. *Dissertation historique et chronologique des monumens de sculpture
réunis au musée des monumens français,* 6th ed. Paris, an X.

Lenormant, Charles. "Du Costume parisien, et de son avenir," in *Le Livre des cent-et-un.*
Paris, 1832, VII, 13–32.

———. *Beaux-Arts—1851—Orsel et Overbeck.* Paris, 1851.

Levitine, George. "L'Aigle épouvanté de l''Ossian' de Girodet et l'Aigle effrayée du
mausolée de Turenne," *Gazette des Beaux-Arts* (December 1974): 319–23.

———. " 'L'Ecole d'Apelle' de Jean Broc: un 'primitif' au salon de l'an VIII," *Gazette
des Beaux-Arts* (November 1972): 285–94.

———. "The Eighteenth-Century Rediscovery of Alexis Grimou and the Emergence of
the Proto-Bohemian Image of the French Artist," *Eighteenth-Century Studies* 2,
no. 1 (Fall 1968): 58–76. LEV-GRI.

———. "Les Origines du mythe de l'artiste bohème en France: Lantara," *Gazette des
Beaux-Arts* (September 1975): 49–60.

———. "L'*Ossian* de Girodet et l'actualité politique sous le Consulat," *Gazette des
Beaux-Arts* (October 1956): 39–56.

———. "The *Primitifs* and Their Critics in the Year 1800." *Studies in Romanticism*
1, no. 4 (Summer 1962): 209–19.

———. *The Sculpture of Falconet.* Greenwich, Conn.: New York Graphic Society, 1972.

———. "Trompe-l'œil Versus Utopia: The Context of Early Nineteenth-Century Primitivism," in *Search for Innocence: Primitive and Primitivistic Art of the 19th Century,*
11–26. Exhibition held at the Art Department Gallery, University of Maryland, 29
October–10 December 1975, College Park.

———. *"Vernet Tied to a Mast in a Storm:* The Evolution of an Episode of Art
Historical Romantic Folklore," *Art Bulletin* 49 (June 1967): 92–100.

Locquin, Jean. *La Peinture d'histoire en France de 1747 à 1785.* Paris, 1912.

Lorenzetti, Costanza. *L'Accademia di Belle Arti di Napoli (1752–1952).* Florence, n.d.

Lucas-Dubreton, J. *Le Culte de Napoléon, 1815–1848.* Paris, 1960.

Lyonnet, Henry. *Dictionnaire des Comédiens français.* Paris, n.d.

Madelin, Louis. *La Colline de Chaillot.* Paris, 1926.

Magnin, Antoine. "Charles Nodier naturaliste," *Société d'émulation du Doubs,* 1909, *Séances du 21 Mars et 23 Mai 1908.*

Marmontel, Jean-François. *Mémoires.* Paris, 1891. MAR.

Marmottan, Paul. *Les Arts en Toscane sous Napoléon, La Princesse Elisa.* Paris, 1901.

Mennessier-Nodier, Mme. *Charles Nodier: Episodes et souvenirs de sa vie.* Paris, 1867.

Merle, Jean-Toussaint, and Périé, Antoine-Hilaire-Henri. *Description historique et pittoresque du château de Chambord.* [Paris], 1821.

Milizia, Francesco. *L'Art de voir dans les beaux-arts,* Général Pommereul, trans. Paris, an VI.

Monglond, André. *Le Préromantisme français.* Grenoble, 1930.

Monnier, Désiré. *Souvenirs d'un octogénaire de province.* Lons-le-Saunier, 1871.

Montaiglon, Anatole de Courde de. *Procès-verbaux de l'académie royale de peinture et de sculpture—1648–1793—D'après les registres originaux conservés à l'Ecole des Beaux-Arts.* Paris, 1875–92.

Montfaucon, Bernard de. *Les Monuments de la monarchie françoise.* Paris, 1729–33.

Nayral, Magloire. *Biographie castraise ou Tableau historique analytique et critique des personnages qui se sont rendus célèbres à Castres ou dans ses environs. . . .* Castres, 1833.

Nettement, Alfred. *Souvenirs de la Restauration.* Paris, 1858.

Nicolas, Michel. *Histoire des artistes, peintres, sculpteurs, architectes et musiciens-compositeurs nés dans le département du Gard.* Nîmes, 1859.

Nivernois, duc de (L.-J. Barbon Mancini Mazarini). *Œuvres posthumes.* Paris: Maradan, 1807.

Nodier, Charles. *Apothéoses et Imprécations de Pythagore.* [1808].

———. "Les Barbus," *Le Temps,* 5 October 1832. Also reproduced in Delécluze, *Louis David, son école et son temps, souvenirs,* Paris, 1855, 438–47. NOD-TEM.

———. *Correspondance inédite,* Alexandre Estignard, ed. Paris, 1876. NOD-EST.

———. "Deux beaux types de la plus parfaite organisation humaine," in *Essais d'un jeune Barde.* Paris and Besançon, an XII [1804], 87–95. Also reproduced in Delécluze, *Louis David, son école et son temps, souvenirs.* Paris, 1855, 74–76. NOD-TYP.

———. *Méditations du cloître,* in *Romans de Charles Nodier, nouvelle ed.* Paris, 1850, 77–86 (1st ed. Paris, 1803).

———. *Le Peintre de Saltzbourg, journal des émotions d'un cœur souffrant,* in *Romans de Charles Nodier, nouvelle ed.* Paris, 1850, 27–74 (1st ed. Paris, 1803). NOD-SAL.

———. *Pensées de Shakespeare.* Besançon, [1801].

———. *Souvenirs de la Révolution et de l'Empire.* Paris, 1850, 2 vols.

———. *Les Tristes, ou mélanges tirés des tablettes d'un suicidé.* Paris, 1806.

[Nougaret, Pierre-Jean-Baptiste, and Leprince, Nicolas-Thomas.] *Anecdotes des Beaux-Arts.* Paris, 1776.

Nouvelle Biographie générale, Firmin Didot fils, ed. Paris, 1856.

Oliver, A. Richard. *Charles Nodier: Pilot of Romanticism.* Syracuse: Syracuse University Press, 1964.

Ossian. Exhibition held in the Grand Palais, Paris, 1974. Text and catalogue by Hanna Hohl and Hélène Toussaint, Paris, 1974.

Ossian, Fils de Fingal, Barde du 3e siècle; Poésies galliques traduites sur l'anglais de Macpherson, Pierre-Prime-Félicien Le Tourneur, trans. Paris, 1810.

Pahin-Champlain de la Blancherie, Mammès-Claude. *Essai d'un tableau historique des peintres de l'école françoise, Depuis Jean Cousin, En 1500 jusqu'en 1783 inclusivement . . . Salon de la Correspondance.* Paris, 1783.

Paillot de Montabert, Jacques-Nicolas. *L'Artistaire: Livre des principales initiations aux Beaux-Arts.* Paris, 1855.

———. *Dissertation sur les peintures du moyen âge, et sur celles qu'on a appelé gothiques* (from the *Magasin Encyclopédique,* March 1812). Paris, 1812.

———. *Théorie du geste dans l'art de la peinture . . . Extrait d'un ouvrage inédit sur la peinture.* Paris, 1813.

———. *Traité complet de la peinture.* Paris: Bossange, 1829, 9 vols.

———. *Traité complet de la peinture.* Paris: Delion, 1829–51, 9 vols.

Pain, Joseph. *Nouveaux tableaux de Paris, ou observations sur les mœurs et usages des parisiens au commencement du XIXᵉ siècle.* Paris, 1828.

Paris as It Was and as It Is, or A Sketch of the French Capital, Illustrative of the Effects of the Revolution. . . . In a Series of Letters, Written by an English Traveller, During the Years 1801–2, to a Friend in London. London, 1803.

Parny, Evariste Désiré Desforges de. *Œuvres choisies.* Paris, 1826.

La Peinture française en Suède. Exhibition held in Bordeaux, 15 May–15 September 1967. Bordeaux, 1967.

Pelles, Geraldine. *Art, Artists and Society.* Englewood Cliffs, N.J.: Prentice-Hall, 1963.

Le Petit Arlequin au Muséum ou les tableaux d'Italie en vaudeville. MS, Coll. Deloynes, XXII, 610.

Polski Slownik Biograficzny, Dunin and Firlej, eds., 1948.

Prault-Saint-Germain, Marcel. *Projet de la seule navigation naturelle et commerciale qui existeroit en Europe et joindroit le Rhin à la Seine jusqu'à Paris, sous la dénomination de: Navigation Bonaparte.* Paris: Desenne, an XII [1804].

Previtali, Giovanni. *La fortuna dei primitivi dal Vasari ai neoclassici.* Turin. 1964.

Pujoulx, Jean-Baptiste. *Paris à la fin du XVIIIᵉ siècle.* Paris, an IX [1801].

Renouvier, Jules. *Histoire de l'art pendant la Révolution considéré principalement dans les estampes.* Paris, 1863.

Répertoire général du théâtre français. Paris, 1818. REP.

Rheims, Maurice. *La Vie d'Artiste.* Paris, 1970.

Rochas, Henri-Joseph-Adolphe. *Biographie du Dauphiné.* Paris, 1856–60.

[Rochon de Chabanne, Marc-Antoine-Jacques.] *La Manie des arts, ou la matinée à la mode,* REP, *Théâtre du second ordre, Comédies en prose,* XIII, 199–244.

Roger, Jean-François. *Caroline, ou Le Tableau.* COL 31, *Comédies en vers,* XIII, 135–89.

Roland, Mme. *Mémoires.* Paris, 1864.

Rosenblum, Robert. *Jean-Auguste-Dominique Ingres.* New York: Abrams, 1968.

———. *Transformations in Late Eighteenth-Century Art.* Princeton, N.J.: Princeton University Press, 1967.

Rubin, James Henry. "New Documents on the Méditateurs: Baron Gérard, Mantegna, and French Romanticism circa 1800," *The Burlington Magazine* (December 1975): 785–90.

Salgues, Jacques-Barthélemy. *Des Erreurs et des préjugés répandus dans la société.* Paris, 1811.

Schlenoff, Norman. *Ingres, ses sources littéraires*. Paris [1966].

Search for Innocence: Primitive and Primitivistic Art of the 19th Century. Exhibition held at the Art Department Gallery, University of Maryland, 29 October–10 December 1975, College Park. Text and catalogue by Melinda Curtis; essay by George Levitine.

[Séguier, Armand-Louis-Maurice.] *Le Maréchal ferrant de la ville d'Anvers, d'après Quérard*. Paris, an VII [1799].

Seroux d'Agincourt, Jean-Baptiste. *L'Histoire de l'art par les monuments, depuis sa décadence au quatrième siècle jusqu'à son renouvellement au seizième*. Paris, 1823.

Silvestre, Théophile. *Les Artistes français*. Paris, 1926.

Sobry, Jean François. *Poétique des arts, ou cours de peinture et de littérature comparées*. Paris, 1810.

Ternois, Daniel. "Ossian et les peintres," *Actes du Colloque Ingres*. Montauban, 1969, 165–213.

Tilander, Gunnar. "Tapet med romantiskt litterärt motiv," *Fataburen, Nordiska Museets och Skansens Arsbok*, 1964, 113–28.

Van Tieghem, Paul. *Ossian en France*. Paris, 1917.

Le Verre cassé de Boilly, et les croûtiers en déroute. Paris, an VII.

Vigée Le Brun, Mme. *Souvenirs de Madame Vigée le Brun*. Paris, 1869.

Vigny, Alfred de. *Stello*, in *Œuvres complètes d'Alfred de Vigny*, La Pléiade, ed., I. Bruges, 1964.

Wackenroder, Wilhelm Heinrich. *Confessions and Fantasies*, Mary Hurst Schubert, trans. University Park: Pennsylvania State University Press, 1971.

———. *Herzensergiessungen eines kunstliebenden Klosterbruders*. Berlin, 1796.

——— and Tieck, Ludwig. *Phantasien über die Kunst für Freunde der Kunst*. Hamburg, 1799.

Watelet, Claude-Henri. *Dictionnaire des arts de peinture, sculpture et gravure*. Paris, 1792, 5 vols. WAT-DIC.

Wille, Jean-Georges. *Mémoires et journal*, Georges Duplessis, ed. Paris, 1857, 2 vols.

Winckelmann, Johann Joacquim. *L'Histoire de l'art de l'antiquité*, Michael Huber, trans. Leipzig, 1781, 3 vols.

Wittkower, Rudolf, and Wittkower, Margot. *Born under Saturn*. New York: Norton, 1963.

———, eds. and trans. [from Jacopo Giunta]. *The Divine Michelangelo*. London, 1964.

Frequently Consulted Periodicals

Bulletin de la société historique d'Auteuil et de Passy.

Gazette de France.

Journal de l'Empire.

Journal des Arts.

Journal des Dames et des Modes.

Journal des Débats. JD.

Journal du Bulletin universel des sciences, des lettres, et des arts.

Journal du Commerce.

Mercure de France.

Le Moniteur Universel.

Index

15. Henri-François Riesener (?), *Portrait of Maurice Quay,* oil on canvas. Louvre, Paris.

16. Jacques-Louis David, *The Sabine Women*, 1799, Louvre, Paris.

17. Jean-Henri Cless, *The Studio of David*, drawing. Musée Carnavalet, Paris.

18. Anon., *Caricature*, lithograph.

19. Charles-P.-J. Normand, *Paris*, engraving.
From Charles-Paul Landon, *Annales du Musée*,
Paris, 1802, III, pl. 63.

20. Jean-Jacques-André Le Veau, *View of Chaillot,* engraving.

21. Antoine Maxime Monsaldy and G. Devisme, *View of the Salon of the year VIII* (1800), engraving.

23. Paul Duqueylar, *Ossian Chanting His Poems*, 1800, oil on canvas. Musée Granet, Aix-en-Provence.

22. Detail of Fig. 21.

24. Jean Broc, *The School of Apelles*, 1800, oil on canvas. Louvre, Paris.

25. Detail of Fig. 24.

26. Raphael (?), *"Calumny" of Apelles,* drawing. Cabinet des dessins, Louvre, Paris.

27. Jean Broc, *Death of Hyacinth*, 1801, oil on canvas. Musée de Poitiers.

28. Pierre-Paul Prud'hon, *Phrosine and Mélidore*, engraving. From P. J. Bernard, *Œuvres*, Paris, 1797.

29. Anne-Louis Girodet, *The New Danaë,* 1799, oil on canvas. Courtesy The Minneapolis Art Institute.

30. Antoine Maxime Monsaldy, Reproduction in reverse of Jean Broc's *Shipwreck of Virginie,* 1801, preliminary drawing (counterproof) for the engraving of the *View of the Salon of 1801.* Cabinet des Estampes, Bibliothèque nationale, Paris.

31. Antoine Maxime Monsaldy, *View of the Salon* of *1801,* showing Jean Broc's *Shipwreck of Virginie,* 1801, engraving, one of four views.

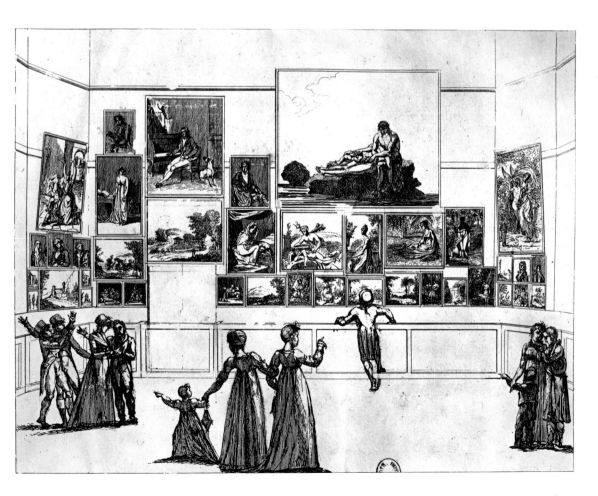

32. Antoine Maxime Monsaldy, *View of the Salon of 1801,* showing Jean-François Hue's *Shipwrecked Family,* 1801, engraving, one of four views.

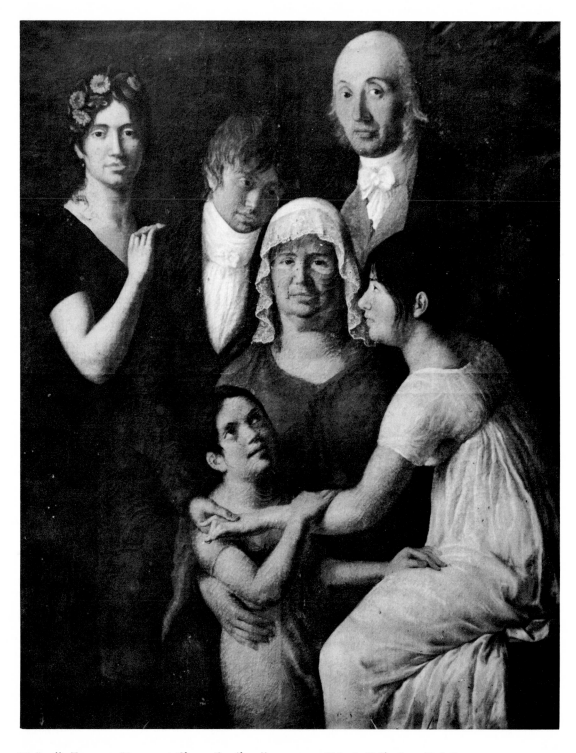

33. Lucile Franque, *Messageot-Charve Family,* oil on canvas. Private Collection, Quintigny.

34. Detail of Fig. 37 (Lucile).

35. Lucile Franque, *Jean-Antoine Gleizes,* oil on canvas. Private Collection, Quintigny.

36. Joseph-Boniface Franque, *Bonaparte as First Consul,* oil on canvas. Musée Marmottan, Paris.

37. Antoine-Jean Gros, *Bonaparte as First Consul,* 1801–2, oil on canvas.
Musée de la Légion d'Honneur, Paris.

38. Maurice Quay (?), *Study of an Unknown Youth,* oil on canvas. Musée Granet, Aix-en-Provence.

39. Jean Broc, *Death of General Desaix,* 1806, oil on canvas. Musée de Versailles.

40. Jean Broc, *Paul and Virginie*, 1820, wallpaper printed by J. C. Xavier Mader and Dufour, detail. Courtesy Musée des Arts Décoratifs, Paris.

41. Jean-Pierre (?) Franque, *Allegory of the Condition of France Before the Return from Egypt*, 1810, oil on canvas. Louvre, Paris.

42. François Gérard, *Ossian Evoking Ghosts by the Sound of the Harp on the Shores of the Lora*, 1802, oil on canvas, version of Hamburger Kunsthalle.

43. Antoine-Hilaire-Henri Périé, *The Bark of Charon*, 1810, engraving by
Antoine-Jean-Baptiste Coupé.

44. Antoine-Hilaire-Henri Périé, *Francis I*, lithograph by
Godefroy Engelmann. From Jean-Toussaint Merle and
Antoine-Hilaire-Henri Périé, *Description historique et
pittoresque du Château de Chambord*, Paris, 1821.

45. Joseph-Boniface Franque, *Eruption of the Vesuvius*, 1827, oil on canvas. Philadelphia Museum of Art.

46. Jean-Pierre Franque, *Angelica and Medor,* 1822, oil on canvas. Musée d'Angers.

47. Jean-Pierre Franque, *Madonna and Child,*
1853, oil on canvas. Chapel of Quintigny.

48. Jean-Pierre and Joseph-Boniface Franque, *The Battle of Zurich*, 1812, oil on canvas. Private collection.

49. Jean-Auguste-Dominique Ingres, *Paolo and Francesca da Rimini,* c. 1814, oil on canvas. Musée de Chantilly.

50. Anne-Louis Girodet, *The Return of the Warrior,* drawing. Courtesy Musée de Montargis.

51. Pierre-Henri Revoil, *Childhood of Giotto,* oil on canvas. Courtesy Musée de Grenoble.

52. Jacques-Louis-Michel Grandin, *Blinding of Daphnis,* 1804, oil on canvas. Musée Jules Chéret, Nice.

53. Pierre-Edmé-Louis Pellier (attributed to), *Victory of Odysseus at the Paeces' Games,* c. 1809–1814. Courtesy Musée Magnin, Dijon.